The Cunning of Reason

The Cunning of Reason

Martin Hollis

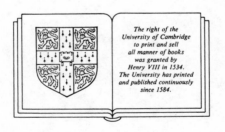

Cambridge University Press

Cambridge
New York   New Rochelle
Melbourne   Sydney

Published by the Press Syndicate of the University of Cambridge
The Pitt Building, Trumpington Street, Cambridge CB2 1RP
32 East 57th Street, New York, NY 10022, USA
10 Stamford Road, Oakleigh, Melbourne 3166, Australia

First published 1987

Printed in Great Britain by
Redwood Burn Limited, Trowbridge, Wiltshire

British Library cataloguing in publication data
Hollis, Martin
The cunning of reason.
1. Reasoning (Psychology)
I. Title
128'.3   BF441

Library of Congress cataloguing in publication data
Hollis, Martin
The cunning of reason.
Bibliography.
Includes index.
1. Reason.   I. Title.
BC177.H65   1988   128'.3   87–14630

ISBN 0 521 24879 5 hard covers
ISBN 0 521 27039 1 paperback

RB

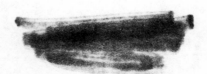

Contents

Preface

A lady once asked Dr Johnson why he had defined 'pastern' in his dictionary as a horse's knee. 'Ignorance, madam, pure ignorance', the sage replied. Readers, seeing that this book is by a philosopher and light on footnotes, may wonder if my grasp of economics, politics and sociology can be relied on. Let me set their minds at rest: it cannot. This is an argumentative text, which poaches not in order to teach experts their business but to borrow from them and enlist their philosophical curiosity. All the same, I shall be presuming on their good nature. Where they disagree, I hope that they will stop to reason with me. Where they could have put the points better themselves, I hope that they will.

If I need not always echo Dr Johnson, it is thanks mainly to friends and colleagues. Shaun Hargreaves-Heap in particular has kindly read the manuscript with an economist's eye and suggested many improvements. This is in addition to the explicit debt of chapter 7 and parts of later chapters to our published articles. Frank Hahn and Edward Nell are two other economists with whom I have enjoyed working and whose company and writings have influenced the text. My chief debt in politics is to Steve Smith and to our joint teaching, which yielded the article drawn on throughout chapter 10. In sociology I owe much to the pleasures of teaching for several years with Bryan Heading and Gareth Jones. Among my fellow philosophers, Tim O'Hagan and Philip Pettit have long been especially helpful comrades. Meanwhile, I am deeply aware that Quentin Skinner's encouragement and marvellous lucidity account for far more of my hermeneutic inclinations than is owned to in chapter 11. More loosely, I have also gained much from the company and writings of Jon Elster, Anthony Giddens, Steven Lukes, Derek Parfit, Amartya Sen, Charles Taylor and Bernard Williams.

In giving thanks, I am not claiming protection. At a time when growing interest in fundamentals lives uneasily with growing specialisation of subfields, the book must take its chance. If its origins are of interest, they lie in my (1977) *Models of Man*, where I argued for Autonomous Man, rather than Plastic Man, as a focus for social understanding. That I gave too little thought there to economic notions of rationality has been underlined by the current surge of rational-man individualism in social theory and political philosophy. I try here to make amends beyond those of the intervening papers cited in the text. It will be seen that I am impressed but not overwhelmed.

Belated thanks go also to the British Academy for helping to support a useful research term in Oxford in the early stages. The delay is due to the dire effects on British universities of cuts and changes in government policy, for which I give no thanks at all. This sentiment is informed by three years as dean of a School of Economic and Social Studies. Dr Johnson opines that 'a man may write any time, if he will set himself doggedly to do it'. Happily, the University of East Anglia thinks otherwise, and I am grateful, finally, for the study leave in which to finish.

I

The sovereign artificer

God speaks to Adam:

I have given you, Adam, neither a predetermined place nor a particular aspect nor any special prerogatives in order that you may take and possess these through your own decision and choice. The limitations on the nature of other creatures are contained within my prescribed laws. You shall determine your own nature without constraint from any barrier, by means of the freedom to whose power I have entrusted you. I have placed you at the centre of the world so that from that point you might see better what is in the world. I have made you neither heavenly nor earthly, neither mortal nor immortal, so that like a free and sovereign artificer you might mould and fashion yourself into that form you yourself shall have chosen.

These ringing sentences come from the the *Oration on the Dignity of Man* which Pico della Mirandola wrote in 1484. They capture a Renaissance humanist vision of man as special in the cosmos, and should catch recent social theorists in two minds. On the one hand God places Adam at the centre of the world and makes him his own artificer. That is just right for an individualism grounded on the idea that man is an active subject, who fashions the fabric of the social world. On the other hand God prescribes no constraints from any barrier. That seems to put Adam beyond the pale of every kind of science. However tempting active subjects may be to political theories of liberty, science needs objects.

    Those last three words would be decisive if social theorists were still mesmerised by Newtonian mechanics and nineteenth-century physics. The social sciences took shape in an age divided from Pico's by the scientific revolution. They inherited a Newtonian picture of nature as a mechanical, law-governed, humanly empty system, whose workings were hidden from the naked eye, rather as the springs and wheels of a fob watch are invisible to those who see only its face. Natural science had triumphed by learning to prise the back off the watch. It had found the forces acting on the cogs and learnt the secrets of the innermost particles of matter. Could the same not be done for human nature and human society?

This question still itched in the 1950s, when I was first exposed to it. By then the prevailing philosophy of science was empiricist, more concerned with the success of prediction and less with structures beyond the reach of experience. Philosophers were thinking of causal laws in terms more of interesting correlations than of necessitating forces. David Hume, quite newly promoted to the pantheon, was responsible for that, and social scientists, although divided about the merits of his analysis of causation, found nothing subversive in his statement of their task. He had published *A Treatise of Human Nature* in 1739 as a foundation for 'a complete system of the sciences'. It is evident, he had said in the introduction, that all sciences have a relation, greater or less, to human nature. 'Even Mathematics, Natural Philosophy and Natural Religion are in some measure dependent on the science of MAN; since they lie under the cognisance of men, and are judged by their powers and faculties.' Hence a science of man, grounded in an empirical study of 'Logic, Morals, Criticism and Politics' would comprehend almost everything which can tend to the improvement of the human mind. Its method was to be 'experience and observation', applied to 'men's behaviour in company, in affairs and in their pleasures'. Its aim was 'explaining all effects from the simplest and fewest causes'.

We reach 1987 without anything at all like a complete system of the sciences. Indeed there is no longer an agreed natural science blueprint by which to test the character of social science. Thanks to Popper, Quine, Kuhn, Feyerabend, Lakatos and others, the thought that science lies under the cognisance of man has undercut common assumptions about scientific objectivity and the independence of facts. Where there used to be foundations for scientific knowledge in unvarnished observation and a hypothetico-deductive procedure for testing theories, it is now argued that there is no 'unvarnished news' (Quine's evocative phrase) and that no observation or test can be innocent of theory. Natural scientists may clock into their laboratories undismayed, but social scientists have never worked under laboratory conditions. If the interpretation of social facts is always the interpretation of interpretations, then the hermeneutic aspects of social science become dizzying.

That is a reference to the hermeneutic or interpretative tradition in social thought, which descends from German idealist reflections on the writing of history. It was never cowed by the insistence that social sciences must be *sciences*, and is now becoming urgent. Its leading category is Meaning, characterised by Wilhelm Dilthey as 'the category which is peculiar to life and to the historical world'. Human life, he said, can be understood only by means of categories which do not apply to our knowledge of physical reality. Meaning, value, purpose, development and ideal are such categories. They all depend on the fact that the connectedness of a life can only be understood through the meaning that individual parts have for understanding the whole. 'Life does not mean anything other than itself. There is nothing in it which points to a meaning beyond it.'[1]

The guiding imperative here is that action has meanings which can be understood only from within. If we ask why the historian, as typical student of mankind, differs from the physicist, as typical student of nature, four instructive thoughts about meaning suggest themselves. (I shall put them in general terms of my own, since I cited Dilthey more out of respect for a founding father than because his actual words remain in circulation.) Firstly *experience* has meaning for people. They find in it signs of order, both natural, as when they classify animals or systematise the movements of planets, and human, as when they respond to a gesture or celebrate the marriage of a friend. They read their experience not only scientifically but also aesthetically and morally. They extract predictions, lessons and ideals from it. They impose themselves

---

[1] Dilthey (1926), vol. vii, p. 224. I have followed the convention of referring to works by citing the year of publication of a standard edition in brackets, e.g. (1926), even when, as here, it is not the year of origin.

and their concerns on it too, and do so in ways which vary between individuals, groups and cultures. An atomic particle is passive by contrast. If it has experience, it kindly refrains from attaching subjective meaning to it. It has no beliefs about the world which need worry a physicist.

Secondly *utterances* have meaning for people. Words and sentences are not just physical disturbances but communications in accordance with rules for their use. They are read and answered in a language governed at least largely by convention. At the same time speakers have both intention and motive in using them. The speaker's meaning and the utterance's meaning can go adrift in ways foreign to objects in nature. Here lie hermeneutic circles of the most daunting kind, which do not trouble the physicist.

Thirdly *actions* have both instrumental and expressive meaning. Both adjectives involve several kinds of meaning, depending on the context of enquiry: what the actor did, intended or aimed to achieve, what the action signified or symbolised and how it was embedded in a network of values or relations are some of them. Since this book is about understanding actors and actions, I shall not linger now. Suffice it to say that political manoeuvre, sexual courtship and religious observance (to pick almost at random) mix intention, motive, convention and propriety in various ways. There is a sort of Bermuda triangle, marked by questions of signs and symbols, of norms and principles and of means and ends, which swallows many a student of mankind. Physicists lose no sleep over it.

Fourthly *ideas* have meaning. People's reading of their situation alters with changes in their beliefs and expectations, as later chapters will insist. Among the ideas which move them are ideas about what moves them. Social theory, being itself in circulation among its subjects, is tied to its own tail. These are matters of meaning in various senses of that nimble term. That molecules have no thoughts about molecules must be a great relief to the physicist.

No quick conclusions follow from these differences between history and physics, but there is enough to pause for. It is not just that the historian needs an insider's view when reconstructing particular episodes in the lives of singular individuals. The suggestion is that an insider view is needed for every study of social life, because the social *is* what it *means*. Because life means nothing beyond itself, a peculiar kind of understanding is called for. This is plausible only if made very sweeping. Any fragment of social life certainly 'means' something beyond itself. The Russian Revolution, for instance, was not a self-contained episode, and especially not one which could be understood just by knowing what the actors had in their conscious minds. Even broad periods of history or complete cultures are set in a natural world and peopled by bodily creatures, as the study of technology or medicine makes abundantly clear. So there is no meaning beyond life itself only if some grand idealist proposition is offered, internalising reality to consciousness and perhaps finding an overall pattern and movement there, too global for individual minds to grasp in their particular time and place.

It will sound as if I am preparing to live up to my Hegelian title by conjuring up a World Spirit to direct History. The Cunning of Reason is Hegel's term for a hidden dynamic or dialectic which sums the consequences of actions in ways unforeseen by the actors. But I have no such grand ambition, witness the outline of the book which I shall give in a moment. I sound the bold idealist alpenhorn only to introduce the tensions which arise if one accepts that meanings matter but denies that nothing else does. The social sciences have always been caught between history and physics (to use a brisk shorthand), and the recent intrusion of hermeneutics into the discussion of objectivity in natural science has not relieved the tensions.

Natural science is happy to take a spectator's or outsider's view of the workings of nature. Explanation naturally takes the form of finding causes for effects, which are systematically linked by causal laws. Thinking in terms of causes, which produce or necessitate their effects and make them inevitable, would do nicely, were it not for epistemologists complaining that we cannot know of such connections. But acceptance of a softer Humean determinism, which (roughly) makes nature regular rather than forceful, does not undermine the idea that objectivity is for spectators. Nor does acceptance that there may be a random streak in nature, which makes complete predictability impossible. The suggestion from Quine and others that the mind can never be wholly self-effacing in what it regards as knowledge of nature is more worrying. But any retreat from a spectator view will be grudging, since (odd cases like psycho-somatic illnesses aside) we still believe deeply that the workings of nature are a test of belief, not an effect of it.

An outsider's view of social life is more precarious. The urge to achieve one in the name of science has produced some uncompromising approaches, like behaviourism, which try to dispense with actors' inner states. But I presume that the actors' desires and beliefs can be allowed to matter for scientific explanation, provided that they have causes and effects. This line avoids direct conflict with cherished beliefs about free will. Indeed, if free action is action which gets the agent what he wants and is done because the agent had so calculated, freedom seems to presuppose a deterministic system of cause and effect. The actors themselves are not always the best judges of what they are doing, why and with what likely consequences. So the social sciences can increase our freedom by explaining us to ourselves and showing us how to achieve more of what we want. Thus microeconomics can plausibly be seen as a theory of rational choice which systematises 'insider' data in conformity with the demands of causal explanation, and hands the results back to the insiders as an aid to better decisions. Why I call this neat view precarious will emerge later.

By contrast, a hermeneutic approach to social life gives primacy to the world from within. It too can be uncompromising. 'The central concepts which belong to our understanding of social life are incompatible with concepts central to the activity of scientific prediction', declared Peter Winch in *The Idea of a Social Science* (1958, p. 94), his robust, well-argued Wittgensteinian assault on causal thinking about action. But in so far as free will is the issue, one should not assume that what a hard-nosed outsider approach denies is safe in hermeneutic hands. If the meaning of action is exhausted by the rules and cultural forms of social life, then Adam is no more the maker of his own history than the atom is of its own explosions. Yet there needs to be more to the meaning of action than what a particular agent took himself to be up to on specific occasions. Otherwise 'understanding' is merely describing or redescribing, and serves at most to set the explanatory agenda. Adam's claim to be a sovereign artificer seems to depend on Meaning being more than the alpha and less than the omega of understanding.

That ushers in some awkward epistemological questions. The

hermeneutic imperative is to understand action from within. How do we know when we have succeeded? How can we tell a better interpretation from a worse one? The answer cannot be meekly to accept the actors' own verdict. For, firstly, there is a notorious Other Minds problem in understanding the actors' own understanding, and it is further complicated if the actors are to be the judges of its solution. This is plainest in anthropology but Other Cultures are just a tuppence-coloured version of Other Minds. Secondly, more goes on in the social world than the actors, singly or collectively, notice and understand. Actors' accounts can be not just incomplete but also mistaken. Many actors are well aware of it – otherwise there would be no research funds for social science.

So we need a vantage point for assessing insider accounts, and one which is epistemologically robust. We need a category which lets the enquirer know when he has identified what the actors are doing and when he has understood why they are doing it. It must respect Adam's sovereign artifice and yet allow a wider view. That sets a riddle: 'When is a science not a science?' The best answer in hermeneutic vein seems to me: 'When it studies rational action'. At any rate, that is the answer to be explored in this book. The category which lets us make most objective yet interpretative sense of social life is Rationality.

The thought is not novel. It occurred notably to Max Weber, whose comments at the beginning of *Economy and Society* provide the best starting point. 'The science of society', he wrote, 'attempts the interpretative understanding of social action.' In action is included 'all human action, when and in so far as the acting individual attaches subjective meaning to it'. By social action is meant action 'which takes account of the behaviour of others and is thereby oriented in its course'. Subjective meanings are not simply private, but are connected with a public system of values. Social action, however, is not just conforming action, since individuals can have goals of their own and calculate the means to them. The proportion of calculation to conformity varies with the form of society, especially across the divide be-tween traditional societies and today's emerging rational–legal Westernised societies. But the key to understanding is to find the rational element in what social agents do.

The theme is not altogether clear, because Weber then lists four types of action, only two of which are labelled rational, and adds that most actions are of more than one type. The four are the instrumentally rational (*zweckrational*), the expressively rational (*wertrational*), the traditional and the affective. Of these, the idea of *zweckrational* action is readily grasped, being the familiar economists' notion of action which embodies the choice of the likeliest means to a given end. Understanding it, however, is not merely a matter of identifying the agent's ends (by reproducing his preferences) and the calculation which resulted in the choice (by reproducing his beliefs and information processing). Weber proposes the construction of an 'ideal-type' of the kind found in microeconomic theory, which lays out an optimal solution to the agent's problem of maximising the value of a variable subject to constraints. The ideal-type serves as a yardstick. Where the agent scores full marks, his action is thereby understood. Where the agent scores less than full marks, his departures need a further explanation, but the ideal-type has done the crucial job of identifying what they are. This method extends to all instrumental choices of action, even if we have no fully articulated theory. For instance the first step to understanding a general's decision in a battle is to ask what the optimal decision would have been. I shall say no more now about the merits and snags of an 'economic' notion of rationality, since they occupy the next chapters of the book.

Action is *wertrational* when the goal is so dominant for the actor that it drives out calculation of means and consequences. Acts of heroism and self-sacrifice are examples and, more broadly, some acts done from duty or principle. Understanding is a matter of grasping why the values expressed had such overriding significance for the actor. This is much less clear, especially since Weber distinguishes *wertrational* from traditional action, which might seem to be its obvious case. Traditional action is defined as 'the expression of settled custom' and glossed as often 'simply a dull reaction to accustomed stimuli'. Is conforming to a norm because it is the norm to be thought of as '*wertrational*' or as 'traditional'? The difference, if any, is further obscured by Weber's remarking that most actions are of mixed types (including the 'affective' type, where the agent is prompted by a simple, unreflective desire). Presumably there is a distinction here between principled action in a largely rational–legal society and norm-governed action in a largely pre-modern one. For the moment, however, I note that there appears to be a second, expressive kind of rational action, whose character will become urgently puzzling as the book goes along.

Obscurities aside, Weber offers to put teeth into hermeneutics by having the social scientist first find the actor's own reasons for action and then judge their adequacy. This seems to me an intensely plausible reading of how microeconomics contributes to social understanding and how, therefore, the category of Meaning can be usefully glossed in terms of Rationality. At the same time, however, he also insists that explanation must be adequate both at the level of meaning and at the causal level. The former requires a method of understanding (*Verstehen*), which starts with 'empathy', or an awareness of what a person is doing akin to perception, and progresses to rational reconstruction through ideal-types. The latter calls for something Humean – causal explanation (*Erklären*) in the form of social statistics to show that what has been found by understanding is also typical of a common type of behaviour.

That sets a puzzle about the relation of the two levels. The idea, I think, is that rational reconstruction yields merely possible explanations, which become reliable only if they have empirical, predictive support. At any rate one common complaint about hermeneutic approaches is that they knit possible caps which fit the actors' heads but provide no way of knowing which cap the actors were actually wearing. Yet, if the final test of an interpretation is at the causal level, then *Verstehen* is ultimately only a heuristic device, a short cut to explanations which are finally in other terms. That would be consistent with the thinking of 'positive' social science, where conjectures and heuristics are welcome from all sources, provided that the logic of validation remains one of predictions derived from causal generalisations and upheld by experience. Weber himself seems to regard *Verstehen* sometimes as a distinct and genuine form of explanation, needing only reassurance at the causal level, and sometimes as an aid to causal explanation. He thus leaves unresolved the deeper puzzle of how an insider's or agent's point of view finally relates to an outsider's or spectator's one for purposes of social science.

I am happy to leave this ambiguity to the end of the book.

Meanwhile these hasty references to Weber have served to set the agenda. Revert to God's promise to make Adam his own free and sovereign artificer, who takes his place, aspect and prerogatives by his own decision. I shall be asking whether this humanism offers terms which a social science can accept by modelling Adam as a rational agent. The challenge is not just to be able to account for individual action within given parameters. 'Sovereign artificers' also make their places and prerogatives – the social fabric itself. Luckily 'Adam' is ambiguously singular or plural. What is not intentionally chosen by individuals singly can be jointly chosen. What is not chosen even in concert may yet be the intelligible sum of the consequences of individual choices. If the idea works, Adam can start the book as an individual rational agent and end it as mankind at large. 'Rational' is the key mystery term, to be decoded as the problems of understanding social action emerge.

With that hint at the theme, I turn now to a sketch of its components, using simple, clean lines to give an aerial view of the stages of the argument. Aerial views can be very misleading about the terrain at ground level. Expert readers will be aware that it is tangled, full of thorn bushes and occupied by argumentative tribes. Others may be lulled into the false security which comes from being handed a marked map in advance of trying the terrain for themselves. They may find that the outline makes better, because truer, sense after the expedition. But, although the clarity of the next few pages is only superficial, I hope that a marked map will give a helpful sense of direction.

There is no mystery about what the term 'rational' means to start with. Chapter 2 sets out a standard anatomy of rational choice by a single individual, intent on maximising his net utility within constraints. The anatomy is borrowed from microeconomics in a form which leads easily into the theory of n-person games. In chapter 3 Eve joins Adam, and it is shown how what is a parameter for each singly can be within their power to fashion collectively. Microeconomics is implicitly a very general theory of social action and even of the social framework. I shall treat *homo economicus* as an ambitious conjecture about *homo sapiens*, which applies wherever people make instrumentally rational choices. Game-theoretic analysis of co-operation and competition not only crosses the apparent divide between the economic and the political or social but also offers to exhibit norms and institutions as deposits from previous games. We have the heady prospect of an individualist, contractarian theory of the social world.

This vision is not remotely plausible if the analysis is confined to the intended and desired consequences of individual choices. Some games solve co-ordination problems. For instance the British convention of driving on the left can be so construed. Other games end with a collective sum of individually rational choices which no one wants, although there is another possible outcome which all would have preferred. Here lies the notorious Prisoner's Dilemma, whose importance is clearly seen if one reads it into Hobbes' *Leviathan* as his account of why 'covenants without the sword are but vain breath'. In deference to Hobbes I term the crux the 'Leviathan trap' and threaten to bring contractarian thinking to an impasse. This is where the Cunning of Reason comes in. Hegel was not the first to spot that the consequences of individual actions can sum to unintended yet systematic outcomes. But his phrase catches my imagination. I do not respond to his suggestion that a World Spirit may be weaving a pattern in history in some amiable, or at least progressive, way. The attraction lies partly with 'cunning' and partly with 'reason'. The cunning springs surprises, which can explain collective mischief produced by individual rationality as well as public good produced by individual self-interest. 'Reason' suits the idea that an apparent snag of rational-choice theory can be transformed into a powerful extension of the theory.

The thought is trailed in chapter 4, where the Cunning of Reason makes the first of three appearances in the book. But I conclude that it cannot be incorporated until we know more about the motivation of a rational agent. Chapter 5 uncovers the Humean philosophy of mind involved in assuming that only desires can motivate and that a rational agent's desires need only be consistent. Taken seriously, these assumptions yield absurdities so large that chapter 6 substitutes a Kantian philosophy of mind for the Humean one. The ideal-type rational agent has good reasons for his desires and beliefs and hence for his actions. He is likened to a Kantian moral agent. This makes it easier to understand how it can be rational to act on principles, and it gives leverage on the jaws of the Leviathan trap.

Having peopled the ideal-type world with agents who have rational preferences, I turn in chapter 7 to a new puzzle about rational belief. A rational agent needs to know the consequences, or likely consequences, of his options. But what if they depend on what other agents will decide to do, which depends on what they expect others to decide? A radical indeterminacy enters, rather as if tomorrow's weather responded to today's forecasts. Expectations are importantly generative, I argue, and cannot be dealt with by including rational expectations in the rational agent's stock of information. Decision infects prediction in a way alien to natural science and unsettling for ideas of probability.

This radical indeterminacy makes nonsense of the initial assumption that rational agents are maximisers. Prompted by Herbert Simon's theory of 'bounded' rationality, chapter 8 makes Adam a 'satisficer', whose search for information is only as complete as it is rational for it to be. This move also leads us into some features of organistions. It becomes urgent that Organisation Man can have radically plural goals and hence 'satisfices' for the deeper reason that he must satisfy several incommensurable claims upon him. The attempt to analyse organisations as if they were individuals starts to go into reverse, with the suggestion that individuals are like organisations. A new Adam emerges, one whose reasons for action derive, partly but importantly, from his social positions and roles. *Homo sociologicus* takes the stage.

That will not be too dramatic a revision, if the Cunning of Reason can do more to organise the social world for *homo economicus*. Chapter 9 takes the business of unintended consequences a step further. Perhaps individual choices, considered collectively, can generate social structures which have their own systematic consequences. If so, *homo sociologicus* can still be *homo economicus* socialised. But functionalist notions of constraints, which serve the dynamics of the social structure, are too strong for Adam's comfort, if he is to survive as a sovereign artificer. There is more promise in the idea that systems consist of rules, which not only constrain but also enable. That sets a difficult question about the relation of rules to choices or, as chapter 10 puts it, of roles to reasons. Adam is there presented as a rational role-player, who has 'distance' within each role and room for manoeuvre between them. Social life is a game created and played by actors, who construct their future from their available past.

It is then time to reopen the question of *Verstehen* and *Erklären*. Chapter 11 resumes the contrast and finds trouble with both halves. It offers to make honest epistemology of a hermeneutic approach by deploying four intensional concepts, those of convention, intention, legitimating reason and real reason. The first two let us identify what actors are doing, and the last two why they are doing it. The quartet is assembled as a final comment on Weber's demand for adequacy both at the level of meaning and at the causal level. The concluding balance between economic and social components of rational action is struck in chapter 12, where the Cunning of Reason is left as little work to do as possible. It is not wholly pensioned off, however, and I end somewhat messily, still holding out for a self which plays the roles, acts from the reasons and intervenes in the consequences.

Conclusion

Think of action as the result of desire plus belief and ask what marks out rational action. A promising answer is that a fully rational agent has fully ordered preferences, perfect information and faultless computing powers. He never misses an option with greater net expected utility. This is to take instrumental rationality (*Zweckrationalität*) as the primary and ideal-type case. Analysis sets off from microeconomics and decision-theory. It generalises from a single agent to several with the help of the theory of games and from economics to social life at large. With the ideal-type worked out, it can then be applied to actual life in Weberian spirit by using it, when it fits, to understand what happens or, when it does not, to identify what needs further explanation.

This ambitious programme runs into several troubles, some remediable, some not. It will not work even in its own terms while its underlying account of human motivation is Humean. But a Kantian substitute restores its prospects. When it comes to generalising from one agent to several, however, a radical indeterminacy creeps in, because expectations are generative. There is often no one outcome which it is rational to expect, since the outcome depends on a regress of expectations. The indeterminacy is partly remedied, however, by there also being normative expectations. But this requires a different kind of agent, one who satisfices not just because of uncertainty but also because of economically incommensurable roles. Yet Adam is not the creature of his roles. He is a rational steward in office and, at the same time, retains a rational partial independence of the history which he helps to make. Singly and collectively he can intervene in the consequences of actions, if he is aware of the Cunning of Reason and its habit of making mischief. Contractarian thinking is thus a powerful tool of understanding, but even its especially forceful economic version implies that the social contract produces what Rousseau calls a remarkable change in man. Rational action is finally the expression of self in a social world.

That is the theme of the book in a stark form, which belies my respect for 'Modern Political Economy' or the attempt to generalise *homo economicus* across the board. So, to start us off, let me say that, if social science is to be possible, God cannot have given Adam a completely unconstrained hand to mould and fashion himself. There have to be some limitations on even a free and sovereign artificer. The theory of rational choice is an elegant, suggestive analysis of agent sovereignty in a constraining world.

2

Rational choice

One merit of an economic notion of rational choice is that it generates subtle, elegant and powerful theorems from very simple assumptions. The theorems fill fat volumes which witness to the claim of neo-Classical economics to be the most theoretically advanced of the social sciences. The assumptions take only a couple of pages at the start of such works and are often so sketchily stated that they seem uncontroversial. Yet more hangs on them than the advanced technicalities of economics. A further merit of an economic notion of rational choice is that it can be applied in other social sciences, where it offers to ground a complete theory of social action and even of social institutions. There are, for instance, 'economic' theories of democracy, friendship, international policy, kula rings, marriage and race relations. These are certainly controversial and raise questions about the assumptions, which also echo doubts about neo-Classicism to be heard within economics itself. So it is worth taking extreme care over the exact assumptions.

I approach the task as a philosopher with warm respect for the technical expertise which economists have and I do not. Respect will take the form of avoiding some hard questions which arise at points where technical supporting theories need to be plugged into the basic model of rational choice before the advanced theorems can be derived. There are, for example, philosophical queries to raise in econometrics, but only if one knows one's way about. The basic assumptions, however, are fair game for anyone, and it soon emerges that they are philosophically charged. In this chapter and the next I shall spell out the notion of rational choice which economists, neo-Classical and of most other persuasions too, bring to the theoretical understanding of action and interaction. I shall do it with as few technicalities as possible, partly so as to bring out its general interest for other social sciences and partly so as to display its philosophical elements.

Let us start with Adam, alone in the Garden of Eden, and contemplating a choice between figs and mulberries. Some slight effort is needed for either, since the fig tree is a mile away in one direction and the mulberry bush half a mile away in another. He prefers figs to mulberries, other things being equal.

The basic elements are all here, although in very schematic form. Adam has an ordered preference among his alternatives, other things being equal. He has perfect information, in that he knows what will be the consequences of each action open to him. Each alternative will give him utility, although he must also allow for the disutility of the effort involved in each. His choice is rational if and only if he does the action whose consequences give him the greater net utility. If the greater effort of one alternative exactly cancels the greater satisfaction which it brings, then he would be equally rational to do either.

The fundamental idea is that rationality is a relation between preferences, action and consequences. The agent aims at the maximal satisfaction of his preferences. His choice of action succeeds provided that there is no other open to him which would have brought him greater net satisfaction. To ensure success his preferences must be fully and consistently ordered. He could not make a rational choice, if, for instance, action a were better for him than b, which was better than c, which was better than a. His information about the consequences must be accurate and he must process it correctly. Otherwise he may arrive at an inferior outcome. The starting point is thus a general proposition that action is a function of desire plus belief, filled in for rational action in the pure, limiting, ideal-type case by specifying ordered desires and true beliefs, correct deliberation and determinate net utilities.

This ideal-type has three sorts of latent presumptions. One is that some variables, which are ignored in the limiting case because they take a value of zero, can be smoothly given other values when the model is applied to more complicated examples. The model has what I shall call 'plug in' points, where technical supporting theories can be added as some of the more restrictive assumptions are relaxed. The second presumption is that there are parameters, within which choices can be rationally made without having to allow for the effect of the choice on them. These I shall call 'cut off' points, because they prevent inconvenient questions about whether economically rational choices are truly rational in some wider sense to be considered later. The third is that the ideal-type case is a microcosm of actual rational choice, in that it is a philosophically warranted abstraction from the choices which flesh and blood persons make, in so far as human beings succeed in being rational agents. I shall next comment on each of these three sorts of presumption.

The limiting case of Adam choosing between figs and mulberries is too simple to be directly useful. What will need to be plugged in? Firstly the model must provide for risk and uncertainty. There is risk when at least one of his feasible actions has more than one possible consequence, each with a definite probability. For instance if all figs look alike but one in ten is slightly toxic, whereas all mulberries are harmless, then the expected utility is the utility discounted for the likelihood of the various consequences. If action a produces either a consequence C_1, worth 100 utiles, 90% of the time or a consequence C_2, worth -10 utiles, 10% of the time, then the expected utility of a is $(100 \times 0.9) + (-10 \times 0.1) = 89$ utiles. These 'utiles' are the units of the old Benthamite felicific calculus and represent what one might call microwatts of inner glow. They need not be taken very seriously, at any rate until I raise the question of what exactly a rational agent is supposed to maximise in a later chapter. The point is only that risk is defined in terms of a specifiable probability distribution whose effect on the calculation of utilities is mathematically precise. Talk of utiles is a neat way of making this clear, without having to go into the niceties of how a sophisticated decision-theory might do without supposing their real existence.

Uncertainty arises when consequences vary in likelihood, but not in a precise way. It is an ordinal concept rather than a cardinal one and is suited to the fact that, in predicting what will happen, we are rarely like someone about to draw a card at random from a pack of known composition. Most decisions are made in the knowledge only that various outcomes are more or less likely than others, or perhaps merely with a degree of comparative confidence in one outcome against others. This sets a problem for decision-theory, which a different sort of book would take very seriously. But, for purposes of presenting a clean sketch of the basic model of rational choice, there is the useful device of working with subjective probability distributions. Uncertainty can be assimilated to risk by assuming that the agent assigns cardinal utilities coherently from his own point of view. By analogy, think how the indefinite and uncertain prospects of a horse race are rendered cardinal by bookies, who convert them into definite odds, in so far as this involves a reckoning of the horses and not just a juggling of the amounts staked.

Adam thus has a subjective probability distribution for the possible consequences of his feasible actions and can arrive at a choice governed by expected utilities. I shall in general presume that this gives enough of a 'plug in' point for the basic model. But one reservation needs to be entered now. Chapter 7 will be about Rational Expectations and will raise questions about the relation of prediction to decision in human affairs. Where what will happen depends on what people expect to happen, it ceases to be plain that individuals can be credited with a subjective probability distribution for outcomes. Until then, however, the assumption will serve.

Secondly, although there was mention of costs in Adam's choice, it needs to be more explicit. The idea is that a simple preference for figs over mulberries is systematically affected by their relative costs. If he would walk an extra half-mile for the figs but not an extra mile, we suppose that there is a notional cross-over point at, say, 0.8 of a mile, where he would be indifferent between the alternatives. The model needs to be able to identify costs in ways which let their inclusion be systematic. This is not always straightforward. For instance the agent may not always know his costs in advance of incurring them. Or he may know what they would be, if incurred, but not be sure that the action would incur them. To complicate matters, costs are at heart opportunity costs. In choosing figs, he incurs the opportunity cost not only of missing out on mulberries but also of forgoing a morning's leisure. If all effort is a cost, then leisure is always a possible choice, with its own costs and consequences.

I shall, in the main, regard questions of cost as technical, in the sense that the basic model need say little about them beyond offering a point where technical answers can be plugged in, as soon as the general reflection that all costs involve opportunity costs ceases to be precise enough. But it is worth noting that what counts as a cost depends on the angle of vision. For example it is not plainly true for everyone that all effort is a cost. The idea that the rational agent always needs an incentive to do anything at all is dubitable. It is connected with the thought that voluntary social relations are instrumental and so engaged in only for mutual gain, which is dubitable too. Also costs vary with the character of the agent, so that, for example, if Adam acquires a taste for walking, or even perhaps a belief that exercise is good for him, distance ceases to be a cost. Matters arising because of the angle of vision are not just technical, and will be taken up again later. But, if we linger now, the model will not be set up. So let us agree that rational choice is, so far, a function of preferences, likelihoods and constraints, as represented by costs.

Thirdly there is more to say about preferences, even at the basic level. Adam is fully informed about his own preferences. The idea is that he can order all the possible consequences of his feasible actions by a series of pairwise comparisons. It can be spelt out in various slightly different ways and, were this a book on economic theory, concerned with exactly which formal axioms are needed for exactly which formal theorems, it would be worth dwelling on the definitions of terms like 'transitivity', 'continuity' and 'independence'. But it will, I hope, be enough for my purposes if I state the idea with the aid of just two concepts and without prejudice to any further requirement of formal economic theory. The concepts are those of completeness and consistency. For each pair he either ranks one above the other or ranks them equally. This gives him a *complete* ordering, since it rules out the kind of indifference which goes with not knowing, or not even having considered, how an outcome would compare with others. For each trio, if he ranks one at least equal to the second, and the second at least equal to the third, then he does not rank the third above the first. This gives him a *consistent* ordering. It ensures that a preference schedule, got by summing pairs into larger sets, never leaves him with a choice between *a* and *b* which varies with the marginal comparisons, which he uses to arrive at it. His preferences, then, are complete and consistent.[1]

The assumption that agents have such fully ordered preferences and know it is wildly implausible. But, as before, we should distinguish two sorts of doubt. If the complaint is that no one in fact has such a comprehensive ranking, then the reply is that the ideal-type case is a limiting case which defines rational choice. For more practical purposes, an agent need only have preferences over a relevant range and of a sort which does not lead him into inconsistency. Similarly, an attempt to argue for *revealed* preferences on the empirical ground that the test of a preference is what people do, rather than what they say after introspection, should be resisted. The theory of rational choice is predicated on *given* preferences and it does not matter in the ideal-type case how the agent knows what they are. These preferences need to be distinct from the behaviour, which they help to explain, if they are to count as explanatory. So it is conceptually neater to treat them as introspected; and practical doubts can wait.

If the complaint is that no one *could* have such knowledge in advance, however, it needs to be taken seriously from the start. The model is set up for, so to speak, shopping in a small super-market. Shoppers have shopping lists which they will rearrange once they know what is in stock at what prices. The model includes enough to guarantee that a fully rational shopper will reach the check-out with a basket of goods which cannot be improved on by substituting anything on the shelves for anything in the basket. That can be defended against charges of unrealism, provided that the idea of a given shopping list is in order. But there is trouble as soon as the model is generalised to

---

[1] The textbooks add a third condition, reflexivity, specifying that he must rank each consequence at least equal to itself (and hence exactly equal to itself). I cannot see why it is useful to say so. It seems to be a condition which has strayed in from formal logic to guarantee that the rational agent is not off his head. In that case, why stop there? Meanwhile notice that I have stated the consistency condition in its weak form, sometimes termed 'acyclicity'. For more casual purposes, there is no harm in thinking of preference in an everyday sense where to prefer *a* to *b* is to rank *a* above *b*. This too is a transitive relation.

any areas of life where the ends are not given in advance of the choice of means. Even in the economic sphere agents want the utility of the services which the possession of goods offers, rather than the goods themselves. Although that is a helpful thought, when one reflects that the actual products on the market change, it also makes the matter of substitutes (and of opportunity costs) much trickier. Think of a shopper who is trying to buy a present for his aunt without knowing what she would like instead, if precisely what she wants is out of stock. Then think of a businessman who is trying to decide what to include in the leisure complex which he is planning without knowing precisely which features of previously successful complexes are the ones which customers value. The shopping-list analogy soon becomes tenuous in the extreme.

Moreover 'utility' covers very varied satisfactions. Even consumption goods range from the bread we eat to the Georgian door-knockers meant to impress our neighbours, from electricity to communion wine. If the theory is to be generalised to life at large, agents must know their preferences for experiences which they have not sampled, for relationships which they have not entered into and for ways of life which they have not tried. They must be able to weigh their self-regarding against their moral concerns. The whole idea that rational choice is instrumental in the service of given goals will become harder to maintain. But here I mean only to give warning. The model extends to any action which can be exhibited as a means to an antecedent goal, provided that the goal can be assimilated to an element in the agent's preference schedule. I shall defend it in this way with fair ingenuity, but shall also contend later that some preferences can only be formed in the course of action or interaction.

Finally among the 'plug in' points there needs to be one for information and its processing. The latter is to be thought of as calculation (for example the finding of formal solutions to maximising problems) or computation (where it helps to represent the agent by means of a computer program). The former consists of rationally held beliefs in a form ready for processing. In the main I shall assume that any puzzles about information and in processing are technical. But two caveats should be entered now. The lesser is that information has costs in time, trouble and expense and, where there is no way of deciding whether it is worth acquiring extra information, short of actually acquiring it, there is a problem which will be raised in chapter 8. The greater is that where expectations depend on what other agents expect other agents to expect, there arises a deep question about rationality which will loom very large in chapter 7. In sundry ways knowledge, or rational belief, does not always behave as a smooth variable with a second derivative, as if imperfections of information could be treated like degrees of friction in a theory of frictionless motion.

Let us take stock. Adam, dwelling alone in the garden, is perfectly informed about the figs and mulberries, the costs of each and their effects on his level of utility. He knows which he would prefer, other things being equal, and he knows just how unequal other things are. Being ideally rational, he makes the choice which maximises his expected utility. The model is not limited to this case, however. It can cope with risk and at least some kinds of uncertainty and with refined problems of assessing costs. It is not confined to cases where the agent has an exhaustive set of preferences and perfect information. In short we have a promising basic idea of rationality as instrumental choice of what maximises expected utility.

One important feature of the basic idea is that it makes the rational agent a bargain-hunter. He never pays more than he must and never gets less than he could at the price. If actions *a* and *b* are equally likely to be effective in achieving a goal and if *a* costs less and has no less welcome further consequences than *b*, then he will not choose *b*. If *a* and *b* have the same costs but different consequences and he prefers those of *a*, he will not choose *b*. These propositions are logically implied in the definition of rational choice. They give the basic idea a useful cutting edge, since they introduce the notion of marginal utility. Even in indeterminate cases, where it is unclear what is the agent's best choice, they guarantee that he will reject inferior ones. The logic of the model guarantees *a priori* that where one choice dominates another, in the sense of at least matching it in some respects and surpassing it in at least one respect, the inferior will be rejected, however slight its inferiority.

This sharp implication cuts both ways, since it is the source not only of some elegant theorems about the mathematics of indifference curves but also of some celebrated puzzles, which will occupy us when we reach the Prisoner's Dilemma. At this stage, however, I wish merely to note it, together with a remark about the agent's motivation. 'Bargain-hunting' may suggest a grasping, penny-pinching, short-sighted selfishness. That is not what the basic model asserts or implies. Adam may turn out to be generous, far-seeing and altruistic; but, even if he does, he will still reject even slightly inferior ways of exercising these qualities. So far utility-maximisation is a very bland notion, and questions about the motivation asserted or implied must wait until chapter 5.

I turn now to the 'cut off' points. The basic model has been introduced by freezing social action in its frame, so that various elements of a social activity can be taken as given. I shall next identify these elements and then end with some questions for later, which arise because the freezing of the film is an artifice.

Closest to the centre of the action is the agent's preference schedule. Rational choice has been defined as choice which is instrumental in securing the agent's goals. These goals need to be made internal to the agent and they need to be fixed, since otherwise expected utilities cannot be calculated. So they take the form of given preferences. In the simplest case they are tastes, as if the economic story started by adding a dash of calculation to what Weber calls 'affections' and others in the Humean tradition have called 'sentiments'. It is in the spirit of things here to quote the Latin tag *de gustibus non disputandum* – 'There is no arguing about tastes.' It seems very obvious how tastes or sentiments move us to action. To the general thought that action is a function of desires plus beliefs, we may add the Humean rider that only desire can move an agent. Given preferences are thus the first parameter and, in assuming them, the model cuts off questions which I shall none the less raise later.

Secondly Adam is alone in the garden so far. One might complain that nothing very revealing will happen until Eve arrives. But, crucially, interaction is not the basic case for the theory of rational choice. When Eve arrives, Adam has to allow for her likely behaviour, when estimating the likely consequences of his feasible choices. She does likewise when deciding on hers. Their interaction is the sum of the choices made by each. In other words any problems of prediction set by risk or uncertainty in a natural environment are merely complicated by adding other agents to the environment. Interaction is analysed as action with the parameters eased to include several actors in the same frame. We shall need to see about that.

Thirdly I have been able to set out the basic model with hardly a word about time. This is partly because the only time considered is 'now', in the sense that Adam is guided only by what he desires now and believes now. It is also because of implicit reference to timeless models in physics, where there are no asymmetries between past and future like those in social life. That is a topic for the chapter on rational expectations, which I shall not broach now.

Fourthly there are no institutions in the Garden of Eden. Choices in economic, political and social life have an institutional framework. For instance a microeconomic analysis of rational choices in the theory of production and consumption sets the market within parameters of government policy and social norms. Two lines of thought are discernible. One is that it is not the job of the theory of rational choice to account for institutions. They are simply features of the agent's environment. The other and more ambitious is that institutions result from previous choices and interactions. My strategy will be to try the ambitious line and fall back on the first only if driven to it.

Fifthly Adam has no technology. This was deliberate, since I shall have little to say about the state of technology as a factor in rational choices and especially in investment decisions. For the questions raised in this book technology and its changes do not raise peculiar problems. But that would not make the matter unimportant, if the aim were a historical theory of social change. Similarly the natural environment is a given parameter and will remain one, even though much human effort is devoted to changing it, rather than merely learning to live within it. Here too there is more to think about than the book will attempt.

This list of parameters makes plain the sense in which the basic model depends on an artifice. It takes a time-slice through a moving world and thus cuts out questions which a full understanding of social action will need to take into account. That is not an objection. One cannot tackle everything at once, and we need to identify the model before asking about its scope. Its scope is a question of which parameters can be accounted for by the model itself, once action has been unfrozen to let us think about a series of actions, and which need to remain as givens for each and every rational action. The basic story has no inbuilt presumption about where the limit comes.

I call it an artifice for a different reason. In freezing action in its frame and simplifying down to a single actor making a pairwise comparison, one seems to suggest ontological priorities. With the act of choice so like a gate in a basic logic circuit, switched one way or the other by the demands of a self-contained programme, there is an air of dealing with basic units. Building on the thought, we are tempted to regard the rational individual actor as a set of preferences and a programme for arriving at instrumental choices consistent over a series. Then we complicate the story by adding other actors and (depending on how ambitious we are) thus analyse interaction, institutions, economies and even entire, changing social systems. Adam is essentially alone, is presently joined by Eve and together they are a microcosm of the social world.

No doubt there is much to be said for taking an instructor's slice through the bustle of life. But it does not necessarily reduce the bustle to its ultimate elements. The best way to learn to tango is no doubt to master one step at a time; but the tango is not an aggregate of separately intelligible steps. I am not trying yet to deny that the artifice yields ultimate units. My point is that it needs long, careful argument to prove it. No social atomism or individualism can be established just by using an elegant expository device.

Nor can the analytical neatness of an instrumental notion of rational choice prove anything about the relation of positive to normative. With action frozen in its frame, rational choice becomes like an adjourned chess position, sent for adjudication. Given the rules and objectives of the game, there is a well-defined adjudicator's question of who wins with best play on both sides. This gives a clear test for the merit of possible moves and hence of the rational choice for the player whose turn it is. Analogously, rational choice theory, aided by game theory, microeconomic theory and other analytical tools, can yield objective solutions to maximising problems for actors with a variety of preferences. That makes it a theory which is both positive and normative, in the usual definitions of those terms. It is positive, in that it reproduces the calculations of fully rational actors, rather as one might discover from the printed record of a chess match why each move was made by asking adjudicator's questions about the preceding position. It is normative, in that the reconstruction presupposes fully rational players and hence is also a source of advice for those whose choices are not the best ones. This aspect of the theory is plainest in welfare economics, where one aim is to arrive at best solutions for a policy-maker seeking to satisfy the conflicting preferences of several actors. But it also applies to any analysis of what a fully rational actor would do, for instance the microeconomic theory of the firm.

The theory of rational choice thus offers to bridge the usual divide between positive and normative. But it does so only in so far as it takes ends (or preferences) as given and merely seeks the most efficient way to achieve them. Suppose, however, that the only way to avoid questions about the rationality of an agent's goals was to assume that whatever goals he has, provided that they are consistent, are rational. Suppose also that, when this assumption was picked out and considered explicitly, it became untenable. In that case the theory of choice would either lose its claim to analyse *rational* choice or be forced into substantive claims in ethics. This daunting possibility is a topic of chapter 6. Meanwhile the point to note is that the freezing of action in its frame also cuts out moral considerations in a way which may turn out to be an artifice also.

Conclusion

The theory of rational choice does a precise job very neatly. It connects concepts of preference, action and consequence so as to give economics a starting point. If 'choice' is extended to any allocation of resources, it may perhaps do the same for our understanding of social action at large. That makes it a hugely interesting theory. But its ambitions are not warranted just by its air of reducing economic or social action to elementary units. A string of philosophically interesting questions attend all the simplifying assumptions which freeze the moving film into revealing snapshots.

The fully rational agent of the ideal-type case has complete and consistent preferences, whose domain is the consequences of his feasible actions. He knows his preferences and enough about likelihoods and costs, so that he can assign expected utilities to his options. He does so within given parameters, which include the preferences of himself and others, the existing framework of norms and institutions, government policy, the state of technology and the natural environment. He makes a maximising choice, in the sense that he always avoids the inferior options. Although not fully determinate, for instance between two equally good options or between options with different points in their favour which will not easily homogenise, this sense gives enough to work with. More loosely, he is a bargain-hunter who never gets less than he could or pays more than he must.

The theorems of microeconomics and other sophisticated implications emerge only when technical supporting systems are plugged in. 'Technical' does not mean philosophically innocent, but my theme does not lie in this direction. A philosopher also finds much of interest in the simplest assumptions of the basic model. The assimilation of preferences to antecedent tastes puts limits on the scope of the theory, when one thinks about preferences which are very unlike tastes (for instance principles) or which change as a result of choices made. The presumption that desire, rather than belief, is the only motor of action is committal in ways which I mean to challenge. So is the presumption that a theory of efficient choice which is unconcerned with the ends pursued can properly be termed a theory of rational choice. There are questions to ask also about the assimilation of belief to information and of deliberation to its processing. That makes for a very mechanical account of cognition, which will come under fire. In short, a different picture of human nature will have emerged by the end of the book.

The broader query about the parameters is whether they can all be absorbed into the model by a series of extensions. Can interaction be treated as a sum of actions? Can norms be analysed as contracts and institutions as deposits? Is the separation of economic from social, and of the market from the political arena, a tactical, expository device, which finally yields to a general analysis, where all social action is subsumed under rational choice? Or are there limits, summed up as a need for rational choice to be made on the basis of givens which must remain given, or at least be accounted for differently? I hope that the chapters which follow will provide leverage.

The immediate question is how to treat social interaction. It is time for Eve to join Adam in the garden.

3

Norms and institutions

Adam, being a rational economic agent, never underplays his hand. The logic of the model commits him to rejecting inferior options. Eve is another. The question of this chapter is how far they and their descendants can get in forming an organised communal life, if any joint activity is to be viewed as interaction among bargain-hunters. If they turn out to need help from God, that will mark a limit to the ambitions of the theory of rational choice. But it is not obvious in advance that they will need any help at all. Analysis offers a route for constructing the complex out of the simple. Action is the expression of individual preference and calculation; interaction the sum of actions; institutions an outcome of interactions. Or so many thinkers have claimed and, at worst, the thought provides a ready way to organise discussion.

Eve's arrival is the cue for the theory of games. As with microeconomic theory, the analysis of games can soon turn very technical and sophisticated. But here too there are some utterly basic moves, which are enough to get the theory moving and to excite philosophical curiosity, even without plugging in the various technical systems needed for advanced purposes. Let us start with the idea of a 'game'.

A 'game' in the theory of games is not what we ordinarily mean by the term, and needs a formal definition. There are Wittgensteinian reasons for doubting whether we in fact ordinarily mean anything definite or univocal. But I shall risk picking out one recurrent strand of family resemblance among everyday games, since it is notably absent from the starting point of game-theory. An everyday game is often a rule-governed or norm-governed activity whose material results, under some other description, could be more efficiently realised. The material results are a by-product, in other words, and incidental to the point of the activity. By contrast, game-theory works in the opposite direction. The players are out to get the best results for themselves, and are willing to introduce or keep to rules and norms only if doing so improves the outcome. The results need not be material, since the value of an outcome is assessed by its utility to the agent and 'utility', as in the previous chapter, covers any form of satisfaction. But the players' attitude to the rules is instrumental. They play the game for what they can get out of it.

A 'game' in game-theory has three formal requirements:

(1) Two or more *rational agents* each with a choice of *strategies* (i.e. agents, as defined in the last chapter, each with a choice of what were there called feasible actions).
(2) An *outcome* which is the combined result of the strategy of each agent.
(3) A *pay-off* to each agent, measured by the value of the outcome to each.

Each agent seeks to maximise the pay-off to himself through a rational choice of strategy, although with the previous proviso that agents need not have selfish preferences or take pleasure in doing others down.

It is worth pausing to emphasise the special flavour of these requirements. In game-theory individuals choose strategies: in everyday games players obey norms. That sets a conceptual difference between individuals and players. It is not a complete difference, since players of everyday games also make strategic choices. In chess, for instance, each player, within the parameters of the rules, chooses the move likeliest to maximise his advantage (or minimise his disadvantage). But the rules of chess are constitutive, in the sense that there is no choice of strategy outside them and no measure of the pay-off except by reference to what counts as winning the game. There are also regulatory rules, which guide good play. For example it is a good rule to post knights well forward and centrally, provided that they cannot be attacked by pawns. This is not a rule from the rule book, but a useful rule of play. There is, however, no sense in which the invention of chess solves an antecedent problem of how to shift small bits of wood from place to place. That might make one wonder whether game-theory can help in understanding norm-governed social activities, where the participants are always role-players.

On the other hand it is silly to suggest that the external, previous problem was one of shifting wood. Chess is a pleasant pastime. It emerged in modern form from earlier versions, which were less enjoyable and which perhaps emerged in turn from less-organised amusements. So the rules of chess can be conceived as an instrumental solution to an external problem. Internally the pay-offs are 'zero sum', in that one player wins only if the other loses. But, externally, even the loser has had an enjoyable evening. To generalise, game-theory offers an analysis of the emergence of norms which turns rational individuals into norm-governed role players by a series of logical steps. To start with, each individual acts in the light of what he merely expects that others will do. His actions are not yet 'moves'. Then expectations become not only reliable but also binding. Norms emerge, first regulatory, then constitutive. The crux is whether this is a possible account.

The issue is a conceptual one, not genetic or historical. It is an historical fact that we live in societies governed by normative expectations, and a genetic one that we are capable of games both literal and figurative. It is presumably an historical and genetic fact that we have evolved from creatures without these skills. But I am not trying to explain this transition. My question is whether we need more for understanding institutions than we need for understanding interaction; and more for interaction than for rational individual action. We carry forward from the last chapter a budget of concepts – basically those of preference, information and consequence. Is it enough?

With Adam and Eve we have a two-person game. Call Adam actor A and Eve actor B. Let the game be about whether to pick figs or mulberries, with the former called 'strategy 1' and the latter 'strategy 0', or 1 and 0 for short. This game has four possible outcomes: 11, 00, 10, 01 (i.e. both figs, both mulberries, Adam figs with Eve mulberries and *vice versa*). The pay-off to each depends on how each ranks these outcomes. (Ordinal ranking will suffice for what follows.) Initially, since there is no shortage of fruit and neither player cares what the other does, Adam ranks only his own *1* or *0* and Eve hers. We do not yet have interaction. So let us advance to the stage where each action, in the words of Max Weber introducing social action, 'takes account of the behaviour of others and is thereby oriented in its course'. Let us do it by supposing that Adam starts to care for Eve's company and she for his.

That gives each an interest in both components of the outcome. Suppose that each ranks figs and mulberries equal but strongly prefers that both parties make the same choice. Here is a neat way of tabulating the position.

A's ranking	Outcome	B's ranking
1st=	$\begin{Bmatrix} 1 & 1 \\ 0 & 0 \end{Bmatrix}$	1st=
3rd=	$\begin{Bmatrix} 1 & 0 \\ 0 & 1 \end{Bmatrix}$	3rd=

(An outcome of '*1 0* means A chooses *1* and B chooses *0*.) Now the ranking of each does depend on what the other chooses. What difference does this make to their choices?

At this stage it makes none. I shall not let them communicate, since an ambitious reading of game-theory seeks to find an explanatory understanding of language in it (see Lewis (1969)). If their preferences and pay-offs are exactly symmetrical and they are going to play the game only once, it is a matter of luck whether they reach the first- or third-best outcome. Nor does it help to let each know the other's preferences. So let us unfreeze the frame enough to allow the game to be repeated. Admittedly they are no further forward, if they make opposite choices on the first occasion. But, rather than let them become indefinitely frustrated, let us suppose that one morning they luckily make the same choice. It is essential for game-theory that each now has a reason to repeat the choice on the next occasion. The rational choice apparatus in the previous chapter does not explicitly license this construal, but it does not forbid it, and I shall allow it. In that case the lucky choice becomes salient with repeated play.

A convention has emerged, owing to luck and a desire by both parties for one. With it the expected utilities of actions change and the position becomes:

A's ranking	Outcome		B's ranking
1st	1	1	1st
2nd	0	0	2nd
3rd=	$\left\{\begin{matrix} 1 & 0 \\ 0 & 1 \end{matrix}\right\}$		3rd=

This is a first basic game and its solution. The game is solved by the emergence of a convention, which is stable in that neither player has any reason to depart from it. There is no need for a previous history of other conventions, or for sanctions and enforcements. Adam and Eve have learnt to co-ordinate their strategies and hence to co-operate for mutual benefit.

I shall call the game 'General Will', since it contains the bones of Rousseau's theory of the social contract, whereby equal and rational individuals arrive at collective action by ranking the outcomes by how well they serve the general will. It is only bare bones, since Rousseau's social contract transforms human nature and his general will involves more than mutual back-scratching. But it catches the nub of social contract theories, which assume that human nature is so constituted as to give us a common interest in co-operation. In that case tacit conventions can emerge through repetition (with a little luck) and remain stable without sanctions, because no one has any reason to depart from them. Another example is how two strangers can each take an oar in a rowing boat and gradually fall into rhythm. Any comfortable rhythm will do; no words are needed; once found, it continues. This example is Hume's, and it hints at a further aspect of the game. When A and B have achieved a rhythm, each expects the other to keep to it. So far that means only that each so predicts with success. But it begins to emerge that each is entitled to expect the other to continue and is, somehow, entitled to complain otherwise. If the General Will game contains this aspect of the social contract, it is going to be important.

Call the solution a 'consensual norm'. There is no problem set for the theory of rational choice by summary rules – rules of thumb which summarise common practice in a predictively reliable way. The fact that *1* is the common practice gives each actor with an interest in co-ordination a reason for choosing *1*. No institutional decision is needed, and an institutional habit, which emerges, does so ready analysed. But an element of moral or legal entitlement is suggested by the term 'consensual norm'. *A* is entitled to be surprised if *B* suddenly switches to *0*. Is he yet entitled to complain? I think not. *A*'s good reason to expect *1* from *B* does not imply that *B* is at fault. Although Eve has knowingly given Adam reason to expect a fig expedition tomorrow, she has not committed herself. If Adam spends all this afternoon making a gadget to pick figs faster (one which does not work on mulberries), he is going to be rationally disappointed by a change in her habits. But she as yet owes him nothing.

The short comment is that so far there is no need for a notion of moral or legal entitlement. That arises only when, without one, players have a reason to depart from their tacit conventions. The simplest way to bring this out is to introduce a fresh game. Adam has gone through the process of naming the cattle and the fowls of the air and the beasts of the field as recorded in Genesis chapter 2; Eve has adopted these names and whatever else a language needs. They can communicate and are getting on nicely together. Last night they agreed that today they would make a long expedition to a distant and dusty part of the garden, where there is no water. To improve their collective geography, they agreed to travel separately. They agreed also that one of them would bring a large and heavy gourd of water. But each has forgotten who was to do this service and, since all effort is a cost, each hopes it was the other. It would be better to have two gourds than none, but they only need one. With '*1*' for 'bring a gourd' and '*0*' for 'bring none', the position is this:

A's ranking	Outcome	B's ranking
1st	0 1	4th
2nd	1 1	2nd
3rd	0 0	3rd
4th	1 0	1st

Now follows an absolutely crucial piece of reasoning. *A* reflects that *01* is a better outcome for him than *11*; so, if *B* is going to choose *1*, *A* does best to choose *0*. He reflects also that *00* is better for him than *10*; so, if *B* is going to choose *o*, *A*'s best choice is *o*. Hence *A* does better to choose *o*, *whatever B chooses*. By parity of reasoning *B* decides to choose *o*, whatever *A* chooses. Each chooses *o* regardless and the outcome is *oo*. They end up with no water, even though both agree that two gourds (*11*) are better than none.

This dry result is central to game–theory. It arises directly out of the theory of rational choice, in the sense that *A*'s choice can be rationally determined without regard to *B*'s preferences. An agent who ranks the outcomes in the order *o1, 11, oo, 10* has a *dominant* reason to choose *o*. That is true for each and every agent, and generalises readily to *n* players, who will therefore generate an outcome inferior for all of them, despite the fact that there was a possible outcome better for all. That the reason is dominant follows directly from the remarks about bargain-hunting. Since *A* prefers *oo* to *10*, he cannot aim for *10*. Since he prefers *o1* to *11*, he cannot aim for *11*. That is enough to clinch the matter, rather as it settles the truth of *p*, if *p* is implied by *q* and also implied by *not-q*.

Of many illustrations, fictitious and real, the best known is perhaps the Prisoner's Dilemma, which has also become the generic name of the game. Here *A* and *B* are prisoners in gaol, awaiting trial. They are charged with burglary, which the police can prove, and may also be charged with murder, which cannot be proved without a confession. The police offer each separately the option of turning Queen's, or state's, evidence by confessing to the murder, with the reward that both charges against him will be dropped if he alone confesses. If one confesses, the other gets a life sentence. If both confess, both get ten years (a mitigation for being helpful). If neither confesses, both get two years for burglary. Each has a dominant reason to confess, with the result that each does worse than he need.

Generalising to *n* players, we get the equally famous 'Free-Rider' paradox. If each groups the players into 'Self' and 'Others' and has the fatal ranking *o1, 11, oo, 10*, then each chooses *o* and the outcome is *oooooo* . . . even though *111111* . . . would have suited everyone better. A literal example is where a trust box is installed in a train, so as to reduce the cost of travel for all by doing away with ticket sellers. If all travellers use the box, all benefit. But suppose that each most prefers that he travels free, while others pay,

35

and least prefers that he pays, while others travel free. Then each has a dominant reason not to pay. The train is withdrawn and the free-riders lose their vehicle, through their own self-defeating choices. Analogously it looks as if rational agents will fail to vote in elections, fail to save water voluntarily in droughts, fail to hold back on wage demands which ruin the economy, fail to shun the suburban hypermarkets which bleed their urban environment and fail to conserve the stock of whales on which their livelihood depends. At any rate these are typical cases (at telegraphic speed), often claimed to exhibit the fatal preference order which leads all to defeat their second-best outcome by contributing to their third-best.

A venerable instance with deeper import can be read into Hobbes' *Leviathan*. Here each individual in the state of nature would most like to advance his own interests at the expense of others. But if all try it, there will be a 'state of warre', marked by continual fear and danger of violent death. The life of man will be 'solitary, poor, nasty, brutish and short'. All would be far better served by a state of Peace, which allows commodious living. But Hobbes' state of nature presents a free-rider problem, because, writing '*1*' for 'co-operation' and '*0*' for 'non-co-operation', each has the fatal ranking *01, 11, 00, 10*, with *111111* . . . representing Peace and *000000* . . . representing Warre. That means Warre, unless there is a social contract to secure Peace. Yet each retains his natural dispositions when subscribing to the social contract which it is rational for them to make. So, when we ask whether they will keep the contract, we find the same snag. If we write '*1*' for 'Keep' and '*0*' for 'Break', each again has a ranking of *01, 11, 00, 10*, and the contract collapses. Hobbes' solution is to make the contract enforceable. It takes the form of 'a common power to keep them all in awe', and embodies the reflection that 'covenants without the sword are but vaine breath'. I shall turn to this solution in a moment. Meanwhile Hobbes has so constituted his actors that there is a puzzle about how society is possible. It is a more fertile puzzle, to my mind, than the one symbolised by asking how two strangers can learn to row a boat in rhythm. As a gesture of respect, I shall speak of the fatal ranking *01, 11, 00, 01* as 'the Leviathan trap' and the game among trapped players as 'the Leviathan game'.

At first sight the difference between General Will and Leviathan springs from assumptions about the players' motivation. General Will is the game which captures theories of the social contract which credit human nature with compatible impulses, whereas Hobbes seems to start from human beings so greedy, so keen to steal a march on others, that no one can resist trying for a bit on the side, unless kept in awe. Similarly the Prisoner's Dilemma may seem to depend on there being no honour among thieves and the Free-Rider Paradox on a shocking lack of public spirit. But this way of looking at it confuses rationality assumptions with motivational assumptions. Although the two will turn out not to be finally separable, at this stage they should be kept firmly apart. The difference in the kind of social contract so far arises solely from the difference in the rankings of outcomes which the players bring to the game. General Will solves as soon as one of its possible equilibria becomes salient. The only puzzle set by a social contract theory which makes it basic is why social order is even fragile, when consensual norms should suffice. In Leviathan the players have dominant rational choices which sum to a self-defeating outcome. If this is the basic game for the theory of the social contract, the puzzle is how social order is possible at all. Nothing has yet been said about motivation in either case.

It might be argued that Hobbes is wrong about human motivation on the grounds that social life is full of Leviathan traps which do not in fact produce self-defeating outcomes. Often at least, people help old ladies across the road, take litter home from picnics, patronise their local corner shops and turn out to vote in elections. When the hat is passed round at a charity show, they put something in rather than, Leviathan-style, taking something out. Indeed the very existence of society, as a triumph of Peace over Warre, shows a co-operative spirit in human nature. But nothing about motivation follows. It follows merely that these examples are only *prima facie*. Someone who helps an old lady across the road cannot possibly be a rational agent, whose ranking order is: '(1st) she gets across with no help from me; (2nd) I help her across; (3rd) I stay put and she gets run over; (4th) I make the effort and she still gets run over.'

Conversely it does not support Hobbes' account of human motivation to argue that these examples are indeed Hobbesian when one realises that there are other implicit motivating elements. Perhaps the old lady will tell her neighbours (or mine) whether I helped her. Perhaps I shall need her trust when I have business with her tomorrow. In general, Hobbesian persons will refrain from driving hard, short-run bargains, especially in small face-to-face communities, where today's grasping is punished tomorrow. But, again, this shows only that we are not in fact dealing with a rational agent whose rank order is *01, 11, 00, 10*. If someone playing the first of a series of games does not act as he would if the game were one-shot, then it follows only that the prospect of a series influences the rankings. For instance, if the outcomes which would be ranked *01, 11, 00, 10* in a one-shot game become *11, 01, 00, 10* when the game is part of a series, then the player no longer has a dominant reason to choose *0*. In other words, any solution to the Leviathan puzzle which involves embedding a one-shot game in a series or 'supergame' where preferences are different is not to be seen as a genuine solution.

This last ranking, if each player has it, produces what is commonly termed an Assurance game, since each will choose *1*, provided that he is assured of others' willingness to do the same. A real-life example is the Fleuro-select organisation of horticulturalists. Horticulturalists have a problem which arises because new varieties of seed take time, trouble and expense to produce but are easily pirated the following year. The large growers have solved it by making a mutual promise not to poach for an agreed number of years. The promise is embodied in the Fleuro-select organisation. The Assurance game is common and important, but it is not a version of the Leviathan game. No doubt many apparent examples of the latter turn out to be Assurance games on closer inspection. But the puzzle before us is how a rational agent who is caught in a Leviathan trap can escape. It does not help to point out that the trap is less common than it might look.

I grant that fiercely self-interested agents may be trapped more often than others. No doubt persons who are both stupid and greedy are forever spoiling the ship for a ha'p'orth of tar. But this is because they find themselves trapped more often and not because, once trapped, they have fewer ways of escape. Conversely, saints too can be trapped. In an overloaded lifeboat full of rational saints, all will be drowned as each leaps overboard. In less flippant vein, a community who meekly practise submission can leave all its members worse situated than they need be. Although serious examples are harder to find than for rampant egoists, they do exist, as will become clear as we touch on the topic of positional goods. Meanwhile the point stands that saints are less often trapped, not that they escape more easily. The trap is set solely by the rank order *01*, *11*, *00*, *10*.

Hobbes' solution, as noted, is to introduce coercive norms, the first of which is the Hobbesian social contract itself. With norms established, Leviathan games can often become Assurance games. The norms need to be coercive to prevent the players having the same free-riding reason for breaking them as they had for setting them up. In Hobbes' version they have to be enforced by the sword, and the sword belongs to one single central authority. This yields a political theory in which the state has a monopoly of legitimate power, although with very limited scope, so that individuals can make whatever private contracts they wish. The state's job is not to interfere with private arrangements but to police them. His specific version depends on his specific view of human motivation, however, and I shall not pursue it now. The general point is that it can be rational to make a contract without its being thereby rational to keep it. Norms which govern bargain-hunting are vulnerable to bargain-hunting and need to be backed by reasons not to renege. The sword is not the only possible reason. Milder theories of human nature give the job to enlightened self-interest, natural sympathy or moral responsibility, as we shall see. But some reason is needed.

That poses a subtle but crucial problem. The idea is that, if each player knows that each player ranks the outcomes *01*, *11*, *00*, *10*, then each can see that, unless something is done to change the rankings, the outcome will be *00*; and each therefore has sufficient reason to accept a norm which would make the change. Each also has reason to accept a change in his own ranking as the price of guaranteeing the change in others by means of an effective norm. But, analytically, these reflections are prior to any institutions. So it would plainly be cheating to assume a Legislator or Sheriff, who imposes the norm by fiat. It would also be cheating, less plainly but no less naughtily, to presume that, since coercive norms do emerge somehow, it is as if all had chosen to obey an imaginary Legislator or Sheriff.[1] Each player has to be equipped to change his own ranking himself from scratch. The problem is that, so far, the grammar of the basic model prevents it.

A rational agent with a ranking of 01, 11, 00, 10 cannot fail to choose 0; and, conversely, if he were to choose 1, he cannot have had that ranking of outcomes. The point could be got round by imposing a change of expected utilities from outside, for instance by penalising free-riders and thus making 01 unattractive. It could also be got round by injecting enough irrational or non-rational behaviour to change the situation. But an ambitious theory of rational choice must make the change a rational choice from inside. That means a grammar in which an agent's rankings can range over his rankings. The new ranking must be the outcome of a choice which is rational in the sense that it maximises his utility as represented by the old ranking.

The grammar is already there in part. Eve's preferences can be straightforwardly of interest to Adam. If she develops a passion for nuts, which he hates, there is no oddity in saying that he prefers that she prefers figs to nuts. That might make it rational for him to refuse to go with her and for her to change preference, under this external stimulus, from nuts to figs. Also we already have a limited sense in which preferences can be conditional. In the opening game Adam preferred figs-if-Eve-prefers-figs to mulberries-if-Eve-prefers-figs, whatever his ranking of figs and mulberries, if left to himself alone. But we do not yet have a grammatical licence for 'Adam, who prefers figs to nuts, also prefers that Adam prefers nuts to figs.'

The snag is that Adam has so far been identified with a bundle of complete and consistent preferences, and Eve with another. One bundle can feature in the domain of another. Can it also feature in its own domain? Something must be done to block the threatened inconsistency. There are aspects of the passage of time

[1] For instance Edna Ullman-Margalit in her interesting and lively book *The Emergence of Norms* (1977) undertakes to demonstrate a 'correlation between certain types of situational problem and certain types of norms which facilitate their solution'. The demonstration, she explains airily, 'is considered an account of the generation of these norms' (p. 10). Here the Legislator's work is done by a highly abstract *post hoc ergo* as if *propter hoc*, and is no less naughty for being abstract.

which look helpful. If figs ripen before mulberries, or lose their attraction as the palate matures, then Adam might rationally choose figs today and mulberries tomorrow. But these cases do not involve a change of preferences which he has chosen. So suppose that mulberries need to be picked before they are ripe, meaning that he can have juicy mulberries long after figs have gone rotten, but only if he forgoes the figs which he would prefer now.

The grammar can include a time flag easily enough by complicating the items for pairwise comparison. Adam compares figs-now-and-nothing-hereafter with nothing-now-and-mulberries-hereafter. Someone might ask how the latter could possibly win, given that next week's mulberries give no satisfaction today. For the moment I shall give the short answer that, since I have been careful to say nothing about the possible sources of utility, we may suppose that Adam takes present satisfaction in contemplating next week's mulberries. The point will arise again presently, however. Meanwhile, the answer will do only if complicating the items compared does not prevent a single, coherent order of preferences. It does nothing to show that one's own preferences can themselves be the subject of one's own preferences.

For that we must do more than divide Adam into two bundles, coherent separately but not together. Otherwise he will simply be trapped in Leviathan games played with himself. Given the basic analysis of rational choice, he needs a single coherent set of preferences, which make it rational to choose an action which changes the set. In effect, we shall have to identify a 'plug in' point in the idea of preference which passed unnoticed in the previous chapter but which allows the complication needed.

Let us start by noticing an ambiguity in the idea of a ranking. Is a ranking to be thought of as the tailoring of antecedent preferences to particular circumstances or as the identifying of an order of expected utilities for possible outcomes specific to the case? The distinction is a fine one, and either reading can sound natural. Sometimes it is natural to say, 'Adam prefers figs, but in this case mulberries are so much less effort that he prefers mulberries'; sometimes to say, 'he would rather have mulberries today'. The difference is that the latter takes preferences as so wholly given that no questions arise about the assigning of expected utilities;

the ranking is simply the ordered list of assignments. Consequently the step from identifying the action with the greatest expected utility to choosing it is automatic, in the sense that, if the agent does anything else, either utilities have been wrongly described or he is not rational. This is the reading which goes with the basic model, and the one which I have been using for the most part.

The other is not inconsistent with it, but does start to raise questions of motivation. The agent is credited with a set of dispositional preferences, which provide an initial ranking, *ceteris paribus*, and which are then adjusted for the particular circumstances of their application. This makes it possible to understand how it can be rational to invest in bread tomorrow when immediate utilities seem to favour jam today. The basic model thus extends to the choice of indirect strategies whose aim is greater overall satisfaction of existing dispositional preferences. But that is not enough for purposes of outflanking the Leviathan trap. If Adam is to reject his dispositional preferences, he will have to be credited with a further set of underlying preferences by which to judge his current dispositions.

Formally, the further set can be marked out as 'second-order', meaning that they stand to 'first-order' preferences as the latter stand to outcomes. Thus a preference for figs is first-order and a preference for preferring figs is second-order. But the grammar of the basic model, even when extended as just done, stops us making much of this form of words. If second-order preferences are genuine preferences, then they are so in the same sense as others. It is not necessarily more rational to act on them. For instance, guilt-ridden homosexuals presumably prefer their own sex and prefer to prefer the other; but it might well be more rational to shed the guilt. Second-order preferences are, so far at least, simply in competition with first-order ones, and the theory of rational choice does not indicate how conflicts should be removed, provided that they are ironed out somehow.

Hence the exercise makes sense only in terms of some very general measure of utility, which lets a rational agent compare his life, and its present underlying preferences, to what it would be, if he were to reverse some or all of them. This is what I meant by saying that questions of motivation were starting to arise. For that reason I postpone further discussion to chapter 5. Meanwhile we are now outside the grammar of a model set up in such a way that a rational choice can be determined without asking about the rationality of the agent's goals, provided only that they are coherent.

At this stage, then, we can see how the existence of a coercive norm helps in by-passing Leviathan traps, but not how such a norm can emerge as the sum of rational choices by players already trapped. Take two players each of whom, in the absence of the norm, ranks the outcomes 01, 11, 00, 10 from the point of view of Self. Add a norm to forbid free-riding or to reward volunteers for effort. If the norm is rigorously enforced, the feasible options reduce to 11 and 00. If it is imperfectly enforced, it acts effectively as a price rise or extra risk, which makes 01 less attractive. If it offers an incentive, 10 becomes more attractive. These variants work by disturbing the immediate rankings without upsetting the underlying preferences. Coercion need not be physical. Once the social system is a going concern, social sanctions may suffice. For a real-life example, think of a government anti-litter campaign which involves on-the-spot fines, or occasional prosecutions or village-of-the-year competitions.

But the problem posed was more fundamental. The idea was to show how it can be rational for the players so to interlock their preferences that each came rationally to choose 1 instead of the previous 0. To resume an earlier thought, there is still the suggestion, conveyed by speaking of 'norms', that elements of trust and entitlement are involved in the successful interlocking of preferences. For, although Hobbes may be right to insist on fear as a motive, coercion is not going to be enough to hold off the dominance of 0 for a ranking of 01, 11, 00, 10. So far I have been dealing with games where all players have the same ranking from the point of view of Self. Fear is all very well as a weapon against those seeking to exploit others and hence to police games in which some players have sociable preferences and others anti-social ones. But the aim is to arrive at normative expectations by rational choice. Normative expectations are not mere expectations backed by 'a power to keep all in awe'.

To make this clear, suppose that cowboys entering the OK Saloon are at first forcibly disarmed and the management hires a man with a shot gun to keep it that way. Peace is kept by ruling out *01* and relies on mere expectation. After a time, when the habit is established, the management dispenses with the shot gun. The clientele, however, although by now containing goodies with the Assurance ranking of *11, 01, 00, 11*, still also contains baddies with the original Leviathan ranking of *01, 11, 00, 10*. The former have lost their reason to trust the latter. The question is still whether the baddies are acting irrationally in being willing to break the norm once it has only Reason to uphold it. The game with symmetrical preferences remains crucial.

That suggests a tempting line of argument to show that it is rational for each to choose contrary to a dominant reason for *0*, when both players have the same ranking. Symmetry suggests that each is a sort of mirror image of the other and can count on his reasoning's being matched by the other's. When Adam and Eve must each decide whether to bring a gourd of water, each is effectively deciding for both. Since each prefers two gourds to none, each decides to bring one. The job which would be done by a coercive norm, if there was one, is done by Reason interlocking the preferences, as a coercive norm would.

The attempt fails, however. Adam says to himself, 'Suppose that Eve made her decision five minutes ago. Either she has decided to bring one, in which case I shall not bring another, or she has decided not to, in which case I refuse to be landed with my lowest-ranked outcome.' So he rationally brings no water. Moreover Eve will have foreseen this five minutes ago and will have refused to be landed with her lowest-ranked outcome. It may seem that she can cause Adam to bring a gourd by deciding previously to bring one herself. But that makes a difference only if her ranking has been wrongly described. Since the time factor is irrelevant to the logic, the same counter-argument defeats simultaneous choices of *1*.

The deeper reason is that Adam is not playing games with his mirror image. He is not like someone gazing into a mirror and wondering if he can fool his image into shutting one eye when he shuts the other. To decide to stick his tongue out is to decide that his image will do the same – there are only two possible outcomes, not four. If Reason had the same effect on the Leviathan trap, there would be no trap. In other words the thought that

Adam is playing games with himself is to be construed by analogy with games between distinct persons, whose preferences are similar but distinct. It is as yet unclear what is to be said about the nature of persons, in the context of a theory which seems to identify them with sets of preferences. But symmetry cannot mean mirror-image identity, while the asymmetrical outcomes (*01* and *10*) remain in any sense feasible. Indeed, for the particular example, an asymmetrical outcome reached by a fair or morally proper method may be the best outcome. If so, we should not construe the identity of persons in a way which rules it out.

Conclusion

The step from individual choice to consensual norms is painless. The emergence of the norm is the best outcome for each player and, as soon as luck throws up a salient, each fastens on to it. But, since such norms are stable, because no one has reason to depart from them, no light is cast on what is involved in a norm which is binding. The same goes for norms which govern Assurance games. Where preferences coincide, Adam and Eve can learn to co-operate – or to be one flesh, as the Bible puts it – without straining the basic theory of rational choice. One sort of social contract is unproblematic, at least if we allow language to emerge by the same route, so that it can be expressed and communicated.

But even in the garden life is not all one flesh. A new phase opens with their first dominant, self-defeating choice. If they already have coercive norms, they could by-pass the trap by invoking one. But the institution of a common power, whether in the form of a sheriff or of social pressure, requires more than the General Will or Assurance game. This is because any reason for a player to make a contract in order to escape a Leviathan trap is also a reason to break it. Apparent counter-examples, including the existence of society itself, show only either that rankings have been wrongly described or that the players are not rational. This, however, is not a deep truth about rationality but a logical implication of the model of individually rational choice.

The next step, then, is to introduce the notion of a binding norm, one which each player will keep to because others are entitled to expect it. To do it within the conceptual budget so far provided, Adam must be able rationally to choose a change in his own preferences. The budget does not stretch to this yet. It allows a distinction between immediate and dispositional preferences, or between first- and second-order preferences. But it demands a single fully-ordered set of ultimate preferences, to ground the idea of expected utility and hence of rational choice. 'Preference' seemed an innocent enough concept, especially when introduced with only the vaguest suggestion that utility was a measure of preference. It turns out, however, that we need to know more about it and hence more about human motivation than the basic model appeared to require.

The problem, stated more grandly, is one of what Kant called 'man's unsociable sociality'. Human beings are not so much one flesh that each always most wants what suits each other. Yet they are not so unsociable that they do not care about one another. The theory of rational choice does not include such grand thoughts in any obvious way, but it does throw up the formal analogue of unsociable sociality. Rational actors find themselves cutting off their noses to spite their faces. That does not happen in the General Will game. But I took the name of this game from Rousseau, and he believed it the fundamental form of game only after human nature has been reshaped by his social contract. This point will need to be pursued later.

The next large question is what the basic model says or implies about motivation. But, before raising it, I want to bring in the Cunning of Reason for the first of three appearances which it will make in the book.

4

The Cunning of Reason I: unintended consequences

A traditional Persian carpet, I am told, is woven on a mesh of threads placed upright between the master weaver and his minions. The minions hook coloured wools through the mesh on command, without seeing or knowing the pattern. He orchestrates, but not by working to a blueprint. Even if the commands could be precise enough, it would not be in the spirit of the business. The weaver conjures up the design as he goes along, by giving rough guidance and turning its results into something original and unique.

This is a possible image for the Cunning of Reason, which, in Hegel's phrase, 'makes passions work for it'. Caesar's crossing of the Rubicon brought the Roman Republic to its close and moved history into the next of a series of phases, which led finally to the nation state. Caesar, like other great world-historical individuals, was in tune with 'the will of the World Spirit', but only instinctively. He could not perceive the design which he served. Without him, however, the World Spirit, like the master weaver, would have had to create a different design. The Cunning of Reason is Hegel's evocative term for the larger, unseen movement of the historical process, emerging in the consequences of what historical actors choose.

I have no yearnings in this direction. The book is not a hunt for the World Spirit or an expression of belief that the consequences of the actions of world-historical individuals sum dialectically to anything fine or fitting. But I am engaged by the idea that institutions can emerge as the unintended sum of intended consequences. From the actors' point of view the sum can be benign, perverse or simply unnoticed. In general the Cunning of Reason makes a great deal of mischief at times, and the same may be said of the Unseen Hand, another name which has been given to the summing of consequences. I shall take up the theme three times as the argument of the book develops. On this first occasion the theme is to do simply with institutions as deposits left by a sum of consequences. On the next it will involve a discussion of functional explanation and of the nature of rules. On the third it will be harnessed to the epistemology of *Verstehen*. By then we shall have distinguished unintended consequences into those unforeseen, those unwanted and those unadmitted. Meanwhile these divisions can be left until they are needed.

Consequences can be systematic without being intended, and can be explanatory without being retroactive. The last chapter gave us two ways of creating institutions deliberately. One was to arrive at a salient solution to a problem of co-ordination, which became embodied by repetition in a consensual norm. An institution created from this source is a cluster of consensual norms or mutually convenient practices deposited through convention. Provided that the chosen equilibrium suits all, it does not matter whether the conventions governing it simply emerge or are consciously agreed by covenants in advance. The examples given all happen to be ones where the consensus was among persons with equal power, but the idea will extend to situations of unequal power, so long as there is recognised mutual advantage.

Even so, consensual norms alone will not take us far. Societies will not get far without enforcing some norms. This thought is not beyond the theory of rational choice, once granted a solution to the Leviathan problem. Agents of equal power, each with a dominant choice not to co-operate, will find themselves co-operating to mutual advantage once a coercive norm has emerged. The previous chapter failed to show how each could rationally arrive at the coercive norm, but could explain why each would be rationally content to observe it, once arrived at, provided that others too would be penalised for a departure. While the agents are of equal power, positive and normative run nicely together, since the coercive norm is a fair device for harmonising the interests of each and all. With unequal power introduced, there is a tendency for positive and normative to diverge. For, although a bargain struck between a lion and a mouse can leave both better off than before, the former gets more of a lion's share than may be right. The coercive norm enforces this discrepancy by stopping the mouse trying for more, and may indeed widen it. That opens the way to a normative theory of social choice. Meanwhile, however, the mouse is rational to keep the bargain, given the enforced parameters. By mixing consensual and coercive norms, we have the makings of an individualist account of institutions.

But the Leviathan problem is not always solved to mutual advantage. Here the cunning of reason comes in very helpfully. A famous example is Marx's expectation that a capitalist system, in which all capitalists have a clear interest in keeping profits up, will be marked by a falling rate of profit. If consumers are rational and demand is falling so that producers must compete for it, each producer has an individual interest in undercutting others, by cutting both costs and profits. If the costs include the wages of workers who are consumers, demand falls again and further undercutting becomes rational. Each capitalist acts rationally and the sum of these rational choices is the collapse of capitalism. At any rate this is the result in theory, *ceteris paribus*, and it shows what the Cunning of Reason can do.

In that example the outcome does not stabilise, short of collapse, or rather short of transition to the dictatorship of the proletariat, which leads onward in its turn. But the Leviathan game itself can stabilise with an outcome which gives each player his third preference. Public squalor, symbolised by littered streets and countryside, can be a stable result of each preferring not to contribute, both when others do and when others do not, even though all would prefer less squalor. Here the players need not have noticed that there could be a better outcome for all. They may not have realised that life could be better or that there are further consequences yet to come. Meanwhile, however, the sum of the third preferences is an institution in the sense of being a stable practice, even though no one intended it. It is stable in that, given the parameters, no one has reason to depart from it, whether because no one has appreciated that he has a reason or because no one individually has a reason, at least on the analysis so far.

Norms supplied by the Cunning of Reason after this manner are binding only in the weak sense that each agent can rationally expect the practice to remain stable. They are 'normal' rather than 'normative'. But they are, I think, very common. Shared habits, which go unquestioned or even unnoticed, are a marked feature of social order. I do not mean to imply that they are good for us. That is a question for chapter 9, when the Cunning of Reason makes its second appearance. But I do mean to suggest that the idea of an institution which is a stable sum of latent consequences is a useful extension to the theory of rational choice. The basic model not only deals with what rational agents deliberately bring into existence or abide by but also extends to unwilled or unnoticed outcomes of individually rational choices.

From the capitalists' point of view, the falling rate of profit is a mischief and so, from everyone's, is the public squalor which litter symbolises. But the Cunning of Reason need not make mischief. A theme of market economics is how the individual pursuit of self-interest can sum to the common good. Adam Smith stated it in *The Wealth of Nations* thus:

It is not from the benevolence of the butcher, the brewer or the baker that we expect our dinner, but from their regard to their own self interest. We address ourselves not to their humanity but to their self-love, and never talk to them of our own necessities but of their advantages. (Smith (1970), p. 119)

The butcher, brewer and baker do not intend the good of mankind, and neither do their customers. Yet transactions prompted by self-love sum to a greater general welfare than they would if each aimed at it. An invisible hand is as if at work. More broadly, Smith, Mandeville and others have pointed out that private vices can sum to public virtues. Self-love, greed and other manifestations of a callous egoism can promote the common weal where private virtues would sum to defeat it.

I shall not pause to consider whether good or mischief is the more usual result. The point is solely to establish an interesting gap between what is intended individually and what happens collectively. Thus I would not care to bet on the outcome of a million small occasions when it is rational to replace human effort by a micro-chip. The result may be a general rise in the standard of life and an increased leisure for the pursuit of individuality. Or it may be the destruction of human self-respect and dignity, through removing the need for protestant virtues of effort, thrift and determination. Either way, the rationality of each individual choice is independent of the resulting sum. The micro-chip offers bargains in the form of small steps which improve on previous maximising solutions. No rational actor can refuse more for less. At the start those who adopt the micro-chip are ahead of the game; presently those who refuse to adopt it are behind the game; in the end all rational agents must play. Whether the accumulated change is for the better is another question altogether.

This example shows that a stable equilibrium need not be static in practice. The Cunning of Reason takes time to work. Institutions can emerge by an accumulation of small choices made serially, and can be eroded slowly by serial free-riding. The basic rational choice model is timeless, but only in the logic of its analysis, where the outcome is an implied, as if instant, sum. It extends to serial choices readily enough. In that case the sum need never be completed. At some stage in the series the parameters may change and a new series begin, which tends to a different final state. For instance the British electoral system is, like parts of the American, one of single-vote-single-member constituencies, which squeezes third parties. If the policies of the two leading parties polarise, less committed voters may turn to a third party which offers good prospects of defeating the incumbent, especially if they believe that other voters are doing likewise. Suppose that the third party is promising to change the electoral system to one of proportional representation. Were this to come about, the rationale of electoral choices would change and the political game would continue under new rules. These kinds of dynamics are within the scope of rational-choice theory and the theory of games.

On the other hand it is not plain that a rational-actor analysis will be very interesting. The British electoral system could develop in several ways. Each way is neatly analysable *ex post*, since the model can always assign expected utilities suitably so as to yield any given result (with a spot of help from the Cunning of

Reason, when it comes to summing the consequences). It is not plain, however, that there is much to be said *ex ante*. Whether there is depends on taking game-theory far further than I shall attempt here. Overlapping games among large numbers of players are dizzyingly more complex than any we have yet considered. For instance the analysis of coalitions is extremely complicated, even when austere simplifying assumptions are made. Yet it is clearly promising. In principle complexity should not be a *nolle prosequi*; but, conversely, chapter 7 on Rational Expectations will raise obstacles of a more radical sort. Meanwhile let us note that the basic model can extend to at least simple dynamics.

I do, however, wish to open one line of thought which should be useful to rational-actor models. Fred Hirsch has suggested that many goods are 'positional', in the sense that people want them only on condition that others do not have them.[1] These are goods at least part of whose value lies in their scarcity. Numbered lithographs are a trivial but instructive example. The greater the total of numbered prints made from the plate the lower is the price of each. For, while everyone could own a mere print, not everyone can own a guarantee that not everyone has one. The idea generalises at once to any goods involving power over others, higher status than others, and to advantages, privileges, prizes and exclusivities of all sorts. An especially interesting case is secrets, not only because there is a market in positional knowledge but also because, I shall insist later, rational action would be impossible if everyone knew what anyone knew. A secret known to all is a secret no longer. For a pithy summary of the general idea I cannot improve on Hirsch's remark that 'if everyone stands on tiptoe, no one sees better' (Hirsch (1977), p. 5).

Scarcity for scarcity's sake is the pure form of a positional good. If power and status are examples (as Hobbes suggests explicitly in chapter XIII of *Leviathan*), the pure form is going to be interesting enough. But Hirsch took the idea of social scarcity a stage further, in order to persuade his fellow economists that, within the familiar textbook economy, there was a whole 'positional economy' waiting to be explored. To pure scarcity-value

[1] *Social Limits to Growth* (1977). For further general discussion see Hollis (1985a) and for an application see Hollis (1982).

(which he put down to motives like 'envy, emulation and pride') he added 'incidental scarcity', which is due to the effects of crowding. Here the value of the good happens to vary with the number of people who possess it, because there happens to be a shortage in what is needed for its enjoyment. For instance the pleasures of motoring diminish as the road fills up, but would be restored if an extra road were built. That is a case of incidental physical scarcity. For a case of incidental social scarcity, think how many more musicians or actors could satisfy their talents if there were more paying audiences to go round. The broad idea is that even a contingent bottleneck has the effect of reducing the utility of a good to each consumer with the addition of each further consumer.

Hirsch's purpose was to prove that the limits to economic growth are not merely technical ones typified by limits on natural resources, like oil or trees, and by limits on social resources, like mathematicians. There are also social limits, he argued, which arise because if everyone had what each wanted, the crowding would turn out to make the goods worthless. I shall next add a further dimension to the idea of positional goods and then point out how useful they are in accounting for social change.

The utility of a positional good to its owner depends, so far, on how many other people own it or, to use a word more natural for contexts like the provision of amenities, have access to it. Call this the 'vertical' dimension, to mark the presence of an advantage which the haves gain over the have-nots. Then reflect that the utility of many goods depends on the distribution of complementary goods. For instance the pleasures of being hockey goal-keeper depend on how easy it is to find a hockey team which wants a goal-keeper. The fun of playing the oboe varies with the supply of musicians who play other instruments. Call this the 'horizontal' dimension, and think of it more generally as an aspect of the division of labour in both production and consumption. Whenever the success of an enterprise undertaken by a group of people depends on a division of labour, the utility of each sort of contribution will vary with the effectiveness of the others. Thus the pleasures of playing the oboe are positional not because they diminish as the number of oboists rises but because they diminish if the number (or standard) of other instrumentalists falls.

Granted that positional goods are common, we have two large reasons why their distribution is likely to apply a pressure for change. In the vertical dimension there will always be a tendency to overcrowding as long as it would profit one further person to acquire the good, with any loss being borne by those who already have it. For example part of a townsperson's pleasure in acquiring a cottage in a country village is the enjoyment of genuine village life. The first incomer does not affect the life of the village. With each new one, there is an increasing total effect. But each new-comer need calculate only whether it is worth it to himself to move in. Any general losses are borne by others. In theory at least, there will be further arrivals while there is any net advantage at the margin. The process continues until the village life is destroyed. By this time earlier arrivals have lost their satisfaction and are looking for other places to live. The result of gradual overcrowding is a shift in the goals whose pursuit caused the overcrowding.

In the horizontal dimension there will be a restlessness produced by imperfect matches. In a complicated enterprise like a society, it is very unlikely that all complementary jobs will get done in a way which suits each. Not even massive central planning can manage it; and it takes a visionary faith in free markets to suppose that scarcities vanish if all central planning is scrapped. Corrective action is at best slow. For instance doctors and hospital consultants tend to prefer cities to country areas, prosperous places to poor ones and glamorous specialisms to unglamorous. Corrections, whether by the state or by the market, are constantly outflanked. The provision of a full range of medical care is never static.

Positional goods thus give large scope to the cunning of reason in overresponding to scarcities and in creating new ones. This suits the rational-actor model, because it supplies a source of change in what otherwise would be too static an analysis. But, in the perspective of an individualist theory of institutions, it does so only *ex post*, as noted earlier. I would like to end the chapter by demonstrating the point more formally, by means of a simple 'positional' game.

Take three players, A, B, C, each with two strategies, o and 1. Let the pay-off to each vary with what the others choose. Catch the positional element by assuming that the worst outcomes for each are the ones (*111* and *000*) where all three make the same choice. Suppose, for neatness, that each prefers the outcome where he alone chooses the positionally advantageous *0* to those where he and one other choose *0*. That yields a preference order for *A*:

A's ranking	Outcome		
1st	*0*	*1*	*1*
2nd	*0*	*1*	*0*
	0	*0*	*1*
4th	*1*	*1*	*0*
	1	*0*	*1*
	1	*0*	*0*
7th	*0*	*0*	*0*
	1	*1*	*1*

(I ignore the question of how *A* should rank outcomes where another player gains the positional advantage.) *B* and *C* are assumed to have analogous rankings from their own point of view.

This game has an indeterminate solution. *A* is not in the Leviathan position of choosing *0* regardless, because he ranks *100* above *000*. If he were and the others were too, then no one could gain the positional good, regarded as a sum of independent choices. Yet there is no obvious strategy which all could choose symmetrically, so that someone got the good. Equally there is no reason to expect a particular one of the three outcomes where one player gets the good (*011*, *101*, *110*); nor, for that matter, of the three outcomes where two players share it (*001*, *010*, *100*). Hence the emergence of any of these outcomes can be analysed into its constituent choices only *ex post*. Meanwhile, it is easy to see why there will be a tendency, if the players are left to themselves, for more of them to choose *0* rather than *1* and for them to drift with repeated play into *000*.

Even with a solution to the Leviathan problem, then, we would still need a way of distributing positional goods to general satisfaction. This is not impossible, if the emergent institutions involve some principle of fair chances or of compensation. But it is well beyond the stage reached so far. At this stage I seek only to introduce scope for the cunning of reason to supplement the basic model. The opening stage was to treat institutions as an enduring sum of intended consequences. In the General Will game the institutional sum was satisfactory for all, because it solved a coordination problem. In the Assurance game the sum was more fragile, since it lasted only as long as each player remained confident that others would behave themselves. But at least it was clear where the solution lay, and it was pretty stable. In the Leviathan game the 'right' solution was clear but inaccessible, and we have yet to discover how rational actors will arrive at it. Meanwhile the 'wrong' solution produced by the Cunning of Reason was stable. With the Positional game, we have an interesting indeterminacy which serves as a possible source of social change.

Conclusion

These last three chapters yield a modest but not unpromising analysis of social life as the interplay of rational individuals. Institutions which rely on consensual norms are readily understood. Those which rely on coercive norms are still puzzling, but at least we see why such norms are needed. In general, then, the analysis also covers institutions which rely on a mixture of the two kinds of norm. That leaves much opaque – a situation which I mark poetically by saying that the Cunning of Reason has plenty of useful work to do. The analysis is not unpromising in the sense that some of the opacity will vanish with a more complicated and advanced theory of games, and that some can usefully be left opaque for the sake of a source of unplanned social change. I especially commend the topic of positional goods to individualist theories with social ambitions.

This modest advance is as far as I can go without opening the topic of motivation. The Leviathan trap is still closed. In preamble, I would like to point out how modest the notion of a norm is so far. The consensual norm is backed by simple mutual preference for a salient. The coercive norm is backed by force (including social sanctions). Neither norm involves trust, and even the solution to the Assurance game, which lasts while players trust each other, does not squarely raise questions of moral obligation.

Furthermore all norms so far considered are regulatory rather than constitutive. They emerge as ways of regulating what players already want to do by helping (General Will and Assurance) or hindering (the Leviathan problem). A constitutive norm, by contrast, would create the activity which it governs. If we need this kind of norm, we shall have to dig deeper.

To explain that distinction, I revert to General Will. I borrowed the name from Rousseau because his social contract is essentially co-operative. But Rousseau himself took a drastic view of what is required for co-operation. His social contract transforms human nature. It produces a 'remarkable change in man' from a 'narrow, stupid animal', guided by instinct, physical impulse, desire and concern for himself alone to a 'creature of intelligence' steered by justice, duty, right and other-regarding principles. It replaces natural liberty, to grab what one can in the state of nature, with civil liberty, limited by the general will and the legal titles of owners to their property. As slavery gives way to moral freedom, what were slaves become men. The institutions of civil society not only constitute activities, of a kind which have no place or meaning in a state of nature, but also constitute the inhabitants of civil society, who are humans with human possibilities, instead of animals.[2]

It is worth connecting Rousseau's claims for a civil society, constituted according to his idea of the social contract, with his remarks about the free-rider problem or Leviathan trap. The problem arises, he says in book I, chapter VII, because the members even of a just civil society retain their individuality:

Despite their common interest, subjects will not be bound by their commitment unless means are found to guarantee their fidelity.

For every individual as a man may have a private will contrary to, or different from, the general will that he has as a citizen. His private interest may speak with a very different voice from that of the public interest; his absolute and naturally independent existence may make him regard what he owes to the common cause as a gratuitous contribution, the loss of which would be less painful for others than the payment is onerous for him.

Falling into this trap, Rousseau continues, 'he might seek to enjoy the rights of a citizen without doing the duties of a subject'. That

[2] *The Social Contract*, book I, chapter VIII.

is a beautifully lucid statement of the problem which we failed to escape or by-pass earlier. Rousseau's own solution exploits the relation of 'man', 'subject' and 'citizen' so as to allow the backslider to be compelled to do his bit for the good of all including him and thus, in a daring phrase, 'to be forced to be free'. The solution has had many critics. But, to my mind, it does at least suggest a strong reason why the problem is not to be solved by invoking a repeated series of games or 'supergame'. I too shall presently distinguish between morally free choice and enlightenedly self-interested choice.

The Cunning of Reason, construed as a neat name for the various ways of summing consequences so as to create patterns and spring surprises, is a useful adjunct to the basic model. So far its work is too great and too unsystematic for comfort, as will become clearer when the theme is resumed in chapter 9. None the less we see how the pattern on the front side of the carpet can go beyond the conscious intentions of those inserting the individual threads at the back. We have an idea of emergence compatible with individualism.

5

Motivation

In the Bible story mankind is descended from Adam and Eve, after they had been beguiled by the serpent and expelled from the garden. When giving Adam the run of the place, the Lord God had expressly forbidden him to eat of the tree of the knowledge of good and evil: 'for in the day that thou eatest thereof thou shalt surely die'. The serpent, being more subtil than any beast of the field which the Lord God had created, persuaded Eve otherwise. 'Ye shall not surely die', he insinuated; 'your eyes shall be opened, and ye shall be as gods, knowing good and evil.' What happened next is a puzzle. She saw that the tree was good for food (although so were plenty of others) and pleasant to the eyes (as if that mattered) and a tree to be desired to make one wise (how did she know what she was missing?). So she ate and gave to her husband, who ate also. They thus learnt that they were naked and made themselves aprons of fig leaves. Retribution soon followed.

This story has elements too difficult for the basic model of rational choice and I shall go at it obliquely by trying out a simpler one. Perhaps mankind is not descended from Adam and Eve. Dwelling outside Eden at the time was a group of homunculi, who may have created the first society and been our true ancestors. Their names were Solitary, Poor, Nasty, Brutish and Short, let us suppose out of respect for the famous bleak passage describing the state of nature in chapter XIII of Hobbes' *Levia-*

than. But another account is given by Hume, who makes them out to be quite kindly little fellows, endowed with natural sympathy. Either version would suit the theory of rational choice, depending on just what the theory needs to assume about human motivation.

The current view is, I think, that the theory needs to assume nothing. The rational agents' preferences must be complete and consistent, but need not have any particular content or shape. To call an agent rational is to say merely that he reasons correctly in identifying the action likeliest to satisfy his preferences. This view has come to replace an older one that *homo economicus* needs some substantial psychological apparatus. F. Y. Edgeworth said firmly in his *Mathematical Psychics* (1881) that 'the first principle of economics is that every agent is actuated solely by self-interest'. In that case a substantive egoism is an intimate component of the dismal science, and there are still economists who agree. But the trend has been towards replacing self-interest first by a very general notion of utility and then by a schematic and formal notion of maximisation. What set off as a selfishness ascribed to human beings fades into a characterisation of the type of mathematical solution sought for sets of equations. I shall oppose this tendency, however, by arguing that a rational economic agent cannot be conceived as all process and no substance. Edgeworth was wrong about the first principle, I shall contend, but right about the need for something like it.

Edgeworth himself thought his first principle nothing grander than a convenient approximation, which happened to fit the areas of commercial life which he intended to study. Also notice that the term used is not 'selfishness' but 'self-interest'. That at once creates an ambiguity about the meaning, the status and the scope of what is often called 'rational-man individualism'. This chapter is a search for the motivational assumption which will allow the basic model as much flexibility as possible, short of destroying the rationale for its elegant formal techniques. In the language of an earlier chapter, I want to preserve the 'plug in points', so that microeconomic theory retains its power, while easing open the 'cut off points', so that the model can generalise beyond pure microeconomics. This attempt is needed not only for the exporting of microeconomic theory but also for that theory itself, given the impasse reached in considering the Leviathan trap. To make it I shall start with a blunt egoism as the motivational assumption and work it gradually loose.

Begin with the first homunculus, Solitary, a pure egoist. Even he need not be crudely selfish or short-sighted. He can be kind to animals and helpful to old ladies, provided that what moves him is the satisfaction which *he* expects from the result. He can give half his dinner away to others today, provided that he expects a better dinner back tomorrow. The crudest version of egoism worth considering is one which identifies costs and benefits as costs to the agent and benefits to the agent, and then insists that no agent will be moved to action unless his benefits outweigh his costs. This is not implausible in itself, and it is a popular reading of what the basic model presupposes.

It does, however, block one tempting exit from the Leviathan trap. Solitary has a dominant reason to choose o when his order of preferences over the outcome is $o1,11,oo,1o$. Suppose that, although this ranking accurately reflects the benefit of each outcome to him, the *total* benefit of 11 is greater than that of $o1$. For instance it is a slight nuisance for Solitary to remove his own litter after his picnic on the beach, but the total utility of a clean beach to all users is greater than the utility of a beach spoilt by Solitary's litter. Plainly beaches are sometimes left clean. So it looks as if there must be people about who do not reason like Solitary. That might also explain why people do usually vote in elections, save water in droughts and keep the social world moving, in apparent defiance of their dominant choices.

Call a person who sets the costs to himself against the benefits to all an altruist. (That is a slightly odd name, if an altruist is thought of as someone interested only in the good of others; but it is the usual one for rational-choice purposes.) This gives us a second homunculus, Poor, as a claim about motivation. At first sight it is a straight empirical question whether more of us are like Solitary or like Poor, and one whose empirical answer is that there are plainly enough like Poor to keep the wheels turning. But this is to misconceive the situation. The defender of pure egoism has two main replies, both showing at least that the question is not simply empirical.

One is that Poor is not truly an altruist. Here, for instance, is a remark by Peter Blau, whose *Exchange and Power in Social Life* is firmly wedded to belief that economics presupposes egoism:

An apparent altruism pervades social life, people are anxious to benefit one another and to reciprocate for the benefits they receive. But beneath this seeming selflessness an underlying 'egoism' can be discovered... A basic reward people seek in their associations is social approval and selfish disregard for others makes it impossible to obtain this important reward. (Blau (1964), p. 17)

One should distinguish here between a general presumption that people seek 'important rewards' for themselves in all their transactions and the specific hypothesis that 'social approval' is one of them. Even the latter is not a simple matter of fact but an interpretation of behaviour premised on the former. For, even granting that people commonly do what brings them social approval, it does not follow that they are doing it for the sake of the approval. That requires the general presumption, for which no evidence is offered, beyond showing that all behaviour *can* be described as a search for important rewards. The 'underlying "egoism"', in short, is not so much discovered as administered.

Blau thus upholds a *psychological* egoism, which is sure to fit, and does so by maintaining that apparent altruists are really egoists. The martyr goes to the stake not for his faith but for pie in the sky, or, if that is too crude, to avoid the social disapproval which recantation would bring. But beneath this seeming psychology, a *philosophical* egoism can, I think, be discovered. The other reply to the suggestion that the world contains people like Poor is that Poor and Solitary are not in basic competition. Both are moved to seek whatever rewards are important to them. If the martyr's faith is important enough to him, he will go to the stake for it; and the theory of rational choice is set no problem in assigning his utilities accordingly. This strikes me as a much better reply and one more in keeping with the recent tendency of economists to say as little about motivation as possible.

Although, on this account, Poor and Solitary are not in basic competition, there is still room for dispute about how common other-regarding motives are. That sounds like an empirical matter, which, I dare say, invites a sporting compromise, as in this pleasantly game-theoretic observation by F. M. Cornford:

It is quite a mistake to suppose that real dishonesty is at all common. The number of rogues is about equal to the number of men who act honestly; and it is very small. The great majority would sooner behave honestly than not. The reason why they do not give way to this natural preference of humanity is that they are afraid that others will not; and the others do not because they are afraid that *they* will not. Thus it comes about that, while behaviour which looks dishonest is fairly common, sincere dishonesty is about as rare as the courage to evoke good faith in your neighbours by showing that you trust them.[1]

But the matter is less empirical and the stakes higher than it might be convenient to suppose. Solitary holds the key to Hobbes' version of the social contract and Poor to Hume's. In Hobbes' version human nature starts as strictly self-regarding, whereas Hume credits us with enough natural sympathy for one another to avoid the threat that the social game is zero-sum. This difference is not to be settled by observation or cosy compromise and it brings sharply different political philosophies with it. Yet the dispute is not basic. It is possible to disagree with both of them.

Even allowing that we have natural sympathies and can take pleasure in the pleasure of others, it is a further step to show that we act for the sake of that satisfaction. Hobbes and Hume agree that there cannot be action, unless motivated by desire and done in order to satisfy the desire. This proposition is buried so deep in the theory of rational choice that it hardly seems to be there at all, and is so broad that it seems to be quite non-committal. But it is there and will turn out to be far from non-committal. In particular, it involves interpreting all sorts of actions, which we tend to describe by contrasting desires with reasons, as a contest between different desires. For instance action on principle is possible only if there is a desire to act on principle or if 'principle' is translated into a desired aspect of consequences. Similar interpretations need to be given to action from duty, action in pursuit of truth or action arising from the requirements of role. I shall try to show that this is a piece of philosophical mischief, which not only creates oddities, when an economic approach is applied to other areas of social life, but also distorts the understanding of econ-

[1] *Microcosmographia Academica: Being a Guide for the Young Academic Politician* (1908), p. 20.

omic action. It is, moreover, the source of trouble with the Leviathan trap.

Let us begin with a more careful look at the idea of a preference order. 'Preference' is the rational-choice term for 'desire' and seems to be wholly non-committal both about what people desire and about what it is to desire something. But this is an illusion. The preferences of a rational agent, as so far presented, are *given*, *current*, *homogeneous*, and *determining*. I shall next work through this list, raising doubts in order to show that the four epithets together amount to an assumption which is at least contentious and indeed false.

In introducing the model, it was very natural to speak of Adam's preferences for figs over mulberries as *given*. People vary in their tastes, just as shoppers vary in what they put on their shopping lists. Tastes may vary over time, but they last long enough to account for choices, without needing to be explained. Similarly the shopping list is a parameter for explaining what the shopper chooses, and it is natural to add that a coherent shopping list is a necessary condition of rational shopping. On reflection, however, tastes and shopping lists are special cases. Most specific desires are premised on beliefs of many kinds and would change if the beliefs changed. For instance a desire to visit the zoo might not survive if a person discovered that the zoo was closed or that the animals were cruelly treated. Whenever it makes sense to ask why the agent prefers x to y, and to expect a reason, the preference is not exactly given.

A preliminary reply is that economists, who speak of preferences as given, mean only that it is not their job to explain the source of preferences; that is a task for psychologists, sociologists or others. But this move will not serve for all cases. One often needs to know how an agent would respond to a change in his situation or in his beliefs about the situation. Not to consider the effect on his current preferences would be a mistake. So would failure to notice that the results of action are prone to affect the desires which prompted the action. For example clever advertising can get people to buy things which then lead them to fresh wants (or to acquire the wants which the advertiser had fooled them into supposing that they had already). The freezing of preferences is an analytical device which is useful only for initial textbook purposes, where it may not matter under what description the agent wants x or what beliefs about himself, his current wants and the world about him are involved in his wanting x.

A better reply is that 'given preferences' refers not to surface or immediate wants but to dispositional ones. Where the agent wants x for the sake of y, it is the desire for y which counts. At the limit, each agent has a very general desire for his lasting well-being, to which all specific preferences are a means, and one which depends on the state of his information. Thus Adam's given want is a satisfying meal, and his preference for figs on a belief that he will find them more satisfying than mulberries for the purpose. This echoes the utilitarian contention that each person pursues happiness and that all specific choices are a means to that end. A snag of going to the limit is that so broad and blank a description of what is given about desire seems to rob desire of its explanatory power. Presumably each person's happiness needs to take a more specific form, even if a dispositional one – a point to which I shall return. But the utilitarian contention does at least reinforce the Humean proposition that only desire can move an agent.

Given preferences, then, are a requirement of a theory of rational action which regards rational choice as the use of instrumental reason in the service of the passions. Explanation needs desires with which to stop. These final desires are given, not so much because they have no further explanation as because their explanation makes no difference to the actions. Later in the chapter I shall point out what this implies for the analysis of principled action and, in the next, what difficulties it creates for understanding the relation of desire and belief.

Secondly the rational agent's desires must be *current*. That seems plainly right. How can he possibly be moved by a desire unless he has it here and now? Yet what is obvious at first blink is so odd at the next that it needs spelling out. Offhand, people are often moved by last week's desires or by tomorrow's. They are moved by hypothetical desires into taking precautions or making investments. They are moved by the past, present and future desires of other people, including perhaps those who have died or not yet been born. Indeed, were the rational agent movable only by what he wants at this very moment, it is hard to see that he could ever choose to boil an egg for eating in four minutes' time. Adam could not take two paces towards the nearest fig tree or be influenced by Eve's wish for a walk in the moonlight. These points will cause trouble for a Humean philosophy of mind. But, initially, they are met with the reply that of course distant desires can move an agent, provided that they enter in at the gate of present desire. Adam needs a present desire to satisfy his past or future desires or Eve's past or future desires. Since agents do have indirect as well as direct present desires, however, there is no instant problem.

This leads to the third feature of preferences, their *homogeneity*. A preference order has to be complete and consistent. For any x and any y, the agent prefers one to the other or ranks them equally, but cannot have no ranking at all. There must be a common coinage which overcomes the threat of incommensurability. This coinage need not be biassed to the selfish, short-term or material. Adam does not have to prefer pushpin to poetry or his present comfort to Eve's future welfare. But he does have to be able to order whatever can enter through the gate of present desire. What is the neutral common coinage which measures all comers against each other? The answer so far has been 'utility', but it is time to declare that in using the name I have only been muttering an ontological spell.

If rationality were solely the choice of means to satisfy *any* complete and consistent set of preferences, there could be some very peculiar rational agents. Suppose someone were to order his preferences by describing his options in German, listing them alphabetically and declaring a preference for whatever was higher up the list. That would give him fully ordered preferences and he could then arrive at expected utilities in the approved way so as to decide whether a 50% chance of *Gemütlichkeit* was a better bet than a 70% chance of *Geschlechterfahrung* as a way of spending the evening. Why exactly would that be a dotty way to proceed? The old answer was that, since utility is connected with his real interests and measured by a subjective flow of psychic satisfaction, he cannot expect to maximise his utility by working from a shopping list guided by the German alphabet. A purely formal notion of utility or preference would be denied this old answer, with dotty results.

So the theory of rational choice requires more of preferences than that they be complete and consistent. A preference order must be an order of *preferences*. The point of the italics can be brought out by asking how preferences are to be identified. Suppose Adam chose mulberries yesterday and figs today. Is this the same preference with different discounts owing to a change in the situation or is it a change of preference? To answer we need to know how Adam is ordering his list. What features of situations does he regard as relevant? What does he include in the services of goods as a plus or a minus? We also need to realise, however, that Adam's account is not an infallible guide (as pollsters have learnt to their sorrow when trying to predict tomorrow's votes from today's declared intentions). Adam's preference order involves a mixture of intentionality and inference. It has to have a rationale, if it is to be a guide to what he will choose (or would choose or would have chosen) on other occasions. Consistency implies some kind of good(ish) reason for preferring x to y.

A rationale is also important because the theory of rational choice is interested in individuals only in so far as they are typical or depart from what is typical in an orderly way. Otherwise it would make no sense whatever to begin the microeconomic textbook with Adam (or Robinson Crusoe or any other exemplar). The 'individual' in economics is not a particular person or a randomly selected one. He is not even the average man, in the sense in which the average man earns £150 a week or fathers 1.8 children. He is all mankind's rational epitome. In setting the benchmark, the textbook is assuming a rationale to the way in which preferences are ordered. They are an expression of something in the individual's nature and hence in human nature. Some opaque but substantive claim is being made about human motivation, so that Adam can be typical of how humans each and all manage to have homogeneous desires.

A preference order thus has a locus in the agent's present dispositions and a direction towards his 'utility'. Meanwhile preferences are, fourthly, *determining*. This is clearest for the ideal-type case where the agent has perfect information, faultlessly processed, and his choice is determined by his order of preference. Here the informational or belief component of the decision is thought of as universal, standard equipment and the desire component as what varies between individuals. If we recall that preferences are 'given', then it will be seen that the agent is simply a throughput. I shall argue later that agents are wrongly conceived as throughputs and that there is nothing in the idea of scientific method which demands that they be conceived as such. For the moment, however, I wish merely to note that there is no obvious reason for regarding desire, rather than belief, as the determining component. Off hand, Adam is moved as much by his belief that there are figs on the tree as by his desire for figs. The belief would not move him unless he had the desire; the desire would not move him if he did not hold the belief. Why give motivational priority to the desire?

The answer is once again that the model is covertly assuming the Humean thesis that 'reason alone can never be a motive to any action of the will' (*Treatise* book II, part III, section 3) or that 'reason is and ought only to be the slave of the passions and can never pretend to any other office than to serve and obey them' (*ibid*). If a Humean image is wanted for individual decision-making, it might be one of an old-fashioned grocer's scales, with two pans slung on a crossbar. Desires for and against are placed in the pans, with due allowance for the likelihoods of their being achieved, and the heavier pan wins. This image is deliberately mechanical. Just as the grocer is called on to weigh, not to judge, so too the rational actor is the slave of the stronger passion (other things being equal). There is no call to explain further why he acts on the stronger desire.

Granted that preferences are given, current, homogeneous and determining, the model is bound to construe Solitary, the egoist, and Poor, the altruist, as agents who differ at heart only in their preferences. Both are moved by desire. So it is easy to see what will happen to a man of principle, who fancies that he is moved by duty or by belief in what is right rather than by fellow-feeling. Since this is not a possible kind of motivation, he will have to be found a desire to act from. It will avoid confusion if we refuse to allow a desire to do one's duty. Such a 'desire' would blur the emerging difference between Humean and other accounts of motivation unhelpfully and, in any case, merely be a relabelling of what should not be possible. So the man of principle is either muddled or dishonest. He is muddled if he is led by too much philosophical talk into thinking of principle as what one should do whether one wants to or not, when in fact principled action is really moved by natural sympathy, as with Poor. He is dishonest if principled action is really moved by the discomfort of a bad conscience, as with Solitary. To signal that he is Humeanly suspect, let us take the next name from the list of homunculi and christen him Nasty.

This philosophical manoeuvre to keep Nasty within the Humean pale may seem too insensitive to the apparent difference between duty, which is belief-related, and sentiment, which is desire-related. If so, there may be merit in throwing in a theory of socialisation. If one classes principles with norms of various kinds, then Nasty sets a problem which rational-actor models must face when confronted with traditional and strongly norm-governed societies. A theory of socialisation explains how norms are internalised and so come to motivate individuals. It carries a strong initial suggestion that individuals are the creatures of the particular social system which moulds them and of the central value system which they internalise. I shall dispute this suggestion when we reach *homo sociologicus* in chapter 10. Meanwhile it offers one way of giving a social dimension to an individualist, Humean philosophy of mind.

Philosophically, then, the standard motivational component of the model makes it correct to say 'every agent is actuated solely by self-interest', provided that 'self-interest' is glossed as 'his own current desires'. If that implied as little as seemed at first, it would do no more than clear the way for the maximising character of rational solutions to problems of choice. The rational homunculus would be not so much Brutal as Short. But we embarked on the analysis of motivation because simple maximisers were stuck with the dominant logic which generates self-defeating choices. Has this chapter yet offered a way of escape?

Early in the chapter I floated the thought that Solitary is trapped by a preference order of *01, 11, 00, 10* because he reckons up the benefit of the outcome only to himself, whereas Poor might be moved by counting the total benefit. It will be plain by now that the thought is no help at all. If Poor is moved to choose *1* by the total benefit, then it follows at once that his order of preference is not *01, 11, 00, 01*. In summary, Hobbes hopes to rescue Solitary by giving him reason to subscribe to a coercive norm preventing *01*, and Hume hopes that people are more like Poor, who values the value of the outcome to all. But Solitary cannot stand back from his current desires far enough to tie his hands; and Poor does not have an escape, once the Leviathan trap has closed. No third way is offered by appeal to ideas of principle, since Nasty too is moved by current desires.

I do not mean that agents with what are sometimes called ethical preferences cannot be trapped. For instance utilitarians prefer that all keep promises or tell the truth rather than that none do, and yet reckon that the general happiness is best served if some promises are discreetly broken and some lies told. That makes each utilitarian a free-rider on the institutions of honesty and promise-keeping, with the result that a community of utilitarians would have no such institutions. The point is sometimes used as an argument for rule-utilitarianism, where the institution is mandatory, and against act-utilitarianism, where it is a rule of thumb. But the difference collapses if only current desires can motivate, because the former retains the desire to improve on the results of a universal mandatory institution by secret breaches; and that is just what the latter recommends too.

We are thus no further on with the solution, but can at least be clearer about the obstacles. We need a homunculus who will sometimes treat the result of all agents choosing *0*, when they each have a ranking of *01*, *11*, *00*, *10*, as his reason for choosing *1*. The snag is that no such reason can motivate an agent who is moved only by his current preferences. That is why we have got nowhere with apparently promising moves like working with dispositional preferences, distinguishing between first- and second-order preferences or adding a dash of fellow-feeling. They are all blocked by the point that no one whose current desires lead him to choose *1* can have been trapped in the first place.

Now try working back from the solution. Picture a habitual smoker who works in an open-plan office where smoking is permitted. He would rather smoke than not, but even he finds the fug awful if all the smokers in the office light up and, besides, he has some sympathy for the non-smokers. He would like it best if there were only a few smokers, including him. His second preference is for a ban, his third for a free-for-all and his last for restraint by him alone. On his desk there lies a voting slip, occasioned by a proposal for a ban on smoking in the office. He approves, in general, of deciding questions of collective welfare by ballot and he reflects that smokers are in a majority. (That is why the fug is awful when they all smoke.) But the office rules say that a ballot will be taken only if no one objects to it and only if everyone agrees to be bound by the result.

Suppose (although I have done nothing to prove it) that his rational strategy is to take part in the ballot, to vote for a no-smoking rule and, if it wins and proves hard to live with, to take a smoking cure which kills his urge to smoke. Suppose also that he arrives at this strategy by reflecting not on how much he likes smoking but on whether it is good for him, and not on how much he sympathises with the non-smokers but on how entitled they are to sympathy. These contrasts can be described in two ways. One is as a weighing of some present desires against other present desires, with its being rational to act on the stronger. The other is as a judgement upon his present desires, with its being rational to carry out the judgement. Both ways look possible, but they have different implications.

On the former description, we need to be able to say more about the structure of preferences than has yet emerged. Some very different sorts of desires will have to be homogenised into a coherent, current order with the aid of reflection on consequences. A fair amount can be done in the name of the thought that a rational agent has a preference order marked by reflective consistency. But there is also a limit, since, if only a desire can move a man, then only a desire can move him to reflect and to accept the results of reflection. This will become clearer in the next chapter. The other description requires a standpoint outside present desires. The case for one is especially persuasive when our hero contemplates a smoking cure which will change his current desire for tobacco and replace it with a desire for boiled sweets, which he does not now have. But that is not a conclusive thought, as will also become clear in the next chapter. Meanwhile it does suggest that it may be worth trying to subvert the standard rational-actor analysis of motivation.

To avoid biassing the discussion, let me admit that the mooted escape from the Leviathan trap is not clearly the one which reason commands, or at least not in all cases. It takes the form of complicating the analysis of rational agency so that the agent can take his *01, 11, 00, 10* ranking as a reason for choosing *1*, when he knows that others have similar rankings. But, before he can rationally act on this information about the ranking of others, he needs to know what theory of rational choice the others hold. If they continue the find *0* dominant, his treating the trap as a reason for acting as if preferences were different will merely result in his least preferred outcome, *10*. This means that the proposed complication goes very deep. While one is relying on *0*'s being dominant for a ranking *01, 11, 00, 10*, it makes no difference to the agent's choice what ranking others have, or, *a fortiori*, what theory they hold about choice. As soon as it matters, however, then it also matters who or what these other agents are. For example, if the agent is playing the Leviathan game against a randomising device, then presumably *0* will remain his rational choice. The same presumably goes if the others are intelligent players but hold a theory which favours the choice of *0* in the Leviathan trap. It is only if all are rationally inclined to *1* that *1* becomes a possible exit.

Conclusion

By way of summary, picture a television show where the hero is playing a Leviathan game in which any pay-off will be donated to his favourite charity. All he has to do is to write *0* or *1* on one side of a board. The board is then turned round to reveal a *0* or *1* on the other side. The pay-offs to the charity are these:

01	£1,001
11	£1,000
00	£100
10	£1

If one speculates about the source of the mark on the back side of the board, one can see how the charity might finish up with £1,001, £100 or £1. But it is hard to see how it will come to get the 'right' amount of £1,000. If, for instance, the hero happened to know that the other mark would be a '*1*', then he could not resist the better outcome of £1,001. A robust theory which requires *1*, if the hero knows that the other mark is arrived at by applying the robust theory, is needed; and this chapter has not delivered one.

But I hope to have shown at least that rational choice theory needs to include some committal thesis about what moves rational agents to action. Old contentions about selfishness or self-interest cannot be replaced with a bland, mathematically neat silence. Yet motivation is not self-evidently a matter of desire. It is time to challenge the approach shared by Hobbes and Hume.

6

External and internal reasons

If reason alone cannot be a motive to any action of the will, then an agent who is locked into a preference order of *01*, *11*, *00*, *10* is not helped by reflecting that he might get on better by acting as if he had a different order. Yet the theory of rational choice is not committed to the common presumption that only current desires can move a person. In this chapter I shall argue the case for construing the proposition that action results from desire plus belief in such a way that belief can be a motive to the will. Rational agents act from objectively good reasons, whose merits are conceptually independent of their current desires. When 'objectively good reasons' is taken as I shall propose, it becomes possible for a rational prisoner to escape from the Leviathan trap.

The key question is whether the rationality of action is always relative to the current desires of the agent. It is an old one, whose recent battle lines derive from Hume and Kant. What form must a reason for action take if it is to move a man? The Humean camp holds that reasons for action must be 'internal' to the desires of the agent, whose reasons they are. The Kantian holds that 'external' reasons can be effective.[1] This classic dispute involves whole rival

[1] I thus accept the posing of the question by Bernard Williams in his incisive paper 'Internal and External Reasons' (in R. Harrison, ed., *Rational Action* (1979); reprinted in Williams' collection of essays, *Moral Luck* (1981)), and borrow his use of 'internal' and 'external', 'internalist' and 'externalist'. It is perhaps rash to take so excellent a guide when I do not intend to follow him all the way; but I have no wish to hide my debt to the paper or my admiration for its skill and economy. On the opposing side Thomas Nagel's *The Possibility of Altruism* (1970) supplies a richness of reasoning for which I am also thankful.

philosophies of mind but turns on a very precise point. Indeed the point is so precise and well-worked that the issue resembles the disputed analysis of a chess opening, with each camp having a favoured line and a counter to the other's.

The leading Kantian line is that a man may sit in judgement on his present desires and, when reason demands, decide to act against the balance of his 'internal reasons'. (The phrase 'internal reasons' will be decoded with Bernard Williams' help in a moment.) The best Humean counter-move is that any reason which actually moves a man must be somehow internal to his 'subjective motivational set' (Williams' phrase) and that the Kantian cannot do without a psychological link between reason and action. My Kantian retort will be that, in recognising a reason as good, a rational man makes it his own. Meanwhile the leading Humean line is that action occurs at one time rather than another only because some present desire has force at that time. My Kantian counter-move will be that 'present desire' must be construed here either so narrowly that rational agents become hopelessly improvident or so broadly that the externalist gets all he asks. It is, I confess, hard to avoid the suspicion that the game should be 'drawn with best play', to use the chess analyst's handy term for a game which God could not win against himself. But I shall press for a Kantian win and, with it, implications for other topics which I find irresistible.

To draw the battle lines I shall borrow from Bernard Williams. The question of 'Internal and External Reasons' is how we are to construe sentences of the form '*A* has reason to ϕ.' Two ways are offered. In one 'the truth of the sentence implies, very roughly, that *A* has some motive which will be furthered by his ϕ-ing'. This is the internalist way, inspired by the thought that reason is and can only be the slave of the passions. The other way carries no such implication and makes space for 'external reasons', which can exist unrecognised by the agent and can come to move a man simply by being recognised by him.

The internalist construal derives from Hume but, out of respect for the complexity of Hume's own views, Williams dubs it 'sub-Humean'. It is right in spirit, he thinks, but not ready for battle in the simple form just given. Improvements are readily worked in, however, firstly by reducing the authority of A's current beliefs and desires. Thus A can want to drink a cup of liquid but not have a reason to do so, if he does not realise that the liquid is poisonous. For he would not in fact further his desire for a reviving drink by taking a swig of poison. Equally A may be mistaken about his own desires. If he has an unacknowledged desire, which would be furthered by ϕ-ing, then he can have an unacknowledged reason to ϕ. These extensions of the simplest model are well anchored in his existing motivational set and hence uncontentious.

A motivational set need not be static. A man can acquire new motivations through new information or further deliberation, provided that he already has a motivation to deliberate from. Furthermore, 'motivation' can be taken pretty broadly, with 'desire' read merely as a formal label for whatever can move a man. A motivational set 'can contain such things as dispositions of evaluation, patterns of emotional reaction, personal loyalties and various projects as they are abstractly called, embodying commitments of the agent'. Such desires need not be selfish; 'he will, one hopes, have non-egoistic projects of various kinds and these equally can provide internal reasons for action'.

The sub-Humean model is thus made flexible without the dropping of the principle that a reason for action must depend somehow on an existing desire. Indeed it is now so flexible that the externalist is in for a thin time. For instance it is often held that a person can have needs which he is unaware of and which hence seem not to belong to his motivational set. That looks like ammunition for the externalist. But, with the sub-Humean model now ranging over unconscious motives, a need is a source of external reasons only if the agent 'really is uninterested in pursuing what he needs; and this is not the product of false belief; and he could not reach any such motive from motives he has by the kind of deliberative processes we have discussed'. These conditions are so strong, says Williams, that they will seldom be known to be true.

Then how about duty, that stern voice which can cut across all our desires? For example might a man from a military family have a duty, and hence a reason, to become a soldier, even though he had not the slightest wish or feeling of prior commitment to deliberate from? If so, duty would indeed be an external reason.

But there is still the further puzzle of how an external reason could possibly come to motivate him. A 'psychological link' would be needed. The obvious link would be his coming to believe the truth of the external reason statement. But, since he could come to believe it only by deliberating from an existing motivation, the link consists in the emergence of an internal reason. Thus the externalist finds that his best examples either turn out to be suppressed internal reasons or could succeed in motivating only if addressed to a motivation already present. In sum, Williams concludes, 'external reason statements, when definitely isolated as such, are false, incoherent or really something else misleadingly expressed'.

So much for summary. Williams' line is, I think, strategically and tactically best for Humean philosophers of mind. The anchor point is that only desires (or members of a 'subjective motivational set') can move a man. With that fixed, there is evident scope for interplay among desires, in response to rational deliberation, with reason acting as an intelligent and ingenious slave of the passions. I make no attempt to stop Williams at source or to suggest that his tactics could be bettered. But I do not grant that external reasons can be all but banished in this way.

A preliminary comment is that Williams is not altogether a friend of the usual theory of rational choice, even at its most flexible. That theory treats desires as complete antecedents of actions, as identifiable causes operating *ex ante*, whereas Williams, to judge from his other writings, thinks of agents as characterised by 'projects' which inform their lives. A project is not a blueprint, to be enacted after rational deliberation. It is more like an operatic theme, which unfolds and develops as a life takes on texture and shape. So the rationality of action is not wholly instrumental. There are expressive elements too, and the more this turns out to matter the more wary the stock theorist of rational choice should be of a sophisticated Humean defence. But most of what Williams offers can be accepted with thanks, and this comment will keep until later.

My response will be to set a 'sub-Kantian' model against his 'sub-Humean' one. The simplest version would be this: A has a reason to ϕ if A's interests would be furthered by ϕ-ing. 'Interests' here no more means egoistic interests than 'desires' in

77

the sub-Humean model means egoistic desires – if Williams can say it on behalf of Hume, I can also say it on behalf of Kant. The crux is the difference in vantage point involved in appealing to interests rather than to desires. The sub-Kantian model allows for the monitoring of desires in ways which the sub-Humean thinks out of court. It is a further question whether the sub-Kantian is to regard A's interests as special to A or to some group or sort of persons which A belongs to or is to regard them as common to all mankind or even to all intelligent beings. Thus it is often held that it is in the interests of a rational agent to act morally and that to be moral is to do what is impersonally and universalisably right for everyone so placed. There is much which might be discussed and disputed here, but there is no need to do it before the sub-Kantian model can be proposed. It is enough to claim that A has interests which are conceptually independent of his desires.

To establish a sub-Kantian model in full, three moves are needed:

(a) Actions classed as rational by one model and irrational by the other are correctly classed by the sub-Kantian.
(b) Actions classed similarly by both models are construed at least as effectively by the sub-Kantian.
(c) External reasons can move a rational man.

Let us start with (a) and the familiar case of the junkie, hell-bent on his next fix. He certainly 'has some desire the satisfaction of which would be served' by his getting it and so promises to be acting rationally by the test of the initial sub-Humean formula. But Williams' reformulations make it harder to decide whether there is truly a reason for him. He may be mistaken about his desires or about the best way to satisfy them or about the consequences. He may have some second motivation which will be frustrated and which yields better reason to change his ways. Even if he consistently and persuasively denies that he has any deeper motivation, for instance, to preserve his health, we might still be inclined to insist that 'really at some level he *must* want to be well'. So the story needs to be told with caution. But it should be easy enough to navigate round all conditions except the last. Suppose him to be well informed about the consequences but too firmly addicted to care. Suppose that no substitutes or clinics are to hand. Suppose that other projects of his, although perhaps important enough to give him pause, clearly weigh less with him in the balance. Suppose in short that his subjective motivational set has all the sort of self-conscious reflective consistency that Williams demands and he is still overridingly an addict. Will he not have a sub-Humeanly sufficient reason to take his next fix?

Well, there is the final clause. But Williams states it rather oddly, as if it applies only if the junkie has *no* interest in his health. I take it, however, that the point is not that a motivation has been completely overlooked but that a balance has been wrongly struck. At some level the junkie does want to be well, but this desire is undercut or overridden by others. Put thus, the final clause is less easily invoked by a sub-Humean. The purpose – indeed the merit in many ways – of insisting on internal reasons is to respect the actual motivations of the actor. Respect means that there can be no further complaint about an actor who has achieved a self-conscious reflective consistency. There is no more external sense in which weights can have been wrongly assigned to existing motivations. The actor's most general project cannot be irrational, provided that it is consistent, after the usual discounting for cost, likelihood and so forth. If this is to be a significant thesis, there must be clear, and indeed common, cases where the fact that the project is the actor's own is decisive. Relativity must be to the actor's actual motivational set and not to some idealised version. Hence the final clause either adds nothing to what was supposed in the previous paragraph or gives the game away.

The difference between sub-Humean and sub-Kantian is hard to isolate because the overlap is greater than Williams makes it look. People's desires usually have much in common with their interests. If the junkie were simply preferring a short life and a gay one to a long and drab measuring out of his life with coffee spoons (as T. S. Eliot puts it) then there would be no need for squirming on the internalist account. But this would not imply that the externalist has no leverage. It would mean merely that there was no clear external reason to think the choice of a short life contrary to his interests. To isolate the difference, we need a case which forces desires and interests further apart. This will make it clear that the crux concerns the proper and improper ways of striking a balance of reasons.

Consider some drastic choice which involves planning the whole shape of a life. For instance Adam can either try to become a successful novelist – a painful process with long odds but glittering prizes – or easily become a petty clerk, with low but assured satisfaction. Quantified notionally, his direct choice is this:

	Utiles	Likelihood	Expected utility
Novelist	100	10%	10
Clerk	5	100%	5

He could, however, go at it indirectly. There is a brain operation which would put novel-writing almost beyond him and, anyway, make even the prizes less satisfying but which would greatly raise the joys of being a clerk. This changes the terms of choice to:

	Utiles	Likelihood	Expected utility
Novelist	50	4%	2
Clerk	25	100%	25

(The numbers are there simply to make the choice more graphic; nothing depends on cardinality.) On the simplest sub-Humean account, Adam's rational choice, given his present desires, is to be the novelist of the first table, just as the junkie's is to take the next fix. But Williams' refinements, which give the junkie better reason to abstain, may make it rational for Adam to have the operation. Do they?

At first glance they plainly do, since there is a higher expected utility for the clerk of the second table than for the novelist of the first. Were the indirect strategy less radical, there would be no doubt about it. A course of training, for example, or marrying a publisher's daughter might change the chances of success. Conversely there may be milder ways of enhancing the satisfactions of a clerk's life, like joining the office social club. In other words the expected-utility figures are negotiable by operating indirectly both on the likelihoods and on the utilities. It is perhaps unclear where the line falls between recalculating the terms of the direct choice and changing the terms by indirect strategy; but, in one way or another, there is room for manoeuvre. There is no deep puzzle yet about the idea of engineering some change in one's own subjective motivational set. The brain operation, however, threatens to change Adam's identity (whatever exactly that may mean) and thus, in effect, involves him in interpersonal comparisons of utility. There seems, offhand, to be some limit to the change in the motivational set which can be contemplated without destroying the balance of reasons.

To divide internalist from externalist, let us so set the limit that the operation offers no path from Adam to Adam*, which Adam, being as he is, can rationally accept from an internalist standpoint. Yet let us suppose also that Adam* would be glad to have had the operation. That suggests, on second glance, that, on the balance of internal reasons, Adam is rational to refuse the operation and try his hand at novels; whereas, on the balance of what must therefore be external reasons, he will choose to forfeit his identity and become a happy clerk. If so, this is an awkward result for the externalist and one which Williams would relish.

The argument is about how to weight reasons in the balance of reasons. It is not (or not yet) as if the externalist were introducing what the internalist refuses to recognise as reasons at all. Both recognise some reason for Adam to have the operation. But the internalist weights it relatively to Adam's existing motivational set and, finding no strong enough desire in Adam for a change of identity, turns it down. The externalist should not, of course, be saddled with recommending brain surgery wholesale. Nor, I trust, is he urging a Brave New World of happy morons on us, as a solution to some famous problems in political theory. But he is willing in principle to weight reasons independently of existing motivations. I shall argue next that he is right.

There used to be a telling advertisement for a pension scheme which made its point with portraits of the same man at five stages of his life. I: He is twenty-five and saying cheerfully, 'I have no idea whether my job carries a pension.' II: At thirty-five he is noting with a slight frown, 'My job has no pension, but...'. III: At forty-five he is admitting, 'I wish my job had a pension.' IV: At fifty-five he is declaring, 'I am deeply worried about retirement.' V: At sixty-five, white-haired and furrowed, he is confessing, 'I really don't know how I shall manage without a pension.' The message, then, is that a pension at sixty-five matters at twenty-five. The question is whether the internalist is in a position to endorse it.

Suppose that Adam, aged twenty-five, has opted for the clerk's job and expects to grow old with his firm. The firm has no pension scheme of its own and the advertisement has just arrived on his desk. If he does not subscribe, he will regret it later; but for the moment and for many years to come he has better uses for the price of the premium. Shall he choose jam today or bread tomorrow? In part it is a matter of calculation. For instance he may die before sixty-five, and the risk needs discounting for. There are other sorts of uncertainty and a familiar element of time preference for immediate satisfactions over future ones. He must work out the real rate of interest on the premiums. This is all by the book and lets him compare one scheme with another in familiar ways – I am not trying to undermine the practical basis of insurance. But in another way the basis of calculation is far from straightforward. Adam I is not merely deciding what to provide for Adam V. He can also affect the motivational set of Adam V and hence the value for Adam V of whatever is provided. That is awkward for the sub-Humean account. Schematically let the possibilities be these:

$$
AI \longrightarrow
\begin{cases}
AII \longrightarrow
\begin{cases}
AIII \longrightarrow AIV \longrightarrow AV \\
AIII' \longrightarrow AIV' \longrightarrow AV'
\end{cases} \\
AII' \longrightarrow AIII'' \longrightarrow AIV'' \longrightarrow
\begin{cases}
AV'' \\
AV'''
\end{cases}
\end{cases}
$$

There are four paths, each giving Adam a different biography. For example Adam I is a bachelor; Adam II is married but Adam II' is not; Adam III has children but Adam III' does not and Adam III'' is a confirmed misogynist; Adam IV is expecting a grandchild, Adam IV' is divorced and Adam IV'' is collecting antiques; Adam V lives with his family, Adam V' has taken up with a fan dancer, Adam V'' is about to be charged with stealing candelabra and Adam V''' is a miserly old recluse. In practice, no doubt, these paths are largely hidden from Adam I, not least because there are elements of luck involved. But even in practice he may have a fair idea of the possibilities and can see how to make each more or less likely. At any rate suppose that all uncertainties have been discounted and that the forks in the paths depend solely on a choice made by the Adam before. (Adam I will decide whether to marry, Adam II whether to have children, and so on). Assume that Adam I can calculate the value of the pension to each of Adams V, V' V'' and V'''.

The proposition that the rational agent maximises his expected utility is starting to look silly. The insurance company is recommending a premium which will produce at sixty-five half Adam's final salary. Is Adam I to try to arrange for whichever of Adams V, V', V''' will get most value from this pay-off? That cannot be right. Adam V''' is a miserly recluse who will live to be 100 on a diet of carrot juice, provided that Adams II', III'' and IV'' have been abstemious too. He is duly glad that Adam I decided not to marry the bewitching Eve, especially as Adam I would have done so were he not trying to maximise the value of the pension. In brief, the fact that Adam V''' is best content is not a sufficient reason for setting off down that path. On the other hand, it is equally odd for Adam I to consider solely the expected utility of Adam I and thus to turn the pension scheme down without more ado. But I shall postpone giving the exact reasons until I have landed the internalist with this solution. So, still taking the puzzle at face value but with uncertainties discounted and time preference allowed for, let us think about picking the path with the greatest total utility.

That sounds promising, especially if this total is greater than that of any path without a pension. Then it seems rational for Adam I to pay his premium and steer his character accordingly. But there is a difficulty about establishing the point of view from which this is a promising solution. The sum (or average) of the utilities of the five stages may be unattractive to most of the occupants. For instance the path involving AIV' has a period of glory with a fan dancer, but its high total goes with a terrible old age. Should a path of $10 + 10 - 20 + 100 - 50 (= + 50)$ really outweigh one of $10 + 5 + 10 + 10 + 10 (= + 45)$? If the question can be taken at face value, we might be tempted to substitute a maximin strategy, picking the path with the highest utility at its worst stage. The reader who catches the echo of recent discussion of Justice will take the point. But that also does nothing to explain the point of view from which Adam's judgement can be made. In effect a new *dramatis persona* called 'Adam-at-large' has entered the story, and we shall need to know more about him.

Before enquiring further, however, I want to identify the difficulty which an internalist faces. At each stage Adam is moved by what weighs heavier in the balance of his internal reasons. Adam's internal reasons at stage I are those of Adam I. Now it may be that Adam I is a soft touch for the insurance salesman because he is burdened with thoughts of decay and death. In that case the internal balance favours paying up. But it need not be so. What it is rational for Adam I to do depends on what Adam I happens to have in his motivational set. Adam I does not have all the desires which later Adams will have and which will make Adam V (or V' or V'' or V''') glad that Adam I signed on. So it is possible that Adam I will rationally do what he knows that Adam V will resent. I do not imply that Adam I is never rational to do what he knows will displease Adam V. Old age has no monopoly of wisdom. The point is that, on an internalist account, Adam I is moved to act by the balance of Adam I's internal reasons. The desires of Adam V come into it only if they happen to weigh with Adam I. So Adam's choice of fun today or a pension at sixty-five threatens to become one between fun for Adam I and a mere receipt from the insurance company for Adam I. Since Adam I will not, it seems, even be around to collect the pension, Adam V's internal reasons threaten to weigh very light with him.

The internalist is soon sunk if Adam I cannot be moved by Adam V's desires directly. In that case the next move is to subdivide Adam I. In the advertisement he has a ten-year span. Think of the decade as ten year-long Adams; then think of each as twelve-month-long Adams, and so on. We shall soon find Adam rationally swilling the cheapest gin today, knowing full well that tomorrow's hangover will be far worse than today's glow. It might still happen that today's heaviest desire needed time and investment for fruition. But that is now unlikely, granted that today's man has all the costs and tomorrow's all the benefits. The more Adam can be subdivided, the more like Aesop's grasshopper he becomes – a thought which I shall return to at the end of the chapter.

'Happen', admittedly, is a tendentious word. Someone may object that, although it is contingent that people's strongest desires are often not for immediate gratification, it is by no means a matter of luck. Were humans constituted like grasshoppers, we would not still be here to discuss it. That is true enough, but not to the point. The question is solely whether it can be rational to act on present desires which are utterly improvident. The simplest sub-Humean model seems to yield the silly answer that it can, provided the improvident desires outweigh the rest. If this answer is indeed implied, then concern for others and even for later stages of oneself will turn out to be external reasons and ones which can evidently move us to action.

Williams' improvements block the silly answer in two ways. One is to require consistency and judgement on the part of a rational agent, so that the balance of internal reasons shall be objectively struck. But there is nothing here to prevent desires which result in utterly improvident action but are assembled with consistency and judgement. A man who knows the effects of cyanide and wants more than anything to know what it feels like to swallow it will still act rationally in taking a spoonful. The other block is to prevent the fragmentation of the self into a series of distinct selves, each being, so to speak, distinct persons. Each of us has dispositional elements – capacities for love, hate, sympathy and other Humean motives – which need preamble and time for consummation. Each of us also has a 'project' on which his identity is staked, and this project gives shape and contour to his subjective motivational set. The self, then, is neither substance nor series but a construct marked by a project. The weightings and weighings which result in rational action, if well conducted, are expressions of the shape of a life. Internal reasons are finally internal to an agent's identity.

This is the message which I get from Williams' work and I am all for it. But it makes no sub-Humean sense to me at all. A passive, dispositional account of the agent's identity does not, I agree, do justice to our ways of reshaping ourselves for what we take to be good reasons. But a constructive account which makes the agent self-directed reopens the questions which Williams claimed to have closed. Projects are mutable. Adam I has a choice of several, some pleasing to Adam V, some displeasing and some cutting out Adam V altogether. To avoid chaos there will certainly have to be some appeal to a point of view which I dubbed earlier 'Adam-at-large'. But to define Adam-at-large in terms of a mutable project is to reintroduce the contingency which caused all the trouble with Adam I. There will have to be something about the sort of shape of this overarching project which sounds uncommonly like guidance of external reasons.

To sum up this detour, then, there is a puzzle for sub-Humeans about delayed gratification. It arises because a rational agent will presumably provide for some desires which he foresees but does not yet have. A sub-Humean agent is moved only by present desires. A present desire to provide for a future desire, if present at all, is likely to weigh lighter than a desire for jam today. If the agent knew that the world would end tomorrow, he would be likely to choose jam today; and, once the self is segmented into distinct motivational sets, it is as if the world were about to end. The threat posed by fragmenting Adam into five decades applies at every moment of Adam's life. It is not lifted by building dispositional concerns, like sympathy for later stages of his life or for other people, into the agent's constitution. If it is at least partly blocked by introducing the idea of a grand project, that, it seems, is only because the idea of a grand project gives the game to the external reasons theorist.

That brings us back to Adam-at-large as an element in deciding rationally between possible paths. The three options so far are the maximum utility for Adam I, the maximum for the whole path and the maximum for the least favoured stage (maximin). How does it help to consider Adam-at-large? The reply which seems finally best to me is that it does not help at all, unless we stop thinking solely in utilities. With Adam-at-large we enter the realm of identity, as Williams maintains. Expressive, rather than instrumental, rationality will finally be the crux. But that reply will cause trouble of various kinds and I shall lead up to it by showing that the snags caused by thinking solely in utilities are worse.

If Adams I, II, III, IV and V are to be treated as separate claimants on a varying stock of utility, we have a nasty analogue of the future generations puzzle. Let 'A' in the pathway diagram stand for 'generation'. Plainly AV, V', V'' and V''' are different sets of people, with earlier generations deciding which of the possible later sets shall become actual. In this posing I cannot myself see why a generation has any internal reason to invest in a tolerable life for its successors. A notion of rational-choice-behind-a-veil-of-ignorance yields the absurd image of all these possible people making suggestions for deciding which of them shall remain merely possible. An assumption that everyone has a streak of natural sympathy, which extends to persons who need never be conceived, is a flimsy dodge. Somehow an element of community over time or communal interest will have to be worked in and, in terms of a scheme where internal reasons relate to the utilities of separate individuals, community will have to be a source of external reasons. Although I cannot pursue the future generations puzzle now, I hope that no one will want to construe the parts of Adam's life by analogy with this version of it.

The point of introducing Adam-at-large, then, is so to link Adams I, II, III, IV and V that each can act rationally against the balance of immediate internal reasons. This would not be achieved by leaving the five Adams as separate claimants on the total utility and adding a sixth Adam as a sort of umpire. That is because the umpire would be deciding not between five actual claimants but between an indefinite number of possible ones. Adam-at-large will have to be the only person and the other Adams suitably downgraded. Yet there remains a perfectly good sense in which 'Adam I' names a subjective motivational set, within which the balance of internal reasons favours the present satisfaction of present desires. That sense was established when we considered the clerk *vs.* the novelist and saw that the balance of internal reasons took the existing tariff of utilities as given. The function of Adam-at-large is to review the principles by which the balance of internal reason is struck. He is there, if you like, to set the exchange rate, without which the value of an internal reason cannot be measured. The sub-Humean model, however flexible, cannot function without a given measure of value, and hence has to take as given what, to my mind, varies over time and with the choices made. If we take seriously the demand that an agent always have an existing motivation to deliberate from, then there has to be a bias towards the present state of the self. Conversely, if an agent is to act against the balance of present desires and remain sub-Humean, he will have to be credited with a desire to do the rational thing; and it is too late to deem this a 'desire' available to Humeans.

87

If Adam is to be able to act rationally – or, indeed, at all – against the balance of his internal reasons, he will have to be able to be moved by a belief. The sub-Humean obstacle, according to Williams, is that belief alone cannot move to action; nor can a belief be rational unless acquired by deliberation, which works from a previous motivation. The time has come to work this obstacle loose. I shall next try to do it *ad hominem*.

Williams means us to assent to his argument, having found it rationally persuasive. He cares how he wins our assent. His message is that his case supplies good reason for any and every rational person to assent, whatever his previous motivational set. Otherwise there will finally be no epistemic difference between justified belief and approved belief, a result with consequences too horrid to mention. But, if the case supplies good reason for *everyone*, then either everyone already has suitable internal motivation or the good reason is external. Yet, since the desire in question would be a desire to assent to the conclusion of a sound argument with true premises, it is simply a special case of the 'desire' to do the rational thing, which Humeans distrust. Besides, I doubt if everyone does have the internal motivation required. There are plenty of bigots who have invested too much in their prejudices to be willingly moved by rational argument. Since Williams thinks that they have no less reason to grant his case than do open-minded persons, he sounds like the pedlar of an external reason. If so, the better his case, the easier it is to refute, because, the better it is, the more it overrides any internal reasons which bigots may have for dissenting!

Perhaps sub-Humeans should acknowledge a possible desire to do the rational thing after all. There could be room for one in a motivational set which already 'can contain such things as dispositions of evaluation, patterns of emotional reaction, personal loyalties and various projects, as they may be abstractly called, embodying commitments of the agent'. But first we must ask how such things get into a motivational set. Williams speaks at that moment in the paper as if they were either innate or caught like measles. That is all very well, if we are content to think of agents as the intelligent instruments of their own passions. But it will not do once the agent has been ascribed a self-direction, which distances him from his passions. The natural model of action is then rational deliberation, where agents arrive at beliefs neither by whim nor by inner impulse nor through socialisation but by recognising the merit of good reasons. Rational assent occurs because the rational person, in recognising a good reason, makes the reason his own.

Assent is a humble action, but an action nonetheless. So an account of how a rational man assents, which requires no motive beyond a notional desire to accept what is warranted, will generalise. In recognising that there is good reason for him to ϕ, the rational man acquires good reason to ϕ. Sub-Humean objection to this simple denouement falls under two heads. One is that there being good reason for him to ϕ is some function of his existing motivational set. But I have already dealt with that as best I can by showing, in effect, how a reason may be good relative to his new motivational set, while remaining outweighed in the balance of his old one. The other is that not even having acquired good reason is enough to produce action; I turn next to that.

Action occurs at a time and place, whereas good reasons are apparently timeless. For instance I have had good reason to write this chapter for at least a year without acting on it until now. In general the rational reconstruction of action, which is so central to rational–man hermeneutics, often fails to explain why actors act when they do. Hence the timing of action seems to depend on the state of motivation rather than on the recognition of reasons. I reply, however, that time is a scarce resource and cannot be used in two exclusive ways at once. The rational man is always busy – granted that he may sometimes rationally be busy doing nothing – and his good reason to ϕ becomes sufficient to move him only if he has no better reason not to ϕ. Thus the removal of a reason against can trigger a reason for. (There is, admittedly, the question of *akrasia* or weakness of will, but I need not go into it to make my point.) The trigger to rational action operates on the balance of good reasons, and there is no need to construe it as producing a change in desires. Typically the removal of a reason for doing something else instead or the approach of a deadline can make a good reason effective at a particular time. I do not argue simply that, since a change in beliefs can lead to action, mere belief is therefore enough to move a man. That would be too quick. But I do mean to say that the sort of explanation of the rational man's ϕ-ing at whatever time can also, when tightened, explain the particular time.

The discussion can now be gathered in. Three propositions were earlier said to be needed to establish the sub-Kantian line.

(a) *Actions classed as rational by one model and irrational by the other are correctly classed by the sub-Kantian*

The crucial group are actions against the present balance of internal reasons which the rational agent will be glad to have performed. They divide into those where, as with Adam and the pension, the actor foresees the desire but is sub-Humeanly unable rationally to provide for it; and those, as with the junkie, where he would be rational to create the desire in himself. I think the group crucial because I insist that the rational man is master of his passions and so his own free sovereign artificer. Williams is not in fact hostile to some such doctrine, since something like it is moving him to make the sub-Humean model more flexible. But he makes it too flexible for its origins, I maintain, and thus plays into the hands of the rival camp.

(b) *Actions within the scope of both models are construed at least effectively by the sub-Kantian*

Whenever the balance of internal reasons comes down in the agent's real interests, both models will give the same reckoning. But this is not to put them on all fours. When judging whether a statement is true, we might confine ourselves to judging whether some argument which implied it was valid. If the argument was valid and moreover happened to have true premises, then we would get the right answer. Yet that does not make it unnecessary to consider whether the premises were true. Similarly the sub-Kantian model demands that the agent have good reason for his desires, whereas the sub-Humean asks only coherence and perhaps practicality. That makes for a large difference in how the metaphor of the balance is to be regarded. For the sub-Humean model, it expresses the passivity of an agent whose output is dictated by his discounted preferences. For the sub-Kantian model, it captures the impartiality of the rational agent, whose decision includes judging whether his desires are desirable.

(c) *External reasons can move a rational man*

The stress here is on 'rational'. No doubt a person can sometimes be the slave of his passions and an internalist account will do for him. But it is also possible to decide rationally against the balance of internal reasons; or so I have argued. At first I argued it for the rare case of a person deciding the shape of his life. The objection was that whatever actually moves a man must surely be an internal reason; and I replied that it was so only in an empty and question-begging sense. The key lay in actions which he was sorry to perform but glad to have performed. Once the rare case was granted and external motivation made possible, I then argued that it was in truth a common case, since all provision for future desire instanced it. In other words an externalist analysis of action seems to me to give a better general account of the relation between reason and desire in rational action. This is granted, I submit, as soon as the internalist is driven to admit a desire to act on principle or to do the rational thing.

The argument has been formal and has given no serious clue to the nature of 'real interests'. In particular I have carefully not said whether all people have the same real interests or whether each is special. This is a deep question in ethics and will be taken up on another occasion. For the moment I shall merely note the formal conditions for rational choice which seem to me to emerge:

(1) ϕ-ing is the best (i.e. most effective, discounted) action to realise state s.
(2) It is in actor A's overall real interest to realise s.
(3) These conditions are A's own reason for ϕ-ing.

Formally 'real interest' is a dummy so far, but we can see what job needs doing. There has to be a source of reasons for judging that what is rational relative to a given motivational set remains rational when options of varying the set are allowed for. To fill in the dummy, I shall need to locate the actor in social relations with others and to connect the shape of his actions to his identity as a social person. That task is postponed for the moment.

Conclusion

The book is intended both to secure a robust sense in which Adam can be the sovereign artificer of his own life and to leave him the subject of a social science which respects the logic and power of decision-theory. The switch from an internal to an external reasons account of rational motivation is crucial on both counts.

As an aid to sovereignty, it opens a gap between desires and interests, which leads into the political theory of liberty. If we were confined to a language of internal reasons, we would have to describe people who succeeded in enacting their reflectively consistent preferences as free agents. Happy slaves, well adjusted to an enduring system of slavery, could not be suffering from false consciousness. They get what they want and want what they get. Yet that ignores a major dimension of the exercise of power, the manipulation of wants. To instil coherent, satisfiable wants in people is often to exercise a very real power over them. I do not mean to imply that wants thus instilled are necessarily 'false', or that such power has to be malign. But I do insist that enduring contentment is not a sufficient test of liberty and hence that there is a further question about reasons for wants, requiring a language of external reasons.

The serpent may or may not have fooled Eve, but he certainly engineered a change in her subjective motivational set. On the political theory side I draw the moral that an agent can act on false beliefs about external reasons or on true ones, and that it will need a substantive theory of ethics to decide which is which. My own guess is that such a theory will disconnect the idea of alienation from its internalist reading as the frustration of present desires and connect it to ideas of identity, citizenship and community. That calls for a positive theory of liberty (or theory of positive liberty), which may be thought to end in totalitarianism. But J. S. Mill was willing to risk the first step by propounding his account of individuality, and his case for thinking in terms of fully fledged individuals, who are concerned for others as a matter of course, is not to be dismissed. Meanwhile there is also a moral for the explanation of action. I picture Eve as moved by belief to want a knowledge of good and evil, whose value she could not assess until she had acquired it. If this is a possible picture, it calls for large revisions in the standard theory of rational choice and explanation, as will emerge in the next two chapters. Here is a preliminary comment.

Weber suggests that, to understand action, one must first assess it by the test of what a fully rational agent would have done in the circumstances. The test establishes both what can be understood through the agent's own good reasons and what is still puzzling, because the agent did not have good reasons. Supposing Weber to be right, it will make a difference what is included in the test. On an internalist account, the agent is assessed only for consistency of preferences, accuracy of information and correctness of calculation. On an externalist one, there is a further question about the rationality of preferences, which spills over into the choice of means. For instance both accounts make it irrational to prefer brown eggs to white if the reason is an unjustified belief that brown eggs are better for one's health. But the internalist would be content if the reason were an aesthetic preference for brown. That sounds only sensible until one asks whether it is rational to prefer Spanish oranges to South African if the reason is a dislike of apartheid. Here the externalist insists that the issue is not 'dislike', as if apartheid were a matter of taste, but the moral character of the regime and hence an objective property of the oranges. Once the issue is seen in these terms, it also affects the evaluation of possible actions as the means to a goal. This is not a comfortable result, because it lands us with objectivism in ethics. What the internalist thinks of as 'ethical preferences' now fall under the heading of beliefs rather than of desires, and economics becomes a moral science in earnest. But, I submit, we shall have to live with the idea that rationality depends on the truth about interests which do not boil down to tastes of any sort in the end.

Having aired this daunting thought, I revert to the Leviathan trap. An agent with a preference order of 01, 11, 00, 10 has a dominant *internal* reason to choose 0, even if he happens to know that the other player has a similar order. He can, however, have an external reason to choose 1 if he can be moved by the belief that 11 is a better outcome. For this to be a good and sufficient external reason, there are two conditions. One is that the belief is true (or at least held for objectively good reasons). This requires a point of view more impersonal than the one from which *01* suits him better than *11*. For instance *01* is unfair or does less for the total happiness or gives him some other test of the general interest by which to assess his own real interest contrary to his current desires. The other is that he can expect the other player also to accept the external reason. An external reason to contribute to *11* is trumped by the knowledge that the attempt will result in *10*.

The latter condition is a formal way of saying that to defeat the Leviathan trap we need a moral notion of trust. The norm which opens the trap is neither consensual, in the sense of a mutually convenient salient, nor coercive, in the sense that breaking it is too risky to be worth it, but moral. What makes it an escape, as opposed to a sign that preferences have been wrongly described, is that it operates through reason as a lever on desire. But, unlike purer moralists, who define the right course of action as what would be for the best, if all complied, I am leaving the rational agent influenced by whether the outcome will be *11* or *10*. Morality is an Assurance game on the whole, and, although I do not wish to rule out occasions when a moral agent should choose *1* and damn the consequences, I do not rely on them to defeat the Leviathan trap.

As a last, oblique comment on the dispute between external and internal reasons, the appendix offers a fable about the snags of prudence.

Appendix
The Ant and the Grasshopper

All summer long the Grasshopper consumed and the Ant invested. 'You are acting very irrationally', the Ant warned, 'and you will be sorry when winter comes.' 'I shall be very sorry', replied the Grasshopper with a chirrup, 'but I am not acting irrationally. To be rational is to do what one most values at the time, and I value present delight above its cost in future sorrow. Surely you too would rather sit in the sun and sing?' 'Much rather', said the Ant, 'but to be rational is to do what best promotes one's interests over a lifetime. Future grief has constant weight (where there is no uncertainty about it). So, being rational, I must keep busy investing against winter.'

Winter came and the Grasshopper was hungry. He appealed to the Ant for help. 'I wish I could', said the Ant; 'there is nothing I would like better. But, being rational, I cannot prefer your interests to mine, and you have nothing to offer in return. Are you not sorry you sang all summer?' 'Very sorry', the Grasshopper sighed, 'just as I knew I would be. But now is now – I acted rationally then. It is you who are irrational, in resisting your present desire to help me.'

The Ant reconsidered but found that he had only just enough in store to last him until it was time to start investing again. 'Now is every time', he explained, 'but I can help in one way. Do you know the leaves of the Epicurus plant over there? They are nourishing and delicious. I would eat them myself (and save the trouble of making my own granary), but it makes insects very ill after a time and, being rational, I cannot abuse my lifetime's interests. For you, however, the present ecstasy would out-weigh the consequences, silly fellow.'

So the Grasshopper sampled an Epicurus leaf and found it excellent, but was soon in agony. 'Is it worth it?' asked the Ant. 'No it *isn't*', the Grasshopper groaned, 'but it *was*.' 'Then I have bad news for you – there is an antidote.' 'Quick, quick', begged the Grasshopper. 'It is no use to you', the Ant lamented, 'since taking it makes your present distress far worse, even though it works rapidly thereafter.' 'Bad news indeed! I *cannot* invest. Farewell!'

The Grasshopper expired, and the Ant lived on into grey old age without ever once doing anything which caused him a moment's overall regret. 'It is hard never to be able to do what one most wants to do', he mused arthritically, 'but then the life of a rational being is a hard life.'

Moral: *It is hard to be wise, but there are many ways to be foolish.*

7

Rational Expectations

The role of rational belief in rational choice is strengthened by switching from a Humean to a Kantian account of reasons for action. Instead of just serving the passions, it directs them by requiring the agent to ask what would happen if everyone so placed did the same. This is usually regarded as a moral requirement, plausible if the topic is what life would be like in a world where all did what they should, but irrelevant if we are trying to model a world where all allocate resources rationally. I have been attempting to undermine the distinction by suggesting that there is something amiss with a theory of rational choice which allows each individually rational allocation to sum to an outcome foreseeably inferior for everyone. That invites some sort of universalisability as a test of rational choice. Even so, however, I doubt if readers are so far inclined to construe belief about what it is rational to do on a model of belief about what it is moral to do.

One deep reason for reluctance is a conviction that rational belief and moral belief have a quite different relation to matters of fact. Even in the present nuanced state of the philosophy of science, it remains crucial that believing something so does not

This chapter owes a special debt to Shaun Hargreaves-Heap, beyond the general acknowledgement which I made in the preface. He introduced me to its topic in the first place and schooled me in some economic theorising, which, although largely implicit here, is set out in our joint article 'Great Expectations'. The present chapter and parts of the next two are, in effect, a version of the philosophical theme of that article.

make it so. Rational belief is belief suitably attuned to an independent world, whose states and events are a test. Even if there are no theory-neutral facts, nature is not thereby turned into human handiwork. A modern King Canute cannot stem the tide by reconceptualising it; a modern Newton is still conscious of casting pebbles into an unknown ocean. Although belief can be rational yet false, it is very much geared to prediction and must adapt to failures of prediction. Moral beliefs, on the other hand, seem to have a very different logic and epistemology, marked by the familiar distinction between positive and normative.

The social sciences have inherited a healthy respect for nature and, with it, an ideal of the scientist as observer, whose theories of probability and evidence are detached aids to prediction. Uncertainty can have only two sources. One is that there may be a random streak in the workings of nature, so that even Laplace's 'supreme intelligence', who knew all the forces acting, could not project from any state of the world to every other state. The other is human ignorance, whether because we have a finite information store or because neutral measurement is impossible or because the ontology of nature includes structures and forces at which we can only conjecture. Rational belief cannot cope with randomness, beyond resting content with probabilities which allow for it, but is a systematic assault on ignorance.

Whatever its merits as an approach to understanding nature, this presumes that the social world sets no radical further problem for the analysis of the rational belief. I propose to argue that it does. The question of the chapter is what to make of the undoubted fact that what social actors do depends on their expectations. I shall tackle it by introducing two theories from economics, one of Adaptive Expectations and the other of Rational Expectations, which try to allow for this human peculiarity without upsetting the role of prediction in science, and I shall then urge that expectation is a creative force quite foreign to the natural world. That will add a new and interesting dimension to what is at stake in the dispute between a Humean and a Kantian theory of action.

Every day the radio issues shipping forecasts and traffic forecasts. They sound similar in form and purpose. A force-9 gale is building up over the Faroe Islands, and prudent ships will avoid

it. A nine-mile tail-back is building up on the city by-pass, and prudent cars will steer clear of it. But there is a difference. If all ships
are prudent, there will still be a huge gale over the Faroes, but no
one will be caught in it. If all cars are prudent, there will be no jam
on the city by-pass, and any very prudent or very imprudent
motorist will have a clear road. I propose to take this
difference very seriously indeed. To do it, I need to borrow
ideas from economics without getting into deeper technicalities
than I am competent to discuss. So I shall first cast my theme
as an allegory about weather forecasting in a world where
forecasts affect the weather. The allegory will at least indicate
why I think the usual account of rational belief needs radical
revision.

Let us start with a backdrop of the kind of weather picture
which ends the British television news. There is a map of Britain
peppered with suns, clouds, lightning flashes and other little
symbols to show how things have been today. Then an expert
moves the symbols around to show what we can expect
tomorrow. Today's pattern is descriptive, and tomorrow's predictive. The one is got from the other with the aid of a sophisticated theory, coupled with information about what has been
happening lately here and elsewhere. Putting aside any thought of
a random streak in the weather, we can think of tomorrow's map
as if it were an attempt to peer into an unknown foggy landscape.
The landscape is there, but the fog prevents the forecaster seeing
quite what is in it. So he fills it out by assuming that it is fairly like
similar landscapes which he is familiar with and differs from
them systematically. Or, if you prefer, think of the landscape as
fog-free but of the forecaster as moving through it and trying to
predict what lies ahead. He adapts his expectations as he acquires
new information about what has happened lately and about how
his own earlier expectations turned out.

The point of thinking in terms of an existent landscape, and
either making it foggy or having the forecaster move through it,
is to stress that probabilities are epistemic. They change as human
evidence changes. The difference between past, present and
future matters greatly to the forecaster, but not in the least to the
landscape. This catches the sense in which science finds it natural
to make timeless models of a changing world; and weather fore-

casting (if one remembers that it involves theory, not merely induction) is a neat image of scientific method at work.

Now bring in another aspect of science, control. Suppose that we learn to control the weather a little. Suppose that, although the process is too tricky and expensive to allow complete command even for the British Isles, the government can intervene some-what. It cannot manage tropical heat in February, but it can lay on sunshine for vital events like major cricket matches, the Queen's Birthday Parade or general elections. But will it? That is a new question for the weather forecaster. Formerly there was just the matter of what nature (probably) has in store for tomorrow. Now it is one question what will happen without intervention and another what interventions there will be. But there is no great problem while the questions remain distinct and interventions local. Forecasts continue to be made in the old way, but are declared subject to *ceteris paribus* clauses, with a promise to update them at the end of *Today in Parliament*. It is as if the traveller through the landscape had acquired a very small howitzer for blasting away a few rocks up ahead, but nothing powerful enough to affect the broad continuity.

Then a daring young meteorologist claims to have made a startling discovery. Weather depends on what people expect it to be. He has been researching on an isolated, sparsely populated island in the Faroes and has found that, if he can get almost every-one to expect a force-9 gale, there will be one. But the key word is 'expect'. Gales do not occur just because people *want* them; only if they *expect* them. At first, however, even this somewhat nuanced claim is received sceptically, despite striking cases where the islanders were fed a false forecast and the weather turned out as they had been led to expect. Most pundits are inclined to the milder explanation that islanders are really guided by uncon-scious atavistic hunches, which are more reliable than the usual professional forecasts. This, indeed, will always remain a poss-ible hypothesis. Meanwhile, however, the pundits become so heated that the affair spills into the Sunday papers. Every bar is full of people pointing out that the weather is just what they ex-pected, whenever the forecast gets it wrong. Some pundits begin to wonder whether people at large are better informed than the Meteorological Office, which issues the official forecasts.

The Met. Office pooh-poohs this idea, but starts to worry about something else. One effect of public interest is to increase the membership of a religious cult which claims to have the ear of a weather god. Prayers have a marked effect, they say, provided that they are offered by sincere members who are agreed in what they are asking for and do not expect large dislocations in the climate. None of this would be very worrying were it not that the cult starts to attract public research funds which would have gone to Met. Office research projects. Thoroughly alarmed, the Met. Office hastily commissions a report from the Church of England on coelestial motions, weather gods, heresy and related matters.

The report, when it comes, is, however, pretty reassuring. Although unable to be definite about the existence of any god, the modern church sees nothing special in this new one. The cult members are not claiming more than marginal influence. At most they have special access to better information about what the weather god will decide. Moreover their god is presumably the same god to whom the Church of England has always prayed for good harvests and calm voyages. Vicars have never hesitated to insure their fêtes against rain (or other acts of God) just because the fêtes are holy, or supposed that concerted prayer would save the need for paying the premium. In short, government grants for meteorological research should continue to be given to meteorologists.

Thus encouraged, the Met. Office reaffirms its standard theory of Adaptive Expectations with only a small amendment. The standard theory is a Bayesian one, governing the adaptation of probabilities to changes in evidence. It requires the expected value of a variable to be adjusted for differences between its expected and actual variables on previous occasions by an amount which diminishes with distance in time. (Thus a change in the weather pattern is absorbed gradually, and probabilities adapt to it fully only when information from the previous pattern is old enough not to make a significant difference.) The small amendment is to include a further adjustment governed by the cult's expectations, weighted according to the accuracy of their previous ones. Its effect is to take out modest insurance in case religious expectations do truly have a mild influence on the weather.

Critics, however, led by the daring young meteorologist from the Faroes, soon complain that the Met. Office is missing the point. The new hypothesis is that weather really and truly depends on what people expect. To take it seriously is to recognise that weather therefore depends on what people expect people to expect. This introduces a fresh twist, well caught by Keynes' analogy between the economy and a beauty contest, where the prettiest girl is the one most people think prettiest. In a competition to forecast the winner of the beauty contest

each competitor has to pick, not those faces which he himself finds prettiest, but those which he thinks likeliest to catch the fancy of the other competitors, all of whom are looking at the problem from the same point of view. It's not a case of choosing those which, to the best of one's judgement, really are the prettiest, nor even those which average opinion genuinely thinks the prettiest. We have reached the third degree where we devote our intelligences to anticipating what average opinion expects average opinion to be. (Keynes (1936), pp. 154f).

This is in contrast to a beauty competition where each judge simply votes for the girl he finds prettiest himself and whose rationale is that the winner wins because she is prettiest. In Keynes' version the winner is prettiest because she wins. Apply the thought seriously to weather, and a radically different meteorology is required.

This time the Met. Office tries much harder and comes up with a theory of Rational Expectations, which pays more attention to the possible effects of expectations upon outcomes. It is derived from a theoretical analysis of an ideal-type case where everyone whose expectations matter knows that expectations matter and knows what everyone else expects. This is dubbed the 'Rational Expectations Hypothesis'. Initially the Hypothesis seems to be merely a postulate that no agent makes systematic errors; and it is unclear that this is a novelty. After all, agents with Adaptive Expectations are also supposed to eliminate systematic errors (thus leaving only random ones). But queries about the learning procedure by which errors are removed presently identify a bold innovation. Each rational agent is being credited not only with rational beliefs about previous trends but also with a meteorological model which includes the expectations of other agents.

The theory explores the ideal-type case, where each agent has a correct model, which includes the correct model in the heads of all agents. This promises to be very interesting for cases where some agents have an incorrect model, as soon as weather is seriously held to vary with expectations of it. Meanwhile the Rational Expectations Hypothesis sets up the ideal case.

Already, however, there is a query about the idea of a 'correct' model, even when all agents have a correct model in their heads. To answer it, the Met. Office borrows a standard reply from economics. As suggested by S. M. Sheffrin (1983, p. 11), summing up the discussion among economic theorists, a correct model is one where 'the subjective probability distributions of the economic actors equal the objective probability distributions in the system'. This is neat and clear up to a point. One sees readily what it would mean for, say, the chances of drawing a black ace at random from a shuffled deck of cards. The objective probability is 1 in 26, and to assume rational expectations is merely to add that each gambler knows this (and knows why). But it is less plain what it can mean if 'the objective probability distributions in the system' depend on expectations, instead of *vice versa*. In a paper which was the starting point for recent discussion J. F. Muth (1961, p. 316) worded the crux thus:

I should like to suggest that expectations, since they are informed predictions of future events, are essentially the same as the predictions of the relevant economic theory ... The hypothesis can be rephrased a little more precisely as follows: that expectations of firms (or, more generally, the subjective distributions of outcomes) tend to be distributed, for the same information set, about the prediction of the theory (or the 'objective' distribution of the outcomes).

These are tantalising sentences. Muth realises that he cannot just define subjective/objective probabilities by reference to either epistemic or physical probabilities. Thus the physical probability that an unseen card at the bottom of a shuffled pack is red is 1 (if it is) or 0 (if it is not); but the economy is not yet in any definite outcome state. The epistemic probability of a red card is evens; but this statement belongs to a calculus where expectation plays no part. So, ingeniously, he exploits the plausible idea that a correct theory is one whose errors in prediction are random and not systematically either above or below the actual values of variables. (Where errors are systematic, a better theory could correct them.) Hence agents with fully rational expectations are agents guided by 'the relevant economic theory'. But, unfortunately, this is not only clever but also ambiguous, depending on how one regards the relevant economic theory.

The crux is, so to speak, the direction of fit between expectations and events. The Rational Expectations Hypothesis is central to what is usually termed New Classical Macroeconomics – the recent attempt to generate a macroeconomics from micro foundations by supposing that macroeconomic agents are invariably the standard rational agents of microeconomic theory. The attempt emphasises the scope and limits of production as a determinant of what can happen next and does so by giving all rational agents a model with this emphasis in their heads. (The drift may be clearer if I add that the attempt is congenial to what are often called 'supply-siders' and its conclusions especially congenial to 'monetarists'). An economy starts each period with a stock of resources. Only so much can be produced from this stock, and only so many people employed in producing it. Since money cannot buy more than is produced, extra increases in the money supply can only cause inflation. There are thus 'natural rates' of employment and of the value of money for any level of economic activity, and, although the government can dodge them briefly by artificially stimulating demand, they are not mocked for long. Inflation is their revenge. The Rational Expectations Hypothesis is an elegant theoretical demonstration. In an economy of fully rational agents, each will anticipate the inflationary effects of overstimulating demand and will know that each other agent is doing the same. These rational expectations will combine to raise prices sooner rather than later. Anticipating inflation, rational entrepreneurs will raise their prices rather than their output, and rational workers will demand higher wages rather than agree to do more work. These logical consequences are less visible in an actual, unideal economy, because not everyone is fully rational. But this means only that the informed gain at the expense of the uninformed, with a resulting misallocation of resources.

On this reading rational expectations are those which appreci-
ate the natural rates and the 'relevant economic theory' is one
which embodies this direction of fit. In weather terms, this
school of thought is at the stage where nature sets very severe
limits to the interventions which can succeed. To put it fanci-
fully, misinformed expectations could perhaps cause a heatwave
on 29 February, but nature would take its toll by delaying the
spring. Less allegorically, rational agents form expectations on
the basis of a naturalistic account of human nature and human
society and do not try to achieve more than natural rhythms
permit.

An opposite reading (loosely Keynesian or, very loosely,
'demand side') reverses the direction of fit by giving production
less importance and distribution more. There are still natural
limits on what sorts of purse can be made from a sow's ear, but
they matter less than the expectations of the purse industry. If the
economy is flagging and the government stimulates demand, all
depends on what businessmen and workers expect. If they expect
expansion, there will be expansion. If they expect inflation, there
will be inflation. For an extreme version one might recall Sorel's
Reflections on Violence (1907), where it is argued that social facts
are a myth and no less real for that; a general strike will occur *if and
only if* workers believe that it will. Economists, with their
stronger sense of external constraints, do not carry the idea so far.
Keynes did not suppose that every outcome was possible at every
stage of the business cycle just by expecting it so. But, witness his
beauty contest analogy, he did hold that several outcomes (or
multiple equilibria) were often feasible, with the actual one
depending on which was expected. In weather terms, it is as if
there were indeed a partly responsive weather god.

The difference in the readings may sound like one of degree,
with both accepting some natural limitations and some causal
influence from expectations. Philosophically, however, different
ideas of rational belief are involved. For the New Classical
Macroeconomic reading the Rational Expectations Hypothesis is
at heart simply Adaptive Expectations idealised for a case where
all agents have *complete* information, including information about
others. For instance when fully informed race-goers lay their bets
at starting-price odds, they need to know both how likely each

horse is to win and how much will have been staked when the race starts. The effect of the hypothesis is to ensure that the starting-price odds reflect the merits of the horses. The Keynesian reading, however, opens up interesting questions about the interplay of prediction, intention and decision. At the limit it is as if the horse with the most money staked on it at the start was thereby deemed the winner. If this limiting case is peculiar, so is the other, as we shall see.

To illustrate the interplay of prediction, intention and decision, let us think further about the weather god. He can make tomorrow wet or fine. Which shall it be? That is partly a question about what he intends. But there is also more to it, since today's intentions are not always put into action tomorrow and since his intentions are not formed on a whim. To that extent even his own statement of intention is a prediction, whose likely correctness can be assessed by the evidence of what the members of the cult are expecting him to do. At the same time, however, intending is a performative verb. What one honestly states to be one's present intention thereby is one's present intention, and the performative quality carries forward diminishingly to the future decision. With no time lag, to intend now is to decide now; with a gap, to intend a later action is to decide conditionally what one expects to do. That makes for a tricky amalgam of an agent's and an observer's point of view, even for a weather god, who represents a single agent forming his own decision.

The amalgam is trickier still if the weather god is a fiction representing the balance of rational expectations on the part of the members of the cult. To form rational expectations, each member singly needs to predict what all members collectively will decide. The decision is a sum of the predictions. In so far as each rational prediction has to fall within the range of feasible continuations, the process of forming rational beliefs is within the scope of a theory of Adaptive Expectations. But, in so far as it involves the oblique self-reference of each agent's expectations about other agents being embedded in the expectations of the other agents, it is altogether more puzzling. Whereas the forming of adaptive expectations can rest content with assigning different probabilities to various feasible outcomes, the self-reference threatens to make nonsense of the idea of probability. It is no good stipulating that each agent has a true model of a world which includes and is influenced by the true models in the heads of all agents until we are clearer about 'true models' in these circumstances. How and why do rational expectations tend to converge?

Observers predict; agents decide. Rational belief is usually analysed in terms of warranted prediction. The puzzle arises because the observers are the agents. To keep it manageable for non-economists, let us transfer the Rational Expectations Hypothesis to politics at election time. Consider a British by-election under the present rules, where each elector has one vote for only one candidate and the candidate with the most votes wins outright. Let there be three plausible candidates (or parties). Assume that each elector has a complete and consistent ranking of the candidates and, if despairing of his first choice, will try to secure the victory of his second. Each knows that all other electors will form and act on rational expectations.

This last condition sounds like an ideal-type assumption of 'perfect information', in the sense that everyone knows what anyone knows. But that cannot be it, as may be seen by first considering a very small electorate where each vote makes a palpable difference. For instance if an electorate of three voters has these preferences:

$$A \quad x, \, y, \, z$$
$$B \quad y, \, z, \, x$$
$$C \quad z, \, x, \, y$$

each voter can apparently elect his second choice. But this, while possibly true of each, if he knows that the others are not tactically inclined, cannot be true of all at once. No one can form rational expectations if all know that all have perfect information. No one can make a rational decision if each needs to base it on the rational decision of the others. A Rational Expectations Hypothesis in these terms prevents rational expectations. It might seem that the rational decision for each is to adopt a probabilistic strategy, for instance by throwing suitably weighted dice. One could then generalise to larger electorates with the dice weighted according to the proportion of first preferences for one's second choice. But that simply begs the question about what 'probability' means here. Otherwise there is no reason to load the dice in favour of the candidate with more first preferences, since even those voters who agree that z is the worst candidate do not just have a co-ordination problem in choosing between x and y. Perfect information here prevents even probabilistic decision-making and so cannot include what is likely to happen.

Is this a peculiarity of very small groups? In an electorate of 50,000 each vote is trifling and, on a Rational Expectations Hypothesis, each voter has a data-base of 49,999 others, who can all ignore his one vote. So each can apparently separate himself into observer and agent, so as to arrive at a decision by means of a prediction about the rest. But this cannot be right either. Take an electorate of twenty-six, conveniently named A to Z. If A's vote were literally of no account, B could form rational expectations by ignoring A and himself and attending only to C to Z. Then C could ignore A, B, and C and focus on D to Z. Then D could focus on E to Z. Then E could focus on F to Z; and so on, until the case reduces either to absurdity or to the one for very small electorates. Rational expectations, in the form of perfect information all round, produce paralysis, however large the electorate. It is worth drawing a parallel with utilitarianism. Utilitarians get on better if they can count on institutions, like truth-telling and promise-keeping, which are not vulnerable to utilitarian calculations. These institutions require that not everyone is a utilitarian, or at least that not everyone knows that everyone is. Perfect information would blow everyone's cover and prevent utilitarianism serving as a guide to rational decision.

It is also worth pointing a moral for the elementary theory of perfect competition, which grounds much in microeconomics. Under perfect competition there are so many small buyers and sellers that no one can affect prices, which are therefore taken as given. Each agent is credited with perfect information, meaning that each knows today's prices and can predict tomorrow's. Thus each can separate himself into observer and agent. Yet tomorrow's prices are not like tomorrow's weather. They do depend on what they are expected to be, however many buyers and sellers there are. Expectations are involved from the very start of microeconomic theory and not merely at advanced stages. What lets the theory of perfect competition assimilate information about future prices to normal weather forecasting is not, as might seem, the large numbers but an implicit imperfectness about the information. If every agent truly knew what any agent knew, the perfectly competitive market would collapse.

The idea behind assuming perfect information in the ideal-type case is to give rational agents enough predictive power to let them rationally expect a particular outcome or at least assign probabilities among those feasible. The effect should be to separate prediction from decision. But it does not succeed. If the outcome truly depends on expectations, then the element of decision is ineliminable. This becomes clear by taking 'perfect information' wholly seriously and finding that it defeats the forming of rational expectations. I shall use the point to infer that social life is possible only if there are elements of what I shall call 'stickiness' and 'lumpiness' in the flow of information. These terms of art will be introduced in the rest of the chapter and developed further in due course.

Bandwaggon effects can occur only if tactical voters rely on there being bandwaggons to climb on – groups of voters whose intentions are unconditional enough to count on. In everyday life these groups occur if there are like-minded voters who do not know or do not care what others are thinking. Not caring produces 'lumpiness' – a process of decision not vulnerable to information because, for instance, the voter has identified himself as a Conservative and intends to witness to his convictions regardless. He is like a non-utilitarian among utilitarians. I shall connect the lumpiness, which occurs when values resist cost-benefit calculations, to satisficing in the next chapter and to normative expectations in chapter 10. For the moment I merely mention it as a fact about some people's political behaviour which makes bandwaggons possible.

In an equally preliminary way, there is 'stickiness' in practice because 50,000 voters do not in fact know what 50,000 voters have in their heads. They may have a rough idea of how many would rank the candidates in each of the possible orders, other things being equal. But they certainly cannot say just how many are inclined to tactical voting, and hence have little idea how unequal other things are. Opinion polls ease the stickiness by reporting – or even perhaps creating – trends in shifts of opinion. But they need not be accurate and do not get the attention of all voters.

Indeed, if the previous arguments are sound, they could not be accurate without a solution to the puzzle of the self-referential regress, and they could not influence all without increasing the instability of expectations. It rather looks as if there is an optimal stickiness, sometimes achieved in practice, although stubbornly mysterious in theory.

It will have been noticed that my remarks about voting have been couched in the Humean idiom of preferences motivating choices in the light of information. Here too we can advance matters by switching to a Kantian idiom. Any Kantian rational voter will reflect that a good reason for him to vote for x (or to switch his vote to y) is also a good reason for anyone else in his position. If the Kantian model of rational choice is a true model, then it is in the heads of all rational voters. So each can count on those like him doing as he does. This restores the influence of individuals, which was apparently threatened by large numbers. When a single individual switches his vote for good reason, it is as if he were switching all the votes of those like him. He does not cause them to switch, but he expresses what they also express. If voters fall into typical groups, then the Rational Expectations Hypothesis, coupled with a Kantian theory of action, ensures that members of groups behave like sympathetic snails. Each typical individual typifies a typical choice and knows it. The electorate is reduced to a few typical groups and the element of decision, which large numbers threatened to submerge in prediction, becomes visible again.

This Kantian reflection does not advance us very far, however. Each agent still needs to know how many others he is typical of and in what respects. For example it might be rational for a group of 500 to switch their votes, when it would not be rational for a group of 5,000 with the very same preferences. Also there will be more typical groups than there are candidates. When, for example, the Liberal vote fragments for tactical reasons, some of it will go Conservative and some Labour. Hence typical Liberals need to think of themselves as subdivided into at least those typical subgroups. Furthermore a typical voter acts as if for those like him only when he acts for typical reasons. If a Liberal suddenly falls passionately in love with the canvassing Labour candidate, his enamoured switch of vote is his alone. Kantian universalisability is not a causal magic which literally turns voters into sympathetic snails. All the same, there is a genuine advance in a theory of action which makes any rational agent who adopts it think in terms of his group rather than of himself alone.

Groups and subgroups are defined by their preference orders (or desires) on a Humean account and by their reasons for action on a Kantian one. Here too I think that a Kantian account is a useful corrective to 'economic' theories of democracy which assume that parties pursue power and voters pursue advantage, almost wholly regardless of what either believe to be right (see Downs (1957)). In the ideal-type case the world under study is peopled by fully rational agents who are moved, I have argued, by good reasons of an organised, not always instrumental, kind. Whatever problems this may set for the relation between the ideal and the actual everyday worlds, it does insist that ideology matters. It matters not only for each agent individually but also for what each expects others to do, given what he knows about their ideology.

Finally there is a further oddity about 'perfect information' which certainly needs a corrective. If all agents were perfectly informed, no one would have anything to learn. They would all know it all already. This simply cannot be a helpful idealising assumption. The social world is entirely populated by people learning their way and is constantly influenced by the fact that some know more than others. These differentials inject an important stickiness into the smooth flow of information, which needs to be reproduced in any model which can claim to idealise our world and to be operative in the heads of rational agents. How this is best done, however, will be plainer after the next chapter.

Conclusion

Shipping forecasts set no special puzzle for a theory of rational belief. They are warnings based on the behaviour of weather, not of ships. If one cared to include an allowance for the success or failure of previous forecasts, that too would set no special problem, because the aim is squarely to adapt expectations to events independent of expectations. Traffic forecasts are quite different, as soon as motorists take an interest in them. In practice they are not widely disseminated, and there are not always alternative routes. But in theory the reflection that they influence the outcome which they predict has striking implications.

These emerge most neatly if one follows the economist's habit of exploring an ideal-type case. Suppose that there is an alternative to the city by-pass, but one worth the trouble only if the by-pass is about to jam. Avoidance is then, given some plausible further assumptions, a positional good, unattainable if each motorist is fully rational and has perfect information about the expectations of all others. Each will rationally use the by-pass if and only if he rationally expects $n\%$ to use the alternative. Tantalisingly, although all would be well if each followed a probabilistic strategy giving an $n\%$ chance of his taking the alternative, 'perfect information' forbids each counting on it. This is a point not about mathematics (see, for instance, Simon (1957)) but about the relation of expectations to social events.

All parties must agree that the set of feasible outcomes is smaller than the logically possible set. Even a Keynesian beauty contest will not be won by an octogenarian competing with teenagers. On a 'natural rate' account, these natural limits to what can happen are strong enough to make it rational to expect a particular outcome, or at least to assign ordered probabilities to those feasible. A Keynesian account, by contrast, insists that expectations are generative, thus undermining the notion of ordered probabilities by reversing the fit between expectations and events. I have argued that expectations do indeed have this creative feature and that what is essentially a collective decision does not reduce to a sum of individual predictions. The self-referential element in the predictions persists in what the rational agents have in their heads.

It looks, then, as if rational beliefs cannot be formed about a social world whose states are a function of rational beliefs. But this result is due to an instructive flaw in the ideal-type case. It stems from idealising away the 'stickiness' and 'lumpiness' of social life in the name of perfect information. The grit, however, is not provided by nature, in the form of, for example, facts of human biology or instinct, in my view, but by aspects of human agency which have yet to be considered.

8

Maximising and satisficing

Maximisation provides the moving force of economics. It asserts that any unit of the system will move towards an equilibrium position, as a consequence of universal efforts to maximise utility or returns. Maximisation is a general basic law that applies to the elementary units and, by the rules of composition, to larger and more complicated collections of those units.

(Krupp (1965), p. 69)

These robust sentences by Sharman Roy Krupp capture an exciting Leibnizian vision of the economy as a system guided by Sufficient Reason towards Pre-established Harmony. Each agent maximises, each larger unit maximises in consequence and, by the rules of composition, the whole heads for equilibrium. By now, however, doubts are starting to obtrude both about the moving force and about the rules of composition. Yet I would be sorry to lose the vision altogether. The next two chapters are an attempt to see how much of it can withstand the substitution of satisficing for maximising and of pluralism for unified harmony.

I have delayed discussing maximisation until now, so as to be able to call on the subversive kind of uncertainty introduced by expectations. While uncertainty is treated as if it were a form of ignorance about what nature will do next, it makes fair sense to analyse rational decisions as those based on subjective prob-

abilities which match objective probabilities. But, if a crucial uncertainty stems from ignorance of what people will do next,
because each agent cannot decide without knowing what others
expect others to decide, it makes abruptly less sense to analyse
rational decision in terms of approximating to the objectively
right solution. When this doubt about the very idea of perfect information is added to some patent practical limits on the information available to a human decision-maker, it is time to think
further about the maximising character of rational action.

Some economists, notably Herbert Simon, have suggested that
the moving force of economics is not maximising but 'satisficing'. Whereas a maximiser succeeds only if he hits on a correct
solution, a satisficer is content with a good enough one. That
might sound like a matter of degree. One might, it seems, picture
the two in a Chinese restaurant. The maximiser reads right
through the long menu and picks the best bargain; the satisficer
settles for the first dish he fancies at the price. The former knows
that he could not have done better; the latter has saved himself
time and trouble. Indeed, in that case, both are really maximisers,
since the issue is one of *net* utility and the satisficer has lower
costs. If so, the stock relation between a theoretical ideal-type
analysis and a practical guide is undisturbed.

But much more is at stake. According to Simon (1976), economics has two conflicting notions of rationality, one of which
does, while the other does not, require a psychological theory of
rational choice. No psychology is required by, for instance, a
theory of perfect competition, where firms and households are
simply assumed to arrive at their optimal behaviour in each situation. If one can assume that agents will always maximise, then it
does not matter how they do it and the situation is everything.
But as soon as one grants, as with imperfect competition, that
agents could not have enough information (because, for example,
the optimal behaviour of each depends on the behaviour of
others), then their psychology becomes important. Attention
shifts from the 'substantive rationality' of the outcome to the
'procedural rationality' of the agent. In Simon's hands the shift
has yielded a distinguished theory of organisations, and of Organisation Man, foreign to the microeconomic textbook.

Witness my earlier chapters, I do not accept that the standard

Rational Economic Man has no psychology. He has plenty of it, in the form of an attributed Humean theory of action, which produces irrational results if applied thoroughly. But I agree that endemic uncertainty makes it impossible to define rationality by reference to a limiting case of perfect information and hence that a rational decision becomes one which is well judged rather than necessarily correct. In what follows I shall first explore some ways in which satisficing is, and is not, radically different from maximising, and then draw a moral for the notion of rational agency in social life.

A Chinese dinner menu is a misleading example because of its suggestion that all the information is there, if one troubles to read it. So let us take an activity where the gaps are more obvious and revealing. Consider house-hunting. Adam and Eve wish to move home and are keen to choose the house which will suit them best. The obstacles to an optimal solution are many. There are more houses on the market than they can hope to visit. The wads of lyrical prose from the estate agents will not do in lieu, because, even supposing it accurate, it does not convey all they in particular want to know. It does not tell them what it would be like to live in the houses described; besides, it often takes a couple of years of actually living in a house to decide how much one likes it. Also they want a structurally sound home, and professional surveys are expensive. Moreover surveyors always cover themselves by speaking gloomily of cracks and movements, worm, rot and decay. How seriously is it rational to take them? Meanwhile there are other house-hunters out hunting, who may snap up the dream home while Adam and Eve dither. On the other hand there will be more houses on the market next week; so it may pay to wait. With such imponderables to worry them, their dream home becomes more and more of a dream, even before they propose a mortgage to their bank manager, who must weigh their finances and those of other customers and consider the housing market at large.

It all means that their ideal house may be already on offer, sporting a 'For Sale' sign, but that they will miss it, because it is in the street next beyond their area of search or because they saw it and failed to realise how ideally it would suit them. To put it more prosaically, information has at least two radical peculiarities. One is that often the only way to decide whether it is worth acquiring is to acquire it. The other is that its acquisition is often irreversible, because it changes both the situation and the agent.

These points are memorably made in legends and myths. Think of the story of Tarquinius Superbus' visit to the Sibyl of Cumae, who was reputed to possess all knowledge, in the form of nine Sibylline books of wisdom. She offered to sell him all nine, sight unseen, but at a price so enormous that he refused. So she called for a brazier and burnt three of the books before his eyes. Then she offered him the remaining six for the whole original price. Again he refused. Again she burnt three books and, still at the original price, offered him the last three. This time he succumbed to her remarkable sales technique and, the legend reports, found that he had made an excellent buy. Clearly all nine at the price would have been an even better buy. But anyone who infers that he would therefore have been rational to buy at the start would be wise to be out next time an encyclopedia salesman calls. In theory information is a commodity with costs and returns, worth acquiring up to the point where the likely marginal return is just not worth the marginal cost. Tarquin is a memorable case of the general proviso that estimating the likely marginal return can depend on knowing what one is missing.

For a reminder that information changes the situation there is Pandora. The gods had given her a box and a stern command never to open it. Although this occurred early on, when the world was still in an age of innocence, Pandora had too much curiosity to resist. The box contained all the ills which could plague mankind, like old age, labour, sickness, insanity, vice and passion. Once out, they could not be recalled. The box, however, also contained hope, to console us for the other irretrievable novelties.

Genesis shows how knowledge can make an irreversible difference not only to the world but also to the knower. The serpent beguiled Eve with an assurance that those who ate of the forbidden tree would become immortal as gods. Although it is not plain why Eve, in her innocence, should either want this immortality or be thus moved to defy the Lord God, she seems to have estimated marginal return above marginal cost. The actual consequence was not immortality at all but expulsion from the garden into a world of sorrow, thistles and toil. It was also knowledge of good and evil, without which, theologians say, we could have no real free will. Whatever else may be obscure, it is clear that Adam and Eve were never the same again. Thus information can raise the sort of points made in chapter 6 on external and internal reasons about puzzles of finding a standpoint from which to measure the value of a choice which changes the internal measure of value. Whether information is worth acquiring can depend on what it does to oneself and one's standards of worth.

It can also depend on who else has it. Much of the information market is concerned with comparative advantage. Think of the trade in secrets – positional knowledge, vulnerable to the obvious point that a secret known to all is a secret no longer. A positional element is very common, for instance in journalism, share-dealing, espionage and house-hunting. A firm's investment strategy is often affected not only by what it knows about its rivals but also by what it knows that they know that it knows. In general the more widely information spreads the less it is worth to the next buyer. But, even so, there is also the comparative disadvantage of not knowing what most others already know. Information is a peculiar good, in short, for reasons which make its marginal value an elusive factor in rational decision.

There is, moreover, the peculiarity that one can have too much of it. The tightrope-walker is safer if he does not look down. The skater may be better off not knowing that the ice is thin. Investment decisions are harder to make if one tries to allow for everything which is likely to happen. For instance a firm needs an estimate of next year's prices in order to make this year's investments. So it constructs a model where future prices are a function of current and previous ones. It keeps the function simple, ignoring complications like shocks to the economy. This is not because shocks are unlikely or because they will not matter, but because allowing for them is too expensive, makes the data too unwieldy or injects more uncertainty than one can act on. With information, as with zabaglione, one can have too much of a good thing.

These reflections suggest that the rational acquisition of new information is a matter of knowing when to stop. Only in some ways is the problem like that of an oil-prospector deciding whether to abandon a bore-hole or to go on boring. The seeker for knowledge has the further problem that he often cannot know what the answer would be worth if he had it. So, although sometimes the only way to assess the value of extra information is to acquire it, it is not always possible to assess it even then. That too is a strong reason for preferring a 'satisficing' procedure, which stops with a 'good enough' partial result, to the pursuit of an optimal result, which supposedly stops at the unidentifiable point where marginal cost is just not worth the likely marginal return. But little turns on this contrast between satisficing and maximising. The maximiser simply retorts that, in the face of such endemic uncertainties, reliance on pragmatic rules of thumb gives the best chance of maximising utility. Suboptimal results are perfectly acceptable, when it is not worth holding out for better ones. Satisficing is simply the reasonable way to maximise in the circumstances, as is clear if one reflects that no rational agent who happened to spot the best solution to a decision problem could reject it in favour of a satisficing solution. The satisficer is no less of a bargain-hunter than is the maximiser and, if handed a bargain on a plate, is bound to prefer it to the findings of an ordinarily more reliable method.

This retort deals with uncertainties of forecasting an event whose value is unproblematic. It covers the case where Adam and Eve know what ideal home they want but are unsure when to settle for second best. It does not cover the case in which they will not know how much they like a house without living in it. Experience is usually irreversible in the sense that it changes both the possibilities and their value to the agents. There is information which can be had only through involvement. Examples range from the trivial – a second bottle of retsina is more attractive once one has got used to the first – to the significant, like the induction of recruits into religions. Questions of the relation between experience, identity and utility were raised for individual choices in chapter 6 on external and internal reasons. They crop up again in the cost and value of information, most clearly for decisions about how to live. The young Catholic who needs to know what it would be like to become a priest cannot find out in the public library. To acquire and understand the information he must invest enough of himself to change his life, even if he finally decides against the priesthood. Earlier, when picturing a life as a series of forking paths, I spoke airily of assigning utilities to the nodes. It becomes clear that there is an information puzzle about knowing in advance what they would be and, indeed, about assigning them at all. Sometimes at least, experience is untransferable and irreversible.

The point applies even more forcibly to whole societies. As information about the outside world permeates a closed traditional culture, the culture changes. Experiments in social living are irreversible. The value of an experiment depends on what happens next. Even if the spread of information leads to a decision to keep to the old ways, it will still have changed the society, whose old ways, therefore, will never be quite the same again.

The puzzle is one about the neutrality of information and of the commensurability of the measures of its value. It is a challenge to the prospects of what one might call blueprint decision-making, where the chooser has a set of well-defined possible end-states and a set of properly costed ways of achieving each. He cannot have fully ordered preferences if he cannot know what the end-state would be like without travelling towards it, and he cannot cost the journey if its schedule of costs depends on where it leads him. The alternative to blueprint decision-making is a satisficing procedure, where rationality is a matter of reaching a defensibly good decision by a defensible process, without having to show that the decision was (probably) optimal by some unitary test. The example of a Catholic deciding the shape of his life may sound too rare and refined to be of general interest for social theory. But it is an example of a challenge which can be put much more broadly, as I shall next try to do.

Whereas a blueprint model requires a unitary decision-maker, very many decisions are taken by or within organisations. Microeconomics heads off trouble on this score by starting with unitary individuals, like Robinson Crusoe or the Adam of chapter 2, and then treating organisations as individuals. Thus a firm has a single aim, like profit maximisation, which it pursues with orderly single-mindedness. A household is a consuming unit which supplies labour to a point which maximises its consumer surplus. The market is an arena where unitary firms engage with unitary households. This idealisation is offered not as a literal description but as a convenient abstraction of theoretical interest and predictive usefulness.

One argument for satisficing models is that they make better sense of organisations, once it is allowed to matter that organisations are not single-minded units. All organisations give different people different tasks. An industrial firm, for instance, is likely to have a production engineer heading a production group, a sales director heading a sales force, a personnel manager with an office staff, and so forth. The firm itself does not care solely about profit. It is concerned also about its employees, their conditions of work, their pensions and even their private lives. Its employees do not care solely about the firm. The sales director, for instance, is concerned about his own team and, no doubt, about his own career and his own family. The conduct of business is thus shot through with plural goals. That would be unimportant if all goals harmonised and the level of profits were a unifying test of success in pursuing them. But this belies the feel of choices made. Management seems often to have to choose between shareholders, customers and workers. Sales directors are not the complete allies of production engineers. Rational decisions seem to be subject to multiple criteria.

Nothing conclusive follows. The firm may still be maximising long-run overall profit and therefore need to care for its employees. The sales force may honestly believe that what suits them is best for the whole firm. Even if it is granted that there are several goals involved, the aim of decisions may still be to maximise a mixture. The question is not whether choices are multifaceted but whether there is a workable commensurability among the claims, so that the firm can decide how much extra profit it is just not worth upsetting the sales force for. Perhaps there is more than one way to maximise a mixture. But that too does not disturb a theory of choice whose key is only that rational agents always reject inferior solutions.

All the same, it is not plain that 'workable commensurability' is a name for maximising when there is such ambivalence about aims. The door is open for further comments. Organisations rarely have clear goals. Their choice of means influences their ends. Firms with different internal organisations behave differently even in the same market. Profits depend on costs, which depend in turn on what people think worth doing. Public-sector organisations are not unlike market organisations in their decision-making, but often do not have a product or a method of costing it. 'Workable commensurability' begins to sound more of a notion borrowed from the political arena, as I shall contend presently, than a guide to the successful use of blueprints.

Here lies a very powerful argument for satisficing, rather than maximising, as the moving force of much economic behaviour. One can maximise the value of several variables at once only if they are so disconnected that attention to one is not at the expense of others, or if they are so integrated that there is a single index to work with. But as soon as aims are awkwardly plural, there is a strong case for thinking in terms of satisficing.

An agent with several primary goals must do well enough to satisfy the minimal claims of each and thereafter may distribute any surplus between them in various ways. To hold out for maximising is to insist that, at least in theory, there is a single test of the final distribution. Endemic uncertainty means that there is not, either in principle or at any rate in practice. This applies both to individuals and to organisations. The stock theory of rational choice gives individuals the single goal of maximising utility. I have been raising doubts about the sense and practicality of this ascription. They are not conclusive doubts but, where they stick, they require a different notion of an individual. As Hargreaves-Heap (1985) remarks, economists who treat organisations as if they were individuals might do better to treat individuals as if they were organisations. For, just as firms involve a division of labour, so too do individuals have a division of roles. For the moment, however, I adjourn discussion to chapter 10 on roles and reasons for action.

So far, then, there are two main kinds of argument for the merit of satisficing models as companions to theories of rational choice. One is that, since an ideal-type defined in terms of perfect information makes no sense at all, an assumption that rational decision-makers maximise has no application. Rationality needs so defining that a rational agent knows, not that he has done very well, but only that he has not done very badly. His confidence comes from having followed a reliable procedure which includes a sensible stopping point. This sort of argument is not radical, because it allows the retort that a satisficer is a would-be maximiser doing his best in the circumstances. But neither is it unimportant, since the underdetermination of rational choice is instantly multiplied by the proviso that a rational agent needs rational expectations about what others will do. If they have several options, then his options proliferate to match. Proliferation then breeds further proliferation.

The second kind of argument attacks the very idea of decision-making as the drawing up of a blueprint which identifies a best goal-state and a route to it. It does so by subverting the assumption of a unitary measure of value for comparing alternatives. For example apparently neutral terms like 'efficiency' are awkward to apply, given the points raised in the previous paragraph, but remain well defined so that, in principle at least, one can usually decide which allocation of resources is more efficient. But if goals are radically plural, then what is efficient in pursuit of one may be inefficient in pursuit of another. Key evaluative terms threaten to lose their neutrality. The threat is far-reaching, since it affects one's view of the nature of political decision-making. On what one might call an Enlightenment view, it is always possible in theory to work out the (or a) rational solution to any problem, since people, singly and collectively, have definite broad goals which harmonise, and hence the only hard questions are technical ones about means. To subvert this view at source, by suggesting that human goals are radically plural, is to challenge not only the merit of modelling political decision on economic decision but also, it will turn out, the usual idea of rational economic decision. Since I am here striking a note for the rest of the book, I propose to elaborate the point by next deploying an Enlightenment view and then putting it to the challenge.

On an Enlightenment view political problems arise from curable ignorance and finite resources. Human goals are given, either because everyone has the same goal, like happiness, or because they are few and obvious, like health, peace and prosperity. Goals are compatible both within and between individuals. The problems are those of means, and a cornucopia whose goods were distributed by and among rational individuals would solve them all. Since there is no cornucopia, one task of natural and social science is to increase the supply of goods.

Nature can be got to provide more, especially if human energies are organised for this purpose and not wasted in social conflict. There may always be limits to growth, but they are not Hirsch's positional limits and, in principle, expansion, technology and efficient allocation of resources can one day yield peace and prosperity for all.

In the meantime wants often outstrip the goods available and conflict with one another. So there is a need for political decision. An ambitious Enlightenment approach calls on government to identify the best solution and impose it. A more cautious one, recognising the limits of current knowledge and respecting consumer sovereignty, confines government to removing imperfections in market allocation. Both approaches conceive of political decision as, ideally, rational decision intended to maximise overall utility. For example welfare economics is standardly conceived as the search for a formula which will convert the preferences of any set of individuals over the possible states of an economy, or even of a whole society, into a social ranking of the states, or at least into an identification of a best state. Despite Arrow's (1951) proof that no formula could be guaranteed to give both democratic and efficient results in all cases, the presumption stands that rational political choice is analogous to rational individual choice.

It hardly needs saying that Enlightenment ambitions, even modest ones, outstrip current expertise. Take, for instance, the siting of a local airport. The decision involves all sorts of elements not obviously homogenisable. There are technical questions of weather conditions, supporting infrastructure, traffic flow and social geography, to name a few from a long list which gets less plainly 'technical' as it grows. There are environmental questions of effects on wild life, natural beauty and the traditions of the countryside. There are the disparate interests of, for example, the local residents and the inhabitants of the nearby city. There are changes going on elsewhere in the country, whose future consequences matter for today's local decision. Somehow the politicians must juggle together the utilities of villagers, businessmen, tax-payers and, indeed, rare toads and butterflies, pick a best site and work out a scheme of compensations for those disadvantaged. Cost-benefit analysis is at present only a dream of how this might be done.

None the less one can still argue that the snag is only ignorance.

In theory one could construct an ideal social map showing the right number of local airports in the right places, with the right set of road and rail links and the right zoning of residential, commercial and open spaces. In that case the problem remains a maximising one in theory. In practice the decision-makers will have to come up with some satisficing solution, for which they can command a loose majority of interested persons and powers. But satisficing is not here an alternative to maximising. It is, as before, a partial shot at maximising, the best shot which ignorance and other constraints allow. As soon as we learn to draw ideal social maps to act as blueprints, decisions will advance from adequate to optimal. By the same token technical advances can solve ethical problems about who should get what by showing how best to pursue the harmonious ends of human life.

Against these Enlightened hopes we may set a rival view of political judgement which refuses to see it as an interim stop-gap, pending improvements in cost-benefit analysis. Political judgement requires the assessing of which claims are legitimate and of what weight they should have. Legitimacy introduces a normative aspect, which, however construed, involves a distinction between efficient solutions and effective ones.

A 'legitimate' claim is sometimes regarded merely as one backed by normative expectations which politicians cannot afford to ignore. For instance, with the next election in the offing, it is no good siting the airport where cost-benefit analysis advises, if the decision will lose the election and then be reversed. This may sound a matter of power politics which could be included in the cost-benefit analysis. But, even if the prime question is whether a decision will stick, there is still a further normative aspect to it. Perhaps the Mafia too have an interest in the choice of site and have the power to subvert decisions which do not suit them. But the undoubted costs of defying the Mafia are not on all fours with those of ignoring the electorate. To call an interest group legitimate is not to say that what it wants is right. But it is to endorse a normative expectation that its wants will be recognised. The kind of entitlement here is akin to legal entitlement. A judge, ruling on a challenge to a will which bequeaths a fortune to the testator's cat, may think the law silly and the bequest immoral. But his task is to rule solely on whether the will is legally proper.

Politicians make law and policy. This involves them in over-riding expectations which are legitimate in the sense of norma-tively established. In the name of principles like justice or of policies on which they were elected, they can play down interests which they think over-represented in order to give effective ex-pression to others. This is an exercise in the art of the possible, a juggling of right, power and expert advice about consequences. Technical expertise has its place, but efficient solutions are not always politically best. 'Best' is a peculiar blend of moral aims and a practical sense of what will work – matters of legitimacy which do not reduce to calculation. Political decision is thus not to be modelled on economic decision.

The most ambitious Enlightenment retort is a flat denial. Bentham, for instance, supposed that the findings of a fully devel-oped felicific calculus would be both morally right and techni-cally exact. The art of the possible, in utilitarian eyes, is simply the proto-science of what will in fact produce the greater happi-ness of the greater number. Utilitarianism is by no means the only attempt to harness a rationalistic theory of ends to a science of means, and I am not trying to show that all such attempts must fail. But they are risky for those who make them, because they grant that ethics is involved in efficiency. For example, any unres-olved doubt about the utilitarian ethics of happiness spreads to utilitarian moral psychology and hence to the claims of the feli-cific calculus to yield genuinely efficient solutions. The scientific attempt to maximise is predicated on a theory of progress which needs demonstrating. Without the demonstration, the expert is left making claims to efficiency which are vulnerable to moral objections. But the risks have always been acceptable to those who look to science for knowledge of how to achieve the general good.

The Enlightenment spirit has not in fact come down to us in such a full-blooded form. Decision-theory, game-theory, gen-eral equilibrium-theory, welfare economics and its other mani-festations are usually accompanied with a firm distinction between positive and normative, which absolves the expert from pronouncing on ends. That points to a marked difference between experts, who identify the way to maximise a stated variable under stated constraints, and politicians, who pick the variables and state the constraints. Indeed the difference is so marked that it may seem odd to diagnose an Enlightenment spirit in the positive/normative distinction at all. But the Enlightenment origins emerge when one notices the arbitrary quality of political judgement on this account. In so far as the politician has reasons for choosing particular goals and specifying particular constraints, the reasons could in theory be formalised and absorbed into the modelling process. In so far as political judgement is irreducibly non-expert it can only consist in the power of authority to decree. In effect, the purely political element is a non-cognitive one of commitment. For the rest, the politician is once again an interim stop-gap for dealing with complexities and nuances which could one day become matters of better information.

However we construe the Enlightenment hopes of a science of happiness, then, we get at least an interim reason to think of political judgement as an exercise in satisficing rather than maximising. Even in the ambitious version, where all problems have calculable optimal solutions in principle, our current ignorance makes it rational for political decision-makers not to try for heaven on earth, especially where the decision would be an irreversible gamble. In the more modest version, where political decisions are the imposing of a non-cognitive value judgement on options offered after calculation, the cognitive warrant for a decision extends only to showing that it was better than some alternatives. Either way, there is a distinction between political judgement and technical expertise, with the former a matter of shrewdness in picking among satisficing solutions offered by the latter.

The moral is that there are choices to make which are underdetermined by the tests of rational decision *in more economico*. No doubt persons of Enlightenment persuasion will try to fill the gap with larger data-bases and subtler computing programs – and good luck to them! Meanwhile, however, even on Enlightenment assumptions, we can ask whether shrewd political judgement is to be regarded as rational judgement. On an anti-Enlightenment view that not all genuine problems are computable even in principle, the question arises straightforwardly. Granted that political judgements are neither arbitrary nor dictated by circumstance, the politician has reasons of, it seems, a sort yet to be discussed. If he is not *homo economicus* and is none the less an agent with (good or bad) reasons, what homunculus is he? I shall attempt an answer in chapter 10.

Conclusion

The present chapter paves the way for a transition from defining a rational agent as one whose reasons for action are of the decision-theoretic kind to defining him as one whose reasons are also associated with roles. The ground for a transition lies in the difference between maximising and satisficing. Since the ground is slippery and the argument important for the strategy of the book, I shall give a more elaborate summary than usual. I opened with a robust claim by Sherman Roy Krupp that maximisation is the moving force of economics and the general basic law which elementary units obey. The arguments for satisficing, as opposed to maximising, models fall into two groups, one modifying Krupp's claim without doing it real damage, the other raising a radical doubt.

The first group points out that perfect information is a will-o'-the-wisp and hence that theories of rational decision-making cannot be predicated on a limiting, ideal-type case where perfectly informed agents make ideally rational decisions. The line of argument emerges readily from the discussion of rational expectations in a world where what happens next depends on what agents expect. There cannot be perfect information where agents are contemplating multiple equilibria and everyone's expectations wait upon everyone else's. To this general snag, we can now add some further reasons why the likely worth of acquiring extra information is often imponderable. Whether it is rational for house-hunters to wait for next week's crop of house advertisements depends partly on whether it is rational for their rival hunters to wait. Information is often a positional good whose value varies with the number of people who have it. Sometimes, as with Tarquin and Pandora, there is no rational estimating of its value without the irreversible experience of acquiring it first. Acquisition can change not only the world but also, as with Adam and Eve's sampling of the forbidden fruit, the agents. Finally there is the wry example of the tight-rope walker who looks down to remind us that extra information does not always make for better decisions.

These points illustrate the formal proposition that information does not have what economists term a 'second derivative' or way of calculating its value at the margin. There are interesting formal and technical implications. But they sum only to a case for saying that the rational agent needs a stopping point in what would be a vain quest for perfect information. This is certainly a strong case for satisficing, in the sense that good enough solutions are the best which are rationally attainable. Rationality becomes a more pragmatic and procedural notion, perhaps to the disappointment of Sherman Roy Krupp but not contrary to the spirit of his belief in maximisation as the moving force. The rational agent is still in the game of improving the balance of utilities, even if the decision to rest content with a balance achieved no longer has the warrant that further rational improvement is impossible.

The second group of arguments injects a radical pluralism into the utility game. The leading suggestion is that organisations do not maximise the value of a single variable (like profit or even utility) but are coalitions of agents with overlapping, distinct aims. So one cannot forecast what an organisation will do in a given situation by ascribing it a single goal and asking what would best achieve it. Instead one must look inside and understand who wants what and how power is distributed. The organisation may profess a single goal, like profit, but one should not suppose that it will do more than satisfice with respect to the declared goal. Whenever there are several ways of gaining enough profit to keep going, one cannot predict or explain its behaviour without knowing what else is going on.

This homely-sounding truth has direct implications for economic theory because of the multiplier effect of expectations. Firms which believe that other firms are single-minded maximising units will behave differently from firms which know that other firms are not. The model of the economy which the

Rational Expectations Hypothesis puts into agents' heads changes correspondingly to one where firms behave as organisations rather than as individuals. That in turn calls for a theory of organisations and hence a rethinking of the relation of economics to sociology. To put it cursorily, the claims of political economy start to prevail over those of orthodox economic theory with the recognition that economic agents are not just makers of purely economic decisions within social and political parameters.

The implications are becoming radical. It is no longer Robinson Crusoe, or Adam choosing between figs and mulberries, who typifies rational agency, but a many-stranded agent with an internal organisation. The individual – or organisation – satisfices not just because he cannot come by perfect information but because the criteria of rational decision are radically plural. Agents whose judgement of what to do involves a balancing act are not the rational individuals of microeconomic theory, and call for an account of rational satisficing, which will lead us into a theory of roles and role-playing. For, although I have been speaking of political judgement in contrast to rational economic choice, I have a wider breed of *homo sociologicus* in mind. Whereas economists, especially those who are known as Modern Political Economists, are prone to regard government as a further case of manoeuvre among rational economic individuals, sociologists are ready with accounts of institutional behaviour which apply to politics and, indeed, to economics. The present chapter has been intended to give them an opening.

Meanwhile the idea that maximisation is the moving force is not yet doomed. Perhaps one can invoke what Krupp calls 'the rules of composition' to show that even the radical case for satisficing models cuts no ice, because the Cunning of Reason can still sum the individual inputs to the sort of collective result which maximising models suggest. The next move is to explore this riposte.

9

The Cunning of Reason II: functions and rules

The suggestion just made in the name of pluralism, in a sense implying incommensurability, is that the declared goals of organisations are suspect as a key to their behaviour. In so far as an organisation professes a single goal, or a unified, harmonious set of them, it will do no more than satisfice. It has to do enough of what it professes in order to remain viable. Its subgroups and individual members share that much of a common interest but, beyond this, they have separate aims. So one should not expect the interplay either of organisations or, for that matter, of individuals to produce a definite, particular outcome. Although overlap reduces the possible outcomes, it does not reduce them to one, even in the ideal-type theoretical case where all agents are rational and act on rational expectations. Radical pluralism implies radical indeterminacy.

This challenge to the explanatory hopes of social science can be met, so to speak, top down or bottom up. An individualistic account of organisations and of Organisation Man proceeds bottom up, with whatever success it can finally achieve by the end of the book. For the moment, however, let us work with social facts – features of social life which have meaning for the actors and are external to each of them – and see whether the indeterminacy left when one considers organisations singly disappears when one views them systematically together. External pressure on organisations as a group will translate as a pressure on each to organise itself internally so as to respond. Then, perhaps, single decisions, which are merely satisficing by the test of professed goals, may be determinate by the test of what the system demands. The challenge of pluralism would thus be met.

This line of thought asks more of the Cunning of Reason than the mere summing of consequences, intended and unintended. It requires at least a tendency for the sum to work out in a way which suits the system. For instance the managerial revolution, by which nineteenth-century capitalists were transformed into twentieth-century managers, went with a systematic divorce of control from ownership. That makes an interesting tale, but one wonders why it came out as it did and not with the proletarian revolution which Marx and others had expected. Without an answer, the suspicion is left that the tale is explanatory only *ex post*. Given the creative effect of expectations, is the poor showing of the proletariat simply due to the fact that forecasters like Marx were in a minority? If not, the Cunning of Reason must inject a direction into the course of events, one discernible *ex ante* by those trying to decide which possible equilibrium to expect.

I shall again refuse any truck with a Persian carpet theory of history which casts a World Spirit as master weaver. But there are two more modest ways of identifying what is systematic about social systems. One is to argue that the parts of any system behave in a way functional for the system as a whole. The other is to argue that social systems are constituted by rules which, in combination, have inherent tendencies. I begin with the former.

There is, or used to be, a grand sort of teleological social theory which does far more than explain individual actions by summing their consequences. It postulates a latent homeostatic system, tending to equilibrium and furthering individual actions which help it along. The equilibrium may be dynamic or shifting and need never be reached; but the tendency to it is a causal power of an explanatory kind. There are four typical components of such a theory:

(1) A primitive concept (or real definition) of a system as a unit, together with criteria for identifying its parts and for specifying whether events in its neighbourhood are internal or external to its normal working.

(2) A goal-state in which the system would maintain itself and

where all motion of its parts could be explained accordingly.
(3) An explanatory schema which explains behaviour (B) in relation to the goal-state (G) by the fact that B is required for G.
(4) A set of requirements for achieving G, such that apparently
different bits of behaviour can be functionally equivalent for
the purpose.

These four components embody a teleology, which lets one
relate events by identifying their contribution to the continued
existence of some unit with parts. This is a point of view which
we grasp readily for the natural world. Let me give an organic and
then a mechanical example. A termite colony survives only if its
huge, solitary queen, buried deep below ground, produces
soldier and worker termites in the right proportions. Too few
workers mean starvation, and too few soldiers mean destruction.
The proportions needed vary with events on the distant surface,
where predators attack the outposts from time to time. Marvel-
lously, the queen responds by producing extra soldiers to fill the
thinning ranks. Why? The teleological explanation is that more
soldiers are hatched because they are needed if the colony is to survive. Notice, however, that there is also an unmarvellous
question of how. The queen's food is gathered above ground
and passes from mouth to mouth down a chain of workers
and soldiers before it reaches her. Each termite leaves a trace
of secretion on it, and the chemistry of worker jaws differs
from that of soldiers'. The queen's body responds to the secreted
proportions.

For a mechanical example think of the solar system balanced
like a mobile in motion. Were a disturbance to upset the orbit of a
planet, other planets would react. Eventually all would either
return to the previous equipoise or a new set of complementary
orbits would emerge and remain stable. Here the idea that the
adjustments occur because they are functional for the system
carries less conviction than with an organic whole. Perhaps our
thinking about organisms carries more of a legacy of the old idea
that everything had an essence marked by an endeavour (*conatus*)
to persist in its peculiar being. But the mechanical teleology does
at least make for a neat mathematics, useful for predicting the
effects of disturbances.

Both examples, and all others known to me, are ambivalent about the teleology involved. It goes beyond the causal explanation of how the system adjusts to a change in its environment or (as with genetic mutations) in the composition of its elements. But it falls short of postulating reversed causation, since it is the present fact that B is required for G, rather than the future goal-state itself, which accounts for B. Necessary conditions fall short of purposes. None the less it is an established form of explanation, marked by a licence to cite an effect in explaining why its cause occurred, and, provided that one retains the ambivalence, a useful one. Transported into the social sciences, it offers interesting scope to the Cunning of Reason, short of postulating a grand design. This is not to deny that it has sometimes been invoked in the service of a complete determinism which denies all genuine human choice in history by subordinating all actions to the forces governing social structure. But it can also be used in a way congenial to the Rational Economic Man individualism which I have been examining, as two instances will show.

The first stems from the efforts of the Chicago school of economists to uphold orthodox microeconomics in its refusal to be concerned about the internal workings of firms.[1] Studies of individual firms seem to prove that actual decisions about output, price and marketing are taken by rule of thumb, often by adding a standard percentage mark-up to costs or by making pragmatic adjustments to last year's budget. They also seem to prove that what departments decide within the firm and what advice they offer to the board has less to do with maximising the firm's profits and more to do with departmental interest than microtheory pretends. In brief, they illustrate one set of arguments for satisficing models put forward in the last chapter. But, the Chicago school replies, look at the scene as presented in the market as a whole. There one finds that firms do in fact adjust to market changes pretty much as if they were profit-maximisers. They do so because otherwise they collapse or are taken over. Even if they do not do it consciously, they survive only if they come to imitate the routines of successful firms which do set out to maximise profits. In the large, therefore, the market works as the textbook

---

[1] I am here drawing on the excellent discussion provided by Jon Elster (1983a), chapter 3, especially pp. 57ff.

says, and it does so by selecting firms which do what is functional in and for a market system.

It might sound as though a determinist suggestion were being made that economic agents are swept along by economic forces regardless. But there is a normative rider. Firms which understand and accept the discipline of the market make better choices. The stock connection between rationality, freedom and prosperity is being upheld in an individualist manner by giving the market a life of its own, rather as if it were a jungle in which one must learn to survive. In saying this, I do not mean to endorse any part of it. It is not obvious that markets tend to an equilibrium or that firms do best by gearing their procedures to the demands of equilibrium. Nor is it obvious that the normative rider avoids an awkward form of determinism. But the example does show how functional explanation can be construed congenially for individualist economics.

It also offers a comment on the question of whether microeconomic theory bears any relation to the real economic world. The answer gives an ingenious twist to Friedman's (1953) contention that, since only the success of prediction matters, there is no reason to be concerned about the realism of a theory's assumptions. The comment is that, since firms survive only if they behave consistently with microeconomic theory, the theory is a useful representation of a functioning market. This is especially congenial for supply-side economists, since it makes it easy to include some natural rates of employment and inflation in the workings of the market and hence in the discipline which rival Keynesians try to refuse. This too I point out without meaning to endorse it.

The other example is the compromise between social structure and individual choice proposed in Talcott Parsons' *The Structure of Social Action* (1968). At the core is a theory of the 'unit act' or of rational choice within social parameters. The social system supplies the actor's goals, his standards of value and his 'mode of orientation' towards them but leaves him a choice of means. The actor picks the means likeliest to achieve his goal, without offending his orientation, in a copybook microeconomic way. The theory is called a 'voluntaristic' one by Parsons, but not in the sense that the system itself is chosen by the actors. The system is a grand homeostatic solution to a set of problems which any social system must overcome if it is to survive. These functional pre-requisites are translated into goals for suitably stratified actors, and choices are suitably biassed towards those which are functional for the system. Although Parsons himself continued to search for a unified theory, his 'unit act' remains instructive. Its dualism illuminates, for instance, the kind of economics which speaks of free markets and market forces in the same breath. Functional explanations, related to an external and constraining structure, coexist with rational-choice explanations. The dualism embodies what Krupp, in the quotation at the start of chapter 8, called 'rules of composition' connecting elementary to system-wide maximisation.

I propose to guillotine the discussion at this point, however, on the grounds that a dualistic compromise is too dangerous, if its aim is to secure a realm for rational choice in the name of individualism. It is one thing to hold that social (or political or economic) systems are external and constraining for *each* individual. It is quite another to make them independent of *all* individuals. In that case social systems, like natural ones, would have powers beyond human influence and, unlike natural ones, would exist only through their control over human consciousness. This may be a possible view, but it is strongly deterministic and leaves human agents only puppet government to pass off as self-government. Certainly it is quite contrary to the spirit of an attempt to explain the emergence of norms as collective solutions to problems of individual choice. The element of choice in Parsons' 'unit act', for example, is exceedingly precarious. If the goals, standard of value and mode of orientation are given externally, there is no reason why the system does not continue the process of biassing the choice, by influencing perception and judgement until the actor is merely the required through-put. If so, it is the norms which explain the desires and beliefs of the actors, instead of the other way about.

Individualist theories of social action need an element of contract or convention in their analysis of norms and hence of social structure. This element need not always be conscious – some norms are simply hit upon and become practices before they are noticed. It need not always be collaborative – some social facts spring from separate individual expectations. It need not be amiable – the Cunning of Reason can work mischief, as we saw. But it has to be there to differentiate social from natural systems. The mechanism which I have proposed is one whereby each agent chooses what those like him have most reason to want, after reflecting on what they expect others to expect. It is causing trouble by leaving outcomes too indeterminate so far; but at least it allows a crucial difference between what is external to each, like norms, and what is external to all, like laws of nature.

Talk of social structure is rich in metaphors, as when it borrows from the structure of termites or atoms. I find myself prone to architectural images, as if social institutions were invisible solids held up by doubly invisible girders. But there are other ways of talking which catch the idea of structure as something systematic and external, while also making it plainer that structures enable as well as constrain. For the rest of the chapter I shall discuss structures as systems of rules, especially rules of a game. The Cunning of Reason, which was initially introduced as a proposition about the unintended consequences of decisions within parameters including rules, now becomes one about the unintended consequences of rules too. Will this perhaps account for direction in the evolution of social systems and so supply a missing piece of the explanatory puzzle?

There is no trouble about finding examples. Take the EEC rules governing agricultural subsidies and meant originally, I believe, to shield small, traditional farmers against modernised agribusinesses in neighbour states. They have made large-scale mechanised farming immensely profitable and so increased the European output that huge butter mountains, wine lakes and other surpluses abound. They have made it profitable to fell trees, pull up hedges and drain wetlands. The effects range from changes in landscape and its fauna to changes in social geography, as the number of people making a living from the land declines. In Norfolk, where I live, for example, villages are fast changing character, as they lose their post offices, shops, parsons, pubs, schools and, in short, their younger generation. Whatever the costs or benefits, it is hardly likely that those making the rules intended the consequences. For less local examples think how rules governing American election campaign finances have influenced not only who is likely to be among the serious contenders but also domestic and foreign policy later; or what the Chinese one-child policy might yield socially, when it results in a clear surplus of males.

The point needs no labouring. It ushers in others very relevant to the theme of the book. To organise them I shall first renew the distinction between regulative and constitutive rules and then ask whether the rules governing social action penetrate so far into social life that a determinate course of events is their, perhaps latent, result. From here on, a Wittgensteinian metaphor of life as a game (or set of games) will start to obtrude. This conception is a nice way of capturing the sense in which social facts are external to each actor without being external to all.

Regulative rules are typically those which let the players of a game play it better or more effectively. They are practical in character, arrived at by experience and, if not merely rules of thumb or matters of useful habit, then executive ordinances designed to faciliate. They govern means rather than ends. The test is whether they direct people to one way of arriving at an outcome for an activity rather than another, as opposed to determining whether the activity is being engaged in at all. For instance the rules of the road in Britain direct motorists to keep left and within a 30 m.p.h. limit in towns. They carry no suggestion that cars cannot be intelligibly driven on the right or that persons whose passage is at higher speeds are not motorists. They merely incline road-users to one of several sets of possible expectations about others and thus enhance the prospect of safe arrivals. Motorists with idiosyncratic opinions will find themselves in court, but will not have failed to be motorists.

Such rules are hugely important to the conduct of social business. Indeed social life would soon collapse without them and, since they are a matter of convention at least as much as of facilitating best solutions, a visiting foreigner needs to be humble about discovering what they in fact are. The presumption behind them is either that we need to learn how best to regulate our activities or that, faced with several workable conventions, we simply need to agree on one. It hardly needs saying, however, that it makes a difference which we pick. Latent consequences can be dramatic, as with the rules regulating farm subsidies. Social life is not lived in self-contained arenas and the rules of one aspect, for instance of religious observance, can produce large effects on others, for instance education or industry. The longer the chain, the less likely it is that the effects were intended.

Whereas regulative rules presuppose an activity to regulate, constitutive rules create one. They are best typified by those rules of a game which declare what the purpose of the game is and what counts as playing it, as with the chess rules which specify the legal moves of the pieces and the conditions for check mate. Many activities can be identified only by way of citing the rules followed by those engaged in them, because the actors take part in a capacity conferred by the rules and their actions have no purpose which can be specified externally. Indeed Winch (1958) argues that all human activities are of this sort, since all actions need criteria of sameness and difference before they can be identified and since such criteria are internal to the activity. Monasteries and monks, for instance, cannot exist without a set of meaning-rules which constitute a form of religious life. In Wittgenstein's lapidary sentence, 'What has to be accepted, the given, is, so to speak, *forms of life*' ((1953), II. 226).

Constitutive rules would be absolutely central to social life, and to our understanding of it, if it were true that all action instances an institution and that all institutions are ultimately self-contained. It would imply, for example, that this book has started in quite the wrong place, because the only version of the social contract worth pursuing is one like Rousseau's, where the creation of society constitutes animals as men, and generates reasons for action which have no meaning outside it. I resist so all-encompassing a claim myself, as will become clear. But one need not be committed to explaining all actions through their internal relations to institutions before agreeing that constitutive rules are important. Nor need one suppose that they are always distinct from regulative rules. It is enough that people often act in an institutional capacity which defines their options. Forms of life are crucial for identifying many social actions, whatever one then goes on to say about explaining them.

I need not labour to show that institutional forms have unintended consequences. For one cogent example take the connections between protestantism and the rise of capitalism.

Whichever way the connections run, the one has had a great unintended effect on the other. It also matters that constitutive rules constitute not only activities but also some aspects of perception and self-awareness. For instance protestant acts of thrift are performed by people who think of themselves as protestants in a world of temptations. Unintended consequences can include shifts in consciousness.

How does a focus on rules help to explain why some feasible continuations are likelier than others? It does so, I think, by making the historical context of social action integral to the actors' awareness. This is a comment on the timelessness of the standard economic model of rational choice. The model is not, of course, blind to context, but it allows for it by varying the actors' information set. Ancients, medievals and moderns differ in their beliefs but not in their internal organisation or, ultimately, in their motivations; witness these memorable remarks by David Hume:.

It is universally acknowledged that there is a great uniformity among the actions of men, in all nations and ages, and that human nature remains still the same, in its principles and operations. The same motives produce the same actions: The same events follow from the same causes. Ambition, avarice, self-love, vanity, friendship, generosity, public spirit: these passions, mixed in various degrees, and distributed through society, have been, from the beginning of the world, and still are, the source of all actions and enterprises, which have ever been observed among mankind. Would you know the sentiments, inclinations and course of life of the Greeks and Romans? Study well the temper and actions of the French and English: You cannot be much mistaken in transferring to the former *most* of the observations which you have made with regard to the latter. Mankind are so much the same, in all times and places, that history informs us of nothing new or strange in this particular. (*Enquiries*, VIII.1.65)

The quotation may seem to rest only on (dubious) empirical observation. But the true Humean reason why mankind are basically the same in all times and places is that the standard dissection of agency into preferences, information and processing holds universally if it holds at all. As we have seen, the same goes for recent rational-choice theory too. Any action is a compound of the analytically timeless and the historically specific. That suggests a gap for a notion of context not merely subordinate to infor-

mation. A thesis about the relevance of rules to the actor's awareness might fill it interestingly. It could give us different sorts of
actors in different periods, instead of the same one sort in every
setting, and hence some lively implications.

This brings us to the edge of a fierce dispute about the scope of
relativism in accounting for cultural variety. One very lively implication might be that the self is a culturally relative object or
construct, present in cultures which shape consciousness in individualistic ways but absent in collective cultures. In that case
rational economic man will perhaps turn out to be a local product
of what Weber called *die Entzäuberung der Welt* in reference to the
replacement of traditional by rational–legal forms of life in
advanced societies. I propose to tread delicately round this mine-
field, confining myself to what can be said about historical, cultural and institutional contexts without implying a substantive
relativism. The dispute itself is fascinating, but not crucial for
present purposes.[2]

If we think of context as a game (or set of games) in which the
actors are players, we get a fresh idea of what options are feasible.
The actors are now choosing from among the moves open to a
player of the game in progress. The constitutive rules of the game
enter into the description the possible moves. The regulative
rules govern what is acceptable as a way of playing and hence
what each player can expect of others. The rules together account
for the players' knowledge of how to go on. This yields an inbuilt
explanation of historical continuity. For example developing
societies cannot make instant leaps forward while commercially
rational actions are not proper moves in traditional games of
honour. The rules of the traditional game have to change first.
For instance the regulative rules governing the making of canoes
adjust to absorb new, imported materials. The adjustment has
latent consequences for the constitutive rules which integrate
canoe-making into the religious life of the society. Gradually the
traditional game can be thus replaced.

---

[2] For recent explorations see e.g. M. Hollis and S. Lukes (1982) and M. Carrithers, S. Collins and S. Lukes (1985). My reasons for rejecting relativism and
for maintaining the epistemological unity of mankind are set out in an essay in
each of these volumes. I shall revert briefly to the topic of the self at the very end
of the book.

In such an account the rules need not be thought of as self-contained. It may partly explain continuity to point out that people accept the new only when they have made sense of it in terms of the old. But it is also a fair point that continuity usually suits those with power. Since power depends as much on acceptance as on a big stick, it is often redistributed by changes in the game. This all makes change a puzzle for a theory which defines context in terms of the prevailing rules. So let us again invoke the Cunning of Reason. Changes in technology can have unintended effects on rules. Changes in rules bring further changes in rules. There is no necessary reason why the system, once disturbed, should tend to its previous equilibrium, if the changes are large enough to make the previous game futile or, indeed, unplayable. We have the makings of a notion of social contradiction, congenial to Hegelians and Marxists, among others. But they are only the makings, without some reason to expect the unfolding pattern to have one character rather than another.

Otherwise we have only the suggestive point that the social framework is reshaped by its own latent consequences. The point has been well exploited by Anthony Giddens, especially in his (1979) chapter 2, where he writes that 'the structural properties of social systems are both the medium and the outcome of the reproduction of the practices that constitute those systems' (p. 69). But we also need a shrewd idea *ex ante* why passage through the medium makes sometimes for continuity and sometimes for change. Since I am upholding Adam's claim to be a sovereign artificer, I wish to maintain that the feed-back is controlled by the actors themselves. They give direction where the Cunning of Reason is blind. I shall end the chapter with the power of the players to change the game.

The sense of 'game' involved is not that of game-theory. There the notion is deliberately bald – little more than definitions of 'strategy' and 'pay-off' to supplement the basic apparatus of rational choice, when agents interact. The aim is an austere abstraction which presents social games as instruments for securing individual pay-offs in ways which lend themselves to an elegant logic and mathematics. No serious attempt is made to capture the expressive aspects of social life or the internal meaning and value attaching to many practices. Nor is there much scope for the actors' critical monitoring of their performances, especially from a moral point of view. For these dimensions a richer-textured notion is needed, more Wittgensteinian in character but, for my purposes, also allowing the players to distance themselves from the game. I shall let it emerge from a discussion of role-playing, rather than try to define it in advance. For the moment let us just consider one way in which games are not static.

Unintended consequences often come to notice, and all societies try to deal with them systematically. This is one task of authority. For instance the game of football has a governing body whose job includes adjusting the progress of the football season, and, if necessary, even the constitutive rules of the game itself, so as to deal with unforeseen effects of earlier decisions and of changes elsewhere in society. This monitoring and governance has an overall purpose which is, loosely, the flourishing of football. With other practices which are not literally games, the purpose may be looser and less a matter of the flourishing of the practice itself. A church, for example, has a higher aim than its own apple-pie order. But it needs to be in good order and spends much effort in adjusting to unforeseen consequences of all sorts. In the political realm, government at all levels from parish to nation is similarly engaged, with, one likes to think, as much scope for interfering with the Cunning of Reason as for adapting to it.

'Men make their own history', Marx wrote, 'but they do not make it just as they please; they do not make it under circumstances chosen by themselves' (1979, p. 103). The constraints are those of nature, previous history, incomplete understanding and disunity. The first two of these are parameters. There are laws of nature and limited natural resources. We inherit a legacy of previous rules and actions, still working as consequences intended and unintended. But nature and the past are not only constraints. They enable us to make our own history with a success depending on how much we understand and how unitedly we try. Understanding is in part a matter of science and technology. But understanding of human beings and human society is as important and bears also on the unity which we can achieve. I see no reason to speak of unintended consequences only in a passive voice which suggests that we can do nothing about them.

By that token there is no way of examining consequences independently of the actors' responses to them. Rules, expectations and consequences are inseparable. Since they enable as much as they constrain, questions of what will happen are questions about what people will make happen. Rules are creative, in that constitutive rules create activities and regulative rules let us pursue them effectively. Expectations are creative through their element of collective decision. Consequences can be put to use, once they are noticed and understood. The kind of understanding needed for the study of activities cannot sensibly be modelled on the sciences of nature.

There is a further point about expectations, which I mention in readiness for the next chapter. I have been using the word mainly in its usual sense for economics, decision-theory and the philosophy of natural science, where to expect something is to believe that it will happen. We also need its other sense, well established in social psychology and sociology, where to expect something of someone is to believe that it should be done. Admiral Lord Nelson's famous signal to his fleet before the battle of Trafalgar in 1805 was 'England expects every man to do his duty this day.' It was not 'England predicts . . .', and Nelson was not laying bets. He was using a language of duty and entitlement. The usual label is 'normative expectation', and I shall have more to say about how normative expectations relate to the rational expectations which we have been considering. They are an important component of the history which men make and of the conditions in which they make it.

For instance the level of employment and of wages depends partly, as noted earlier, on what employers and workers expect it to be. These expectations vary at different times and places. One reason is that what trade unions can expect of their members varies. If the union can count on solidarity, wage cuts are easier to resist. Solidarity is a matter of an effective norm to prevent individual defections. Such norms have a history. They grow from shared experience and their character and strength vary with their origins. Trade unions in the 1980s are influenced by the depression of the 1930s through the lessons deposited in the consciousness of those still alive or those brought up by parents who lived through the 1930s. These experiences influence present expectations. They affect not only rational expectations, in the sense of predictions, but also normative expectations; and they influence the former through the latter. Expectations, in short, take texture from life as well as information from books, and are a living part of what is therefore always a specific historical context of action. The feasible future varies with the available past.

Conclusion

I have been exploring two ways to fill the information gap which emerged because Rational Economic Man cannot form rational expectations about what will happen next, while confined to an orthodox information base and a timeless model of rational choice. Both ways try to give latent direction to the sum of the consequences of individual actions, or, to put it metaphorically, try to work the Cunning of Reason harder. I find both unsatisfactory, but for different reasons.

The first is to borrow ideas of system and function from the study of nature, hoping to cut down the previous indeterminacy by showing that otherwise possible outcomes are not to be expected, unless they suit the dynamics of the social structure. There is much which I could have said about the epistemological demands of the idea that social structure is a real entity with needs and dynamics. But, believing that sentences are not to be multiplied beyond necessity, I asked only what becomes of the human actors. At first sight they are the deluded puppets of the hidden structure. That, however, ignores the demand for a mechanism through which the dynamics work, akin to the chemical chain which controls the queen termite's varying production of workers and soldiers. The only promising mechanism is the actors' consciousness and, once this is admitted to matter, I see no reason for thinking of it as a mechanism. Nor does it help to try a Parsonian compromise where the actors make rational individual choices within structural parameters, since there would be no reason to deny that such mighty forces penetrate into the apparent choices. I submit, therefore, that there has to be a better way of appealing to latent consequences without destroying Adam as sovereign artificer altogether.

The other strategy is to construe the social structure or system as a set of rules constituting and regulating social activities. Rules arrived at piecemeal, whether consciously or not, can and do have all sorts of unintended consequences in combination. This, incidentally, is yet another nail in the coffin of 'perfect information' as a conceivable ideal case. If the combination renders the activity determinate or gives it direction, which becomes determinate when a wider set of combinations is taken into account, then the Cunning of Reason will indeed have disposed of the information gap. This notion of structure has the advantage over the other that it makes good sense to speak of a system of rules as external to each actor yet internal to all. Also, by noticing that rules evolve in a way influenced by the actors' shared experience, we get a promising idea of historical location. The actors become flesh and blood followers of rules, with a knowledge of how to go on which is more concrete than an analytically timeless model allows and yet more general than the mere vagaries of time and place would permit. Contrary to Hume, I suggest that history has at least something to teach us about human nature.

Even so, however, it remains unclear how the actors relate to the rules. Since the image is no longer one of causal forces but one of games and institutional forms of life, there is not the same threat to turn them into puppets. Instead the suggestion is that they are players of roles, governed by normative expectations. This usefully fills in the radical case for satisficing models, which sprang from the fact of plural goals and hence of plural criteria for assessing choices. The satisficer's rules of thumb take on form and direction if they are related to the role-player's imperatives. But an actor who is not the creature of hidden forces may yet be the creature of rules. That would be too high a price for expectations which made social life determinate. The next task is to stop the Cunning of Reason making this new mischief.

10

Reasons and roles

The attempt to regard Adam as *homo economicus* with different masks for different social settings has run into, broadly, two kinds of trouble. One is that there are snags to the model even for the economic realm. In brisk philosophical summary, they crop up in both the belief component and the desire component of rational choice. The expected utility of a choice depends partly on what outcome it is rational for the actor to expect and partly on how much he wants that outcome. But expectations generate outcomes, thus unsettling notions of objective probability, and serial interaction changes preferences, thus unsettling the utilities. In upshot outcomes are too indeterminate for the model and are reached by a process which affects the individual inputs meant to explain it. The other broad kind of trouble is that social relationships need to be more than instrumental devices in the service of individual goals. It is not true that all the world's a shop and all the men and women merely shoppers.

The second complaint has emerged only piecemeal so far, and needs organising into a fresh portrait of Adam. This chapter tries to make sense of social life in a way which applies to economic activity too. Having found that social relations are not just market relations in disguise, let us see whether market relations are social relations. The emphasis will remain on Adam, the individual social actor. The shift will be not from actors to organisations and institutions but from marketeers to role-players, who recognise one another as players of roles. This will, I hope, regain reliability for actors' expectations and hence restore the fortunes of rational-choice theory – a negotiated settlement between the standard *homo economicus* and the standard *homo sociologicus*, whose terms are a fresh notion of rationality. One persistent loose end will, however, be left for the next chapter – the weight to be finally attached to the actors' own view of what they are doing.

To keep the theme focussed and philosophical feet somewhere near the ground, I shall work with a microcosm of the general argument between economic and sociological approaches to social action. The obvious source of one is politics, where the appeal of both approaches is powerful. That much is evident from earlier chapters, where Hobbesian contract theory seemed a natural and promising link between the economic and the social. But it can seem a drawback for contract theories that, even in analysing economic life, they come late to the world which they claim to have arisen through contracts. If marketeers ever stepped pristine from a state of nature, it was long before economists were there to watch. All known markets are ensconced in a social framework of established, enforceable conventions. So, in order to claim that primary motivations are self-interested, the economist has to abstract before he can pretend to describe and then has to defend the abstraction. The same goes more plainly still for political and social contract theories. Even Hobbes, writing with the anarchy of the English civil war fresh to mind, set the state of nature in a misty past, where there was no legacy of English constitutional history to obscure the laws of nature.

Political science does, however, offer one splendid illustrative microcosm, where the action seems to proceed without an encompassing established framework and where the rival pull of economic and sociological models is palpable. The study of international relations is difficult and fascinating in ways which I have no credentials to discuss, but it is unmistakably in the throes of precisely the argument which I wish to conduct for social science at large. I shall begin by saying briefly how this comes about and thereafter address the general theme to questions of decision-making in foreign affairs.[1]

I

The diplomacy of states is among the oldest topics which have caught the attention of writers interested in human motives. But tales of princes, statesmen and generals, even when not just chronicles, have different aims from a scientific study of international relations. Such tales can be worked up into loose generalisations or into handbooks of statecraft. There are evergreen examples as old as Thucydides or as pointed as Machiavelli. But they contain an irreducibly personal element in their sense that diplomacy, like all history, is made by individuals who are not interchangeable. When Henry VIII succeeds Henry VII or Canning takes over from Castlereagh, foreign policy changes with the change in its creator. This remains a very defensible assumption, of course, and one still shared by many writers on foreign affairs, who maintain that the study of international relations cannot and should not aspire to be a science. But others have tried in the last fifty years to apply what they took to be scientific method. Specifically Hans Morgenthau's *Politics Among Nations* (1948) advocated a scientific 'Realism' which set the stage for recent debate about how to tackle the international scene.

This Realism connects with a broadly positivist view of realism in science but, more to my purpose, it also involves a realism about human motivation. In this context Realism echoed a Hobbesian view of human nature and a borrowing of economic theory to go with it. Here, one might say, is one realm where contract theory can get straight to grips. With international law

---

[1] My mentor for the state of play in international relations is my colleague Steve Smith, and any credit for apparent expertise goes entirely to him. The chapter draws gratefully on our joint (1986) article 'Roles and Reasons in Foreign Policy Decision-Making' and on the joint teaching which inspired it. I have, in effect, extracted its philosophical theme, in a way which concedes less to his ideas of science than he might wish and without trying to reproduce his case study of the Iranian hostage crisis of 1980, which we took as our touchstone there. But my debt to him is not thereby lessened. I have also been helped by Smith (1987). For further reflection on some themes of the chapter, see also Hollis (1977) chapters 4–6 and, on self and role, Hollis (1985b).

nascent and anyway no match for imperious nations, we have something instructively like a state of nature, inhabited by states very like Hobbesian individuals. At any rate, Realism presented nations as the self-interested units of a fragile international 'market', each rational in the sense of the basic economic model and willing to accept collective regulation only in so far as it suited them individually. These units behave like firms in orthodox microeconomics, except that the national interest, which each seeks to maximise, is reckoned in power rather than profit. I shall refer to this generalised economic approach to international relations as a rational–actor model.

A rational–actor model is undeniably tempting, especially with some accompanying game-theory. For instance think of the Geneva disarmament talks as essentially a two-person game between the USA and the USSR, who distrust each other (in a spirit of what Hobbes terms 'diffidence' in chapter XIII of *Leviathan*). Each would prefer that both disarmed than that neither did. But each would most prefer that it remained armed, while the other disarmed; and would least prefer the converse. Writing 'o' for 'arm' and '1' for 'disarm', we get a familiar ranking of outcomes from the point of view of each: $o1, 11, oo, 1o$. The Pareto-inferior but unsurprising result is a continued arms race. Nor will treaties put a stop to it, while ineffective inspection procedures mean that 'diffidence' also marks the preferences of each for keeping or breaking treaties: $o1, 11, oo, 1o$ again, where 'o' means 'Break' and '1' means 'Keep'. There is no need to labour the point that a rational–actor model, whose individuals are self-interested nation states, can score several initial successes.

Even where it works best, however, one can still raise Herbert Simon's objection that the internal organisation of the units matters. The arms race illustrates the logic of dominant inferior choices very prettily. But is that why it happens? Might a deeper explanation not be that there are powerful agencies in both the USA and the USSR with a strong vested interest in armaments? There are vast industries (private or state owned) which make arms, and huge local constituencies with political clout, which depend on these industries. There are commanding bureaucracies whose importance would wane if the lion lay down with the lamb. When statesmen call for arms reductions, it is not plain that they voice the national interest, or that they sincerely believe that they do, or that it matters what they sincerely believe. However pretty the logic of games, it fails to prove that the true driving forces are not the domestic agencies, whose interests are well served by the outcome.

Where the first thought was of a 'market' system, whose logic disciplines the behaviour of states, the second is that, within some constraints set by what is internationally feasible, foreign policy is decided *in foro interno* by the agencies of domestic politics. This too has marked attractions, as soon as one notes that foreign policy decisions are often made by small elites summoned to special meetings because they represent relevant agencies. For instance the American President normally convenes about a dozen representatives of the State Department, the Defense Department and his personal White House staff. This is not to ignore wider groups with an interest in the policy, since their concerns are very much in the minds of the small group, which will have to stand up for the decision afterwards. But it is to suggest that the national interest, which states pursue on the rational-actor account, is not a well-defined maximand or (to forestall the retort that satisficing and bounded rationality are what matter) even the one which gives the decision-makers their bearings.

These ideas crystallised in Graham Allison's *Essence of Decision* (1971), which studied the Cuban missile crisis of 1962 and found that American policy was best explained by examining the sectional interests represented at President Kennedy's crucial meetings as the crisis developed. It was striking that the advice given by each of those present varied with the agency which he represented and that the decisions were those which suited the winning coalition of agencies which favoured them. Allison generalised the theme to what he termed a 'Bureaucratic Politics' model, summing it up in the pithy sentence (first minted by Don Price) that 'Where you stand depends on where you sit.' A bureaucracy, for this purpose, is not exactly an organisation of administrative officials, since those present in the elite forum may include the Vice-President, the Press Secretary and others of political importance, and could include persons involved through some more commercial organisation. But 'Bureaucratic Politics' is an evocative term, capturing the point that each decision-maker represents an organised source of pressure, typified by the great offices of state. These organisations have purposes and dynamics of their own, as is the wont of bureaucracies. We are to think of the decision process as the interaction of a small number of officers of state, each giving advice which suits his corner and with an impact determined by the allied power of those with similar interests.

It matters very much whether the units of a Bureaucratic Politics model are bureaucracies or bureaucrats (agencies or agents). The starkest contrast to a rational-actor model would make them bureaucracies, with the human agents cast as mere puppets or mouthpieces of the agencies which send them into the fray. In that case the model should be generalised within an ambitious structural–functional account of social dynamics, where organic or hydraulic forces are at work and the system has some overall tendency to which its parts contribute. But, having dispensed with this kind of metaphysics in the last chapter, I shall not try interpreting the model in this way. As soon as we ask how the invisible dynamics work, we find that we need human agents for them to work through. In less stark but more plausible contrast to the rational-actor model, let us regard bureaucratic agents as rule-followers, subject to sets of rules which differentiate between bureaucracies. In other words let us resume the idea in the second half of chapter 9, where system was construed in terms of rules rather than of functions, and ask what we should say about social agents.

Some concepts from role-theory will help to keep things short. Think of each policy-maker at the crucial moments of collective decision as having an institutional position which accounts for his presence. Think of each position as laying normative expectations on whoever occupies it, thus giving him rules to follow, tasks to perform and demands to fulfil. Think of each actor as obedient to the demands of his position. In brief, think of the actors as role-players and of role as the normative expectations attaching to an official position. If it is true that 'Where you stand depends on where you sit', this small budget of concepts should yield a powerful explanatory scheme.

It is worth pausing to recall the relation between normative expectations and predictions. The former is an insider-concept referring to what others may expect of a person in office, to their entitlement to his acting accordingly and to their right to complain in case of failure. But people in office do neither all nor only what is expected of them. For instance President Nixon used his authority to discredit political opponents by means which almost resulted in his impeachment. Critics, who were shocked, were not necessarily surprised. Prediction is a spectator-concept applied on a different basis. The spectator needs to know what the normative expectations are; but he asks also whether they will in fact be met. He is interested too in matters connected with roles but not part of them. For instance it was perhaps predictable that a President with Nixon's background would fall out with the East-Coast establishment. But the difference is not clear cut. For example Presidents influence American foreign policy in ways sensitive to their standing in the opinion polls, especially in an election year. Is this a proper responsiveness to the voice of the people, an improper courting of political advantage, something which they do in the slightly different role of senior members of their political party or something not subject to normative expectations at all? None the less there is a useful distinction between what one expects of people and what one expects that they will in fact do.

The divergence rules out any simplistic version of the Bureaucratic Politics model. If roles are supposed to be complete lists of duties, then it is simply false that they are performed in full and simply feeble to say that they usually are. But the model becomes plausible as soon as it is granted that roles are not fully scripted in advance of every situation. There are, no doubt, some definitive dos and don'ts. The President has a clear duty to maintain national security and a clear duty not to siphon off White House funds into his private bank account. In between, however, lie permissions – he is neither required nor forbidden to sell wheat to Russia or to veto congressional bills. One could regard permissions as requirements to act when he judges it in the national interest. But this closure of his options would be purely formal and would not make him the creature of his office. On the contrary it would give him a duty to use his judgement, thus making judgement an explicit feature of the model. The same point arises for even the clear dos and don'ts, as is plain as soon as one asks what exactly are the demands of national security or what exactly limits the kind of investigation into the lives of political opponents which he can order the FBI to conduct.

By the same token the model has an answer to the point that persons in office do neither all nor only what is expected of them. A role cannot cover all contingencies in advance. Its content can vary, when it is played with different partners (or opponents). For instance the President should be frank with his staff, frankish with the press and not frank at all with hostile foreigners. A role can have subdivisions, meaning for example that what the President gleans from the CIA is not always to be acted on when dealing with Congress. The person who is President has other roles, ranging from closely related, like chief of the armed forces, through semi-related, like party statesman, to unrelated, like church-goer, father and friend. The model can thus be defended against apparent counter-examples by complicating the cross pressures of role-play and exhibiting action as a response to them.

By now a Bureaucratic Politics model is turning into a broader model of *homo sociologicus* as role-player in all aspects of social life. The suggestion might seem to be that actors are puppets after all, because, wherever a single role leaves them an option, the combination of roles closes it. If one objects that roles often conflict, rather than summing coherently to a single course of action, the answer might be that there are also inbuilt priorities. For instance the President, like Agamemnon, must put his country before his family in case of conflict. But this seems to me perverse. The more extended and complex the model the more scope it gives the actors and the greater the demands it puts on their judgement of what in particular is required of them. That is what Greek tragedy says about Agamemnon, and I see no reason to dissent.

The point emerges readily as soon as one stops thinking of social structure as a set of forces. If institutions are conceived in a language of rules, rather than hydraulics, it is plain that the actors' knowledge of 'how to go on' has more to do with skill in judging the spirit of the rules than with mindless reading of the small print in a handbook. The thesis that social actors are always trying to follow rules prescribed by their social positions is quite contentious enough without a needless rider that they therefore have no minds of their own.

The Bureaucratic Politics model is a special case of a broader institutional role-theory and concerned only with the main plot of the play in a special theatre. But, if I am granted that the apparatus of normative expectations sits rather lightly on the actors as they pick their way through underscripted situations, then it raises a broader question of self and role none the less. The last two sentences use the language of theatre deliberately. An institutional role theory offers a conceptual budget of social positions, normative expectations and obedient actors. Even granted that 'obedient' does not imply 'mindless' and hence that there is still a need for actors, this is not very illuminating. A dramaturgical analogy, as it is often called, promises to shed light on what is involved in playing a role. I think that it does, but in a surprising way.

By one account of theatre a stage is a place where individuals step out of their private lives and into character parts. They pretend to be the *dramatis personae* for the performance and act as the play requires. The text is already scripted; the players don masks for the duration and, when the curtain falls, return to their off-stage lives. At first blush, this is a reassuring account to apply to socal life, if one is recommending individualism. It distinguishes sharply between public and private being and postulates a self behind the mask. The message is reassuring in its refusal to dissolve personal identity into social relationships. It says something significant about role-distance and leaves it open to any actor who is morally offended by the action of the play to resign, throw off the mask and go home.

The implication for the social sciences depends on how literally one takes the analogy between the episodes of social or political life and the pre-scripted scenes of a play. Taken literally, the text has nothing to do with individual choices and the social scientist is like a member of the audience who does not know how the play will end only because he has not seen the script. This is a possible reading of the analogy, but one which buys the distinction between self and role at a recklessly high price. The individual is wholly distinct from the role but totally unimportant. The script is everything. Moreover, if the analogy is meant to illuminate the individual in the play of his own life, then it extinguishes him altogether. For, if the bureau is a stage, then so presumably is the pub, the sitting-room, the bedroom and every other retreat from bureaucratic view. So is the market place, where *homo economicus* turns out to be performing a script too. This reading is a determinist disaster for individualism.

So how about making the analogy one with an incompletely scripted play where the actors supply the ending themselves? The idea is to find a compromise between *homo sociologicus*, who is the character provided as far as the script goes, and *homo economicus*, who is an individual fleshing out the rest of it for whatever private purpose of his own. But that makes no sense at all. In so far as the private purposes obtrude, they spoil the play and, in so far as they remain concealed, they do not matter. If norms and choices are related as public discipline to private motive, then the discipline is what counts and, when the model is again applied to the individual in the play of his own life, he is again abolished.

But there is no need to take the analogy in this way. After all, plays are about social life and cannot be warranted in imposing a determinist view of it merely because of the conventions of drama. If we are trying to extract a view of a distanced role-playing self, we shall do better with a different account of theatre, where actors are thought of not as impersonating characters but as personifying them. Gielgud's Hamlet has the same lines as Olivier's but is different. Great actors become the masks which they don. Their performances are open-ended, despite the complete script. This idea of acting as personification is older and closer to the roots of drama than the idea of dressing up and pretence. It taps ancient fears of unleashing elemental forces, of naming things hidden and of encroaching on the sacred. More prosaically, however, it suggests a proposition about role-distance which I find very persuasive.

Role-distance conjures up images of alienation, disenchantment and frustration, as if the wearer of the comic mask were weeping behind it. But, in this second account of theatre, we can think of it as detached judgement within the play. It becomes, so to speak, presence of mind instead of absence of mind. Gielgud's Hamlet and Olivier's Hamlet are different interpretations of Shakespeare's *Hamlet*, different enacted running commentaries on what the play means. Detachment can be not the cool use of the stage for some private purpose but the monitoring of one's own endeavours to bring the character to life. There is a nice symbiosis between the playwright's tale of how his characters chose to weave the plot and the actors' attempt to be persons who would weave it so.

I need not claim that this is the right account of drama for it to be a promising way to take the Bureaucratic Politics model. It puts the self on the public stage and gives it work to do. The thesis that the actors are wholly obedient to institutional factors remains, of course, contentious. But it is made much more enticing by the idea that obedience is not a mechanical concept. It lets us think in terms of loyalty rather than subservience. For instance a priest who has a mind of his own is not thereby disloyal to his church or to his God, 'whose service is perfect freedom', in the words of the Anglican collect. Indeed priests are normatively expected to think for themselves. The same is true of the person appointed to his office in the councils of state, for whom the model is especially designed. Bureaucracies which send dummies into the fray soon lose out. It is a further question when a model suited to elite decision-making is an apt model for *homo sociologicus* at large but, at least for its own territory, there is everything to be said for marrying obedience with latitude.

In the same vein a puzzle about the relation of the model to the actors' personal view of themselves now starts to look tractable. While scientific method is thought to demand an impersonal eye and stresses the durability of bureaucratic positions at the expense of their occupants, the actors emerge as creatures. What then are we to make of the piles of autobiography which every international crisis leaves in its wake? They testify to the actors' awareness of their parts, both singly and collectively, in shaping the decisions. Each principal records his own thoughts and those which were, he suspects, in the mind of others. Each describes the nuances and difficulties of reaching the right result. Are these documents just flotsam from foregone conclusions, rationalisations by puppets, self-deceptions, meretricious *Treppenwitzen* for use in the next act of the play? Well, no doubt they are not suffused only by fearless honesty. But they can at least be taken seriously, if we may regard their authors as, on the whole, intelligent and loyal officers of state, who are often uncertain in advance what is for the best.

That is only a preliminary word on a later topic. Meanwhile more needs saying about the mysterious element of judgement which I have injected into the proposition that 'Where you stand depends on where you sit.' Since this will be a long chapter, however, I will first briefly take stock.

World politics, given the fragility of international law, looked sufficiently like a Hobbesian state of nature to tempt realists into a rational–actor model whose individuals were self-interested nations. But foreign policy is decided at home, with the parties to the moment of a decision being selected by powerful agencies. Or rather, when one looks closer, and with an eye to the workings of structures, the parties are agents who represent agencies. There is immediately a question about such representation. A Bureaucratic Politics model is unpersuasive, if it makes obedient servants into puppets, and, paradoxically, the more one tries to add extra strings, the more latitude one gives the servants in how they construe their masters' orders. Yet latitude is not disobedience. We take the model as a hypothesis that those who play the roles of bureaucratic politics use their own judgement, but in the service of their bureaucracies.

II

This raises a large question about the nature of the actors' judgement, and I begin with an answer which offers to reinstate the rational–actor model in more appealing form and one closer to its true microeconomic roots.

My remarks about theatre were meant to count against an image of the actor as a purely private *dégagé* egoist. But they did not rule out a rational actor of the microeconomic sort, whose preferences have bureaucratic source and shape. Indeed the revised Bureaucratic Politics model seems positively to invite one. Besides, the basic unit of microeconomics never was the firm, and so there never was compelling reason to translate it as the nation state. The basic unit was always the human individual agent allocating scarce resources, guided by his beliefs and desires. If he will do nicely to fill in the hole where judgement is needed from bureaucrats, we get a neat compromise between the models.

Such a compromise would be like a draw agreed in chess when

both sides still have plenty left to play for, if so minded. Once readmitted, the rational-actor model can be used to doubt whether bureaucrats are truly loyal. The principal actors in foreign affairs do surely have goals of their own and may be picking and choosing among their bureaucratic imperatives, so as to further their own ends. They have their pockets to think of, their careers and their families. Granted that they must satisfice bureaucratically, in the sense of doing just enough to keep their colleagues quiet, they have latitude for the rest. Even in being as loyal as they must, they have latitude in deciding what loyalty requires. In general the thrust of a rational-actor approach is to take the magic out of government and public life by decomposing important-sounding bodies into groups of rational individuals, who negotiate tactical alliances. There is plenty of scope, summed up by suggesting that individual actors do not after all personify bureaucrats but impersonate them.

Conversely, however, it is not plain, from the Bureaucratic Politics standpoint, that even beliefs are independent of role. The 'information' component of microeconomic decision-making includes the agent's perceptions, stock of generalisations and, whenever inferences are not a matter of simple deductive logic, tendencies to favour some sorts of conclusions over others. For instance members of the Defense Department are markedly prone to see communist influence at work and to recommend military solutions. Soldiers perceive like soldiers, think like soldiers and infer like soldiers, one might say. This is hardly surprising, granted that the Defense Department, like all bureaucracies, selects, trains and promotes people who have its interests at heart. It sends them forth only after pickling them in departmental ways of assessing evidence and subjecting them to the pressures of 'group think' (as Smith (1985) argues with the aid of a case study). The rival model is greatly mistaken in taking the microprocessor for an abstraction for how people, especially office-holders, acquire and process information. People in office are as loyal in their perceptions as in their preferences.

It may therefore be too soon for a draw, while each model can still attack on even the strongest flank of the other. But a draw would have the advantage of recognising that the two models have something in common. Both attacks display the kind of scientistic spirit which I have been trying to work loose. The notion of actors' judgement threatens to personalise foreign policy by making it matter who is doing the judging. The initial idea of the Bureaucratic Politics model was that actors are highly interchangeable: *any* Secretary of Defense would give the same advice. That yields the highly implausible suggestion that, were the Secretary of Defense to swap places with the Secretary of State each would behave just as the other used to. To head it off, without conceding anything to the other model, one gives each office-holder an institutional biography. Each has been picked and groomed and so comes to the conference table after a history of role-playing which pre-ordains his attitude to the current crisis. Hence Secretaries of Defense are pretty interchangeable with each other, but not with Secretaries of State. Yet the limits are not hard and fast, since some major swaps are indeed possible. For instance British Cabinet ministers are sometimes transferred from 'spending ministries', like Health, to the tight-fisted Treasury, where they argue fervently against the spending programmes which they had formerly been proposing. Thus, by appealing to induction procedures for awkward cases, the model can argue for a determinism which keeps the individual in his place.

This is not to dispense with psychology altogether. The Bureaucratic Politics model has room for a psychological analysis of how perceptions are shaped by 'group think' and other bureaucratic pressures. It can also countenance a personality variable, to distinguish between, for instance, hawklike personalities suited to the Defense Department and dovelike personalities suited to the State Department. In other words a psychological theory which fills in the detail of how bureaucratic determinants work is positively useful.

A rational-actor model is more ambivalent both about individual judgement and about the claims of psychology. Its initial, ideal-type case postulates a fully rational individual, who assigns expected utilities objectively to the options which are objectively feasible. In so far as this is a coherent idealisation, it goes with what is often called 'situational determinism': anyone knowing the individual's preferences and his situation could predict exactly what he will do. But I hope to have undermined the coherence of the ideal-type case by now. If so, the model apparently needs to fall back on a claim that what counts is the individual's subjective perceptions and assignments of utility. It can resist the move by maintaining that the external disciplines of nature, markets and other arenas weed out those who are insufficiently objective. But I hope to have undermined this too. So we seem to be left with individuals, who matter, and an interest in their psychology. The model, however, can still insist on a universal computing unit and hence get by with a very simple utilitarian psychology, which amounts to no more than an embodiment of decision-theory. Individuals are all interchangeable in this regard, although they do of course differ in their preferences or individual sources of satisfaction.

In chess terms, then, it is risky for both models to try for victory over the other and a draw is an attractive solution. Grant that role-players are groomed for office and even that office influences their perceptions. They still have to work out what best to do in each new situation. They still have to calculate the costs and benefits of several options, all of which would be acceptable to their bureaucracies and some of which perhaps suit their own personal ends better than others. This calls for a *homo economicus*, lodged within *homo sociologicus*. Domestic wrangling about which homunculus has the lion's share of the action can wait, given the advantages of a united social theory, where each model can cover any weaknesses in the other.

I am going to reject the terms of this compromise on the grounds that it misrepresents the actors' judgements. In preparaton, however, I shall first try to show that, even in combination, the models fail to account for a kind of power which some actors possess and which stems from skill in judgement. The topic of power needs to be raised somewhere and I do it now, so as to lead up to a final portrait of the actors to end the chapter. For a framework, I shall borrow Steven Lukes' admirable (1974) analysis of power into three dimensions (although departing from it at the third).

The topic is social power without violence. I shall not discuss the natural power of wind or waves, or the kind of power which grows directly out of the barrel of a gun. My limited target is to understand broadly how the balance of power influences social action and shifts in the course of it. I have said nothing on the subject so far, and the omission is glaring. The distribution of power plainly affects the start of each game, the course of it and the outcome. It is part of the answer to the troublesome question of why some outcomes are likelier than others. Yet games of social interaction do not always uphold the saying that to him that hath shall be given. Powerful actors can lose power as well as gain it. We plainly need to ask, therefore, what the two models make of it. Crudely, is power a resource conferred on role-players by their bureaucracies, which have varying amounts of the stuff? Or does it reside in a system of prices, literal and metaphorical, which lets one actor buy the compliance of others on favourable terms and thus get his own way?

The generic question, as Lukes poses it, is what it means for A to have power over B, where A and B are agents. A natural way to tackle it is to hit on a behavioural test of whether A has power over B; and the natural test is whether an overt contest between A's wants and B's wants would be won by A. Thus, if the State Department can muster enough votes to defeat the Defense Department proposal for some particular crisis, it has more power on that occasion, and, if it can usually do so, it is a more powerful agency in general. Similarly a powerful firm can set prices which suit it or outbid its rivals in a competition for resources. At this first dimension power is the ability to win in overt conflict through, so to speak, sheer weight. That is fine as far as it goes, but, since it does not differentiate the models or require anything subtle from the actors, I shall not linger.

Battles can be won without being fought, however. At Lukes' second dimension A has power over B if A can prevent B's wants reaching the moment of overt conflict and decision. For instance democratic political systems do not enact majority preferences if the majority cannot insist on its wishes reaching the agenda. Power here is the ability to win in covert, pre-agenda conflict, the ability to adjust the rules of the game in one's favour before the game starts. This is unmistakably a major aspect of the workings of power and one which both models are quite at home with. For example the power of the Cabinet Office in Whitehall can be traced through its control of what reaches the Cabinet agenda and in what form. Economists know very well that cartels are happiest when their price-fixing is invisible. But it does not just happen. There is skill involved in fixing an agenda or exploiting a market imperfection. We are looking for hidden actors as much as for hidden resources. They earn their pay or promotion because they are better at it than their rivals. The power to stack the pack exists only where there is skill to use it.

A's power over B is greater yet if A can manipulate B's preferences. This third dimenson is contentious, even when one does not follow Lukes in specifying that the manipulation must be contrary to B's real interests.[2] For instance the British Conservative Party has acquired significant working-class support since the post-war years, when its canvassers called at council estates in pairs or not at all. It is debatable whether this has been a use of power or an exercise in rational persuasion. In the present context, however, I take the question as one about the methods used, rather than about working-class interests. If working-class supporters have come to prefer Conservative policies because they recognise good reasons to do so, then, I submit, no power has been exercised, even though the Conservative Party has gained strength at the polls. If the new votes are cast for bad reasons thrust on the voters by manipulative means, then the party has been exercising power. In other words the test is whether A has subverted B's autonomy. This will in the end raise queries about B's real interests if one takes the view that there is more to autonomy than coherent beliefs and preferences which the agent is free to act on. In other words there is a respected, if disputed, notion of autonomy, which connects it to ideas of positive liberty and calls for true beliefs and desires directed to rational or good ends. In that case real interests are finally involved. But, meanwhile, one can usefully pick out a third dimension short of it, where

---

[2] Lukes (1974), chapters 4–6. Lukes distinguishes there between 'power' and 'influence', depending on whether B's new wants are contrary to or in accord with his real interests. But it seems to me that this difference refers more naturally to the process by which B comes to new wants, and that the character of the process does not depend on how real interests lie at the end of it. Nor is it affected by whether A is truly pursuing his own real interests or is mistaken about them. Power misguidedly used by A to undermine his own interests is still power. This does not dispose of important questions about power and real interests – perhaps a fourth dimension would be useful. Meanwhile it seems to me tidier to advance from a second dimension, where wants are diverted, to a third, where they are reconstituted.

power is the ability to manipulate beliefs and preferences to suit the wielder.

This aspect of power suits a Bureaucratic Politics model, given what was said about grooming and group think. Agencies spend much effort on licking their agents into shape and even more on trying to change the preferences of outsiders. It suits a rational-actor model less well, because it subverts the image of individual decision-makers as universal, cool assessors of evidence and calculators of means. Admittedly firms engage in manipulative advertising and public relations (well beyond the informative, rational persuasion which they claim it to be in public); but presumably it would not be worth spending the money if the world contained only economically rational agents with determinate rational expectations. More broadly, a rational-actor model works best when preferences can be regarded as given, without trying to enquire how the agent came by them, because the basic idea is to treat preference as explanans, not explanandum. Equally broadly, therefore, the Bureaucratic image of actors as stewards of roles has the edge at the higher dimensions of power. None the less the ground is tricky for both models, because manipulation is a matter of skill in judgement by the manipulator and lack of it by the victim. A concept has been introduced which makes the exercise of power an art and is awkward for the usual scientific pretensions of both models.

The moral which I draw from these brief remarks about power is that neither model can explain changes in the distribution of power during the game. The advantage of role-theory is that it goes suggestively behind the parameters of rational choice. It is systematically instructive about the control of information and its processing and about how the game starts long before the rational actors take their places at the table. It uses a normative vocabulary suited to games played under rules and to translating power, regarded as resources lodged in institutions, into the options normatively open to the players. But this leaves it quite unclear how power shifts. It is like an account of the game of poker which explains everything except how a player can finish with more money than when he started. Here a rational-choice theory points out helpfully that players need to figure the odds and, if that were all there is to it, our search would be over. But even in poker expectations are not solely a matter of odds. There is bluff, timing, the reading and sending of signals and the scenting of luck. More skill is involved than calculation can analyse, and much of the money goes with it.

In sum, institutional power is a real feature of social rules, and rational actors allow for it in their calculations. It is plausibly conceived as the accumulation of winnings from previous games. But we shall not know how people win or lose it until we have at last connected the loyal role-player with the rational actor. Autobiographies are incontrovertible evidence that the problem is solved in practice. They are written in the active voice, not in the passive, and are suffused with the authors' conviction that it matters not only what cards one is dealt but how well one plays them. To give them any credence at all is to reject explanatory theories which work by translating the active voice into the passive. So let us now ask directly what can be said about judgement as a factor in social action.

III

Begin with judgement in the game of chess – partly because chess just might yield in the end to a massive computer program which needed no judgement, or might yield only to a program which judged better than grand-masters. It is Kasparov's move at the climax of a tense game against Karpov. He has perfect information about the rules, the position and his own desire to win. Were he infinitely clever and blessed with infinite time, he might come up with the move which God would play against God, and do so because he could prove it such. But being finite and under the time pressure of the ticking clock, he will have to rely on a mixture of experience, theory, imagination and hunch. Besides, he does not have perfect information, because he does not know quite what Karpov is thinking. Also, if he cannot count on finding the move which God would play against God, perhaps his second best strategy is to try instead for the move which Kasparov should play against Karpov. Sometimes it pays to play the man rather than the board, especially if a theoretically inferior move will complicate the game in ways which suit Kasparov better than Karpov. Karpov, of course, will be thinking similar thoughts, thus making the rational choice still harder to find.

That paragraph contains two steps away from the ideal or maximising choice – the move which God would play against God. One is a simple retreat to a satisficing solution for familiar reasons. The other is a suggestion that even a satisficing solution needs a judgement which is not just a cut off point in a sequence of calculations. There is a skill to identifying the crux of a position and to forming a shrewd idea of what might develop from plausible next moves. This skill is something which, so far, computers can neither quite reproduce nor replace. Yet the crux identified and the plausible continuations are objective features of the position, even if it takes skill to spot and act on them. For instance, if Karpov has an isolated backward pawn which threatens to advance and grow strong, Kasparov has an objectively good reason to post a knight in front of it. In describing what Kasparov realises and what he is led to do about it, the appropriate language is that of external reasons, as deployed in chapter 6. There are objective statements to make about what is a good reason for what, if one has the skill to know which they are.

Even in chess, then, with its complete, explicit rules and its well-defined problems, judgement is not all mechanical inference. In social life the parameters are usually fluid, the normative expectations indefinite and the descriptions of the problem-setting up for debate. For instance Nelson on one famous occasion failed to see a prominent signal recalling his fleet, after scanning the halyards for it through a telescope put to his blind eye. He has often been acclaimed for this way of exercising his judgement. Kasparov could not get away with that. (Nor indeed could Nelson, had he not gone on to a victory.) All the same, I shall press the thought that chess and social life are problem-solving games, where the players are in search of good moves – moves which there is objectively good reason to play – with the aid of judgement. The more significant, complex and fluid the game, the more explicitly normative become the adjectives used to describe good moves. Whereas the chess-player may make clever or far-sighted moves, role-players can sometimes manage shrewd, mature or wise ones. But the language remains, I contend, one of objective reasons.

The notion of judgement which I am after is both normative and positive. A particular decision-making game opens with a situation and a problem. For instance the CIA reports that Nicaragua is importing Soviet weapons, and the President, having summoned a dozen principal advisers, asks the Secretary of State for his view of this threat to national security. The Secretary of State must judge quickly not only whether he agrees that there is a threat to national security but also whether he is willing to say so. The former question is positive, in the sense that it is an empirical matter whether the movement of weapons constitutes a threat, and also quasi-normative, in the sense that interpreting the situation involves understanding several sorts of norm. The latter question is normative in the different sense that to accept a posing of a problem is to accept an agenda. If he is at odds with the Defense Department, he will not want the problem defined in terms which invite military solutions; on the other hand to redefine the problem in a way which could seem soft on communism is to risk losing influence over its solution, if the others present still believe in a threat to national security. Meanwhile the latter question is also positive in that, if he makes the wrong move, experience can demonstrate his error.

An object-language containing statements like 'there is a threat to national security' is at several removes from the sort of unvarnished observation-language once deemed basic for science. As for that, I assume that Quine (1953) is right to hold that there is no such thing as 'unvarnished news' and hence that judgements of perception inextricably involve judgement of what concepts to apply. This sounds more plausible for a trained physicist describing what he perceives with an electron microscope than for a boy scout reporting that he sees an owl. None the less the proposition that facts are theory-laden applies to both, and both are exercising some skill in judgement. No further epistemic problem is set by the judgement that an object is a pawn from a chess set or a pillar box for posting letters. Despite the reference to norms or rules, pawns and pillar boxes are object-level furniture and are perceived objects of the social world.

From the decision-making angle, perception, description, interpretation and evaluation form a continuum whose end is qualitatively different from its beginning. A pawn is one thing; a dangerous pawn another. A spectator, or even a player, can know that he sees a pawn without knowing that it is dangerous. Yet the further knowledge involves only further empirical understanding of the game. That goes too, I think, for the judgement that a movement of missiles is a threat to security. Since the rules of the game are indefinite and the activity of other minds harder to read, the judgement is more disputable and its dependence on future developments, were they allowed to happen, greater. But we are still dealing with a continuum of richer descriptions of the state of play.

Richer descriptions are more disputable because they are also more loaded. They activate reasons for action. In the game of defending national security, threats need removing, countering, counterbalancing or otherwise keeping in check. In this game a policy of keeping neutral countries neutral by not trying to interfere in their internal affairs is permissible but not very easy to justify. In the related game of influencing world opinion, however, it is much more likely to be voted through. Policy-makers will therefore prefer descriptions which belong to the game which they prefer to play. When the Secretary of State is asked for comment on a threat to national security, he has to decide whether to accept the game offered or to propose another. This judgement belongs in a higher-order game of deciding what game to play.

In speaking of activating reasons for action, I have two frames of reference in mind. One is the role-playing frame, where the reasons for action derive from normative expectations. That a situation is of a declared sort makes it the particular responsibility of those in some set of offices. They thereby have a reason for doing something appropriate about it. A Bureaucratic Politics model is excellent for pinning down this point and spelling it out. The other frame is a problem-solving one. It will not do to come up with any old appropriate solution. The problem calls for a best, or at least, a good one. A rational-actor model is excellent for studying those aspects of decision-making which are fairly independent of normative context. The models now combine, I suggest, to give us rational bureaucrats in search of solutions, which they can recommend to anyone and especially to those whose particular spokesmen they are.

That deliberately leaves an ambivalence, which could be re-
solved in either direction. The portrait is of social actors as intelligent stewards. Stewards are like the characters in the parable of
the talents in Matthew chapter 25, who were given a stock of capital and later asked to account for what they had made of it. Those
who had used the talents well were praised and made 'rulers over
many things'. The test, however, was solely whether they had
benefited their master. As a parable about social explanation, this
is clear on the point that the servants had only a general objective
and were to use their skill in judging how to carry it out, so as to
be able to justify themselves when called to account. This does
not guarantee, however, that the servants were single-mindedly
devoted to their lord. Perhaps they were just satisficing, while
also making some deals for their own benefit on the side or
because they had moral scruples about the service of a master
known to be 'an hard man, reaping where thou hast not sown,
and gathering where thou hast not strawed'. Intelligence in role-
play remains a quality of the actors themselves, and we are still
unclear what finally to say about them.

In its international relations context a Bureaucratic Politics
model gives only a selective glimpse of the actors. It concentrates
on the manoeuvres of small elites at a conference table. For this
special setting it makes good sense to conceive the actors as loyal
yet rational stewards, helped by the reflection that role-distance
can be detachment within the role. But even here there may be
more to them. They may have other concerns, ranging from a
patriotic zeal for the national interest (as mediated through their
own bureaucracy) to a private regard for their personal affairs.
They may indeed have moral concerns above all these claims too.
None of this is ruled out, especially granted that the conference
table game began long before the conference and is embedded in
other games. The model suggests merely that 'Where you stand
depends on where you sit' is the best hypothesis for the student of
foreign policy-making. I have been presuming that my final version will generalise, but have yet to prove it.

The obvious objection is that crisis decisions by an elite are a
poor clue to everyday social life. I reply, however, that the crisis
element simply concertinas the protracted stages of an everyday
process, which starts with a new situation and progresses by in-

teraction and manoeuvre to an outcome combining everyone's choices. It is true that the roles are unusually well defined. But that makes it especially interesting to find that even precise and explicit roles enable more than they constrain in a novel situation facing intelligent role-players. Looser roles with vaguer normative expectations give more latitude but, I maintain, involve a similar blend of enablement and constraint. In other words, it is revealing to think of everyday life as soap-opera, and of soap-opera as the drama of decision by persons in specific social positions. If this is granted, the crux becomes only whether it is fruitful to think in terms of an elite setting.

My reply to that may be something of an act of faith, but it is a firm yes. In trying to find terms on which Adam can be both a sovereign artificer and a subject for science, I have never presumed that they applied only to graduates. Even the corniest soap-opera presents its characters as men and women who are elite decision-makers in the dramas of their own lives when their roles require them to think what they are doing; and I see no reason to doubt their accuracy on this score. But I have been careful not to suggest that the skills of role-play are equally distributed or uniformly well practised. There are sovereign artificers and there are fools in every walk of life.

Intelligible social action is always intelligent, but not always very intelligent. It is always intelligent in the sense that the actor will have had reasons for it and that the first step in explanation is to recover those reasons. But it is not always very intelligent, in that one may be left wondering why those reasons sufficed. I defer discussion of the issues thus raised to the next chapter. For the moment I will just point out what is implied by the harmless-sounding proposition that rational action involves skill in judgement.

Economic models of action idealise in two senses. One is that they abstract schematically from what people do and from the context, so as to arrive at an anatomy or formula connecting preferences, beliefs and decisions. The other is that the formula lets one distinguish between better and worse decisions. In the former sense all action is economically rational, if the model applies to it at all. In the latter sense some actions are more rational than others. The senses are related by a minimal requirement that agents do not arrive at idiotic decisions. For instance someone who rejects a juicy orange at 5p in favour of a less juicy one at 10p *must* be distinguishing between the oranges in a way which the values to be assigned to variables in the formula should reflect. (Perhaps it matters that the juicier orange is South African.) But it takes a deliberate argument to maintain that every agent is always rational in both senses, because every agent always makes the best decision. One such argument goes that decisions are always fully subjectively rational and adds that there is nothing more objective to be said about their rationality. On the whole, however, economists believe that economics is a source of advice and can tell people how to avoid inferior choices.

In that case there is an explicitly normative aspect to the idea of rational choice. For example, economics teams up with the science of nutrition to work out what sort of diet people need and to show how to plan a suitable diet at various levels of income. Anyone not dying of starvation must have solved the problem of getting a passable diet somehow, whatever their income, but with expert advice they might do better. Choosing a diet is thus a skill, and an explanation of why particular diets are in fact chosen uses a model which can also be employed to suggest rational changes. In this example the notion of a better-value diet is well defined and yields at least partial rankings for diets, which are a matter for expert judgement. But the point is general for models of problem-solving activity. The idealisation used to analyse an actual solution also opens the way to a better one. Otherwise it would have failed to identify the element of judgement at work.

By turning rational 'economic' actors into intelligent role-players I mean to complicate this line of thought without subverting it. The actors still have reasons for action, but they are role-related reasons. Problems arise within particular role-playing games and their possible solutions are constrained and enabled by this fact. Judgement is the role-player's judgement of how best to satisfy the demands of office, perhaps tempered by a refusal to heed only those demands. The effect is to make rationality less a matter of maximising the value of a variable and more one of playing a role or game well. That greatly enlivens the question of whether expertise is what the spectator can learn from the players or what the players can learn from the spectator. For diets, the experts study human metabolism and habits, distil this information and then hand out improved diet sheets. It is not plain, however, that, for most of social life, the spectator judges better than the players. He has more hindsight and oversight but less insight. The aim is an improved insider's view and it calls, somehow, for symbiosis.

This is well understood by chess commentators, who scour the moves of grand-masters for mistakes and improved lines of play, without supposing that they could therefore defeat the masters tomorrow. It is understood by the masters too, since they read the analyses with interest, sometimes arguing with them and sometimes putting them into practice. Although the skills are different, each commentator has to be a passable player and each player needs something of a commentator's detachment. Chess is no doubt a special case here too, since few academics would cut a passable figure in many of the social arenas which they study. Economists rarely make better tycoons than philosophers make kings. But the point stands, because the spectator needs to understand the player's judgements before attempting a view from the stalls.

Conclusion

An analysis of social action might start with a model and then ask what sort of actors are needed to fit it. This is what is done, in effect, by the standard theory of rational choice, with its basic rationalising assumptions and hence its need for bargain-hunting individuals engaged in instrumental social relationships. Although I still think that the social sciences have nothing to touch the elegance of the resulting economics and game-theory, I have tried to show that the model is hopelessly indeterminate. A group of agents acting rationally in the light of their expectations could arrive at so many outcomes that none has adequate reasons for action. The trouble can apparently be cured by adding normative expectations strong and definite enough to turn the bargain-hunters into creatures of norms. But I have tried to show that norms are not definite enough to do it and anyway do not rob actors of discretion.

Alternatively one might work from the other direction by first seeing what kind of actors one wants and then asking what model will suit them. I want social actors whose reasons for action stem from their social relationships but who judge which of the relevant reasons is best. It sounds as if, for modelling purposes, they are a simple blend of *homo economicus* with *homo sociologicus*. The latter renders the former determinate; the former puts the calculation into the latter. But, if each of two models explains how actions are programmed, then they cannot be combined to explain why action is not programmed. Judgement of the kind proposed in this chapter is more like moral judgement than like either ready reckoning or rifle drill. It consists in acting intelligently for reasons which a role-player can justify.

If this is messy, then the reader was warned at the very beginning. Besides, it is not an altogether messy idea that we make our own roles but not in conditions of our own choosing. It is no messier than is required by the general thesis that, where understanding (*Verstehen*) diverges from explanation (*Erklären*), we should seek understanding. This thesis will be defended in the next chapter.

11
Rationality and understanding

Marcus Atilius Regulus commanded the Roman army in the first Carthaginian war, until he lost a battle and was captured in 255 BC. After a spell in captivity, he was despatched to Rome to try to exchange himself for some high-ranking prisoners. To kindle his ardour, the Carthaginians extracted an oath from him that, if the mission failed, he would return to Carthage to be put to death by torture. On reaching Rome, however, he urged the Senate to refuse, since the prisoners were worth more to Carthage than he to Rome. His advice carried the day. Then, unmoved by the pleas of friends and peers, he insisted on keeping his oath. He sailed back to Carthage, where he was returned to prison and kept awake until he died.

Cicero introduces this memorable story into a discussion of duty and expediency, as 'a real event in our history', illustrating his theme that what is truly expedient is what is truly right (*De Officiis* III.26). It will do nicely to examine the notion of rationality as rational role-playing and to pose some epistemic questions about understanding (*Verstehen*) and explaining (*Erklären*). There is also a twist to the tale, as will be revealed later, when we come to the hermeneutic circle. Meanwhile let us ask whether we can understand and explain Regulus' course of action as one rationally chosen by a Roman general in the dawn of the Republic. I shall deploy the answer suggested by the previous chapter, giving it a Weberian frame and thus pointing up some epistemological problems of this style of analysis.

The original economic or instrumental notion of rationality gives grounds for deeming Regulus rational, irrational and non-rational. If we stress that utilities are subjective and that the crux is whether Regulus achieved an optimal match between his desires, beliefs and actions, then we shall be inclined to call him rational. No other option would have been likelier to achieve what he most valued. But this assumes that no queries about a rational agent's motivation arise, or, to put it more accurately, that we can simply infer his utilities from his choices. As soon as motivation is allowed to matter, however, and some kind of reference to self-interest is involved in distinctively economic thinking, we shall be more inclined to call him irrational. No one could rationally prefer death by torture to life in Rome. No one whose interests included his family and the wishes of his friends could have done the sums as Regulus did. An American general who was captured by the Vietcong, was returned to Washington on similar terms and then insisted on keeping his oath would be off his head. But then our world is not the Roman Republic. So perhaps Regulus and the old *mores* fall outside the scope of any economic model. In that case he is neither rational, nor irrational, but non-rational.

None of this is appetising. Take the 'non-rational' category. The action was not 'traditional' in Weber's (1922) sense of 'the expression of a settled custom', if that implies 'simply a dull reaction to accustomed stimuli along lines laid down by settled habit'.[1] For although Cicero presents Regulus within an encompassing moral framework which governed the giving of oaths to legitimate enemies, he praises his virtuous choice to speak against his own mission and points out that few would have done the same. Regulus made a reasoned choice prompted by 'greatness of soul and courage'. To anticipate a later point, I do not see how we can make any sense of the story unless we can find reasons which were probably Regulus' own. But what gets classed as non-rational because it is not instrumentally rational (*zweckrational*) may yet be expressively rational (*wertrational*). Weber's test is whether it is 'an attempt to realise some absolute value: that is the agent may consciously believe in the unconditional intrinsic value, whether ethical, aesthetic, religious or any other, of a par-

---

[1] Translation by Eric Matthews, p. 28, listed in the bibliography as Weber (1978).

ticular sort of behaviour, purely for its own sake and regardless of consequences' (1978, p. 28). That sounds better, except that it overrides an interesting distinction drawn by Cicero between Regulus' decision to speak against his mission and his decision to return to Carthage. The latter was not a choice at all, Cicero says, because no true Roman could have done otherwise after sabotaging the terms of his own oath. 'For the fact of his returning may seem admirable to us nowadays, but in those times he could not have done otherwise. The merit, therefore, belongs to the age, not to the man' (*De Officiis* III.31). The former was a noble, rational action.

Yet Cicero cannot mean quite what he says, because he also cites examples of dishonourable Romans, who gave similar oaths and then broke them. Presumably whether to act beyond the call of duty is one sort of choice and whether to abide by the consequences of one's actions is another. Are both sorts *wertrational* in Weberian terms?

A possible answer is that Regulus acted in a *wertrational* manner throughout, whereas dishonourable contemporaries, who broke their oaths, acted instrumentally both in the making and in the breaking of them. Then it looks as if Regulus acted irrationally from an instrumental point of view but not in a way which matters epistemologically, because he was not attempting to serve his own interests. But this is not Cicero's attitude. He regards the contrast between expediency and right as spurious.

When he came to Rome, he could not fail to see the specious appearance of expediency, but he decided that it was unreal, as the outcome proves. His apparent interest was to remain in his own country, to stay at home with his wife and children, and to retain his rank and dignity as an ex-consul, regarding the defeat which he had suffered as a misfortune that might come to anyone in the game of war. Who says this was not expedient? Who, think you? Greatness of soul and courage say that it was not. (*De Officiis* III.36).

Cicero is arguing that it is always rational and right to do what is *truly* expedient. In that case Regulus acted rationally from an instrumental point of view too, but not because of any assignment of subjective utilities. The truly expedient action is the one with the strongest external reasons.

Modern sympathies tend to be for Weber's separation of *zweck-rational* from *wertrational*, which might seem to correspond nicely to the positive/normative distinction. But Weber himself at once hedges by remarking that most actions are a mixture. Certainly the line is not between reasoned and unreasoned decisions. That is clear in Weber himself from his account of 'Politics as a Vocation' (in (1978)), where he savages the idea that those who act on principle take no account of consequences. It is clear also from our earlier discussion both of principle and of role-play that neither the pursuit of moral ends nor obedience to the demands of a role is careless of consequences. A man of honour may assess consequences by the criterion of honour, but he does not ignore them. Cicero's way of telling the story has at least the descriptive merit of making us realise that the modern distinction between expressive and instrumental rationality is not one which everyone draws.

Cicero in fact separates three kinds of reason. There are those of base, misguided self-interest which move some people to shirk their obligations. There are those which 'belong to the age, not to the man' or, for our purposes, those which stem from norms defining a role. Then there are those of 'greatness of soul and courage', which prompted Regulus to speak against his mission, although honour could have been satisfied by merely putting the Carthaginian offer to the Senate without comment. Admittedly *De Officiis* is an argument in ethics rather than a discourse on method. But there is a moral psychology in Cicero's talk of kinds of reason capable of moving people. Even in a heroic age, he presumes, people can do their duty or fall short or go heroically beyond it. In the terms of my previous chapter, the apparatus of roles sits somewhat lightly on the self if, even in the old Roman Republic, choice of action was underdetermined by social positions.

A notion of understanding (*Verstehen*) which does justice to this variety will not be a simple one. But we have come too far to falter on that account. Weber's distinction between 'direct' and 'explanatory' understanding is the next step ((1978), p. 11). He gives *Verstehen* a primary, initial sense of 'empathy' or direct insight into what action is being performed. By 'empathy' we know directly that a man swinging an axe is cutting wood or that a marksman is aiming a rifle. By 'explanatory understanding' we come to know that the woodsman is earning a living or the marksman seeking revenge. *Verstehen* thus works with a datum level or observation-language of *actions* – happenings specified in terms of what the actor is doing – which avoids some epistemic problems. Knowing what someone is doing does not involve fragile inference from his physical behaviour to the mental state which caused it. It involves simply knowing what intensional concept applies. There are actions which we perceive to occur. Thus we see people shake hands, even though there is a physical story in which hands only touch, and a visiting Martian might not have the action story which we have. No doubt action-descriptions are corrigible, just as claims to see a tree in the quad are corrigible. But, according to Weber, knowledge of intentions is not basically and inherently more problematic than knowledge of physical behaviour. I am going to assume that he is right.

Explanatory understanding is a matter of assigning an action to a complex of meanings in, Weber says, three possible ways. One is 'historical', where we identify the actual motive of a specific individual in a concrete situation. For instance we establish that the marksman is aiming to shoot his brother's murderer, not taking part in a military exercise or hunting expedition. Another is 'sociological', where we treat the action as an instance of a common phenomenon, like vendettas, and hence as being 'intended by the average agent to some degree of approximation (as in sociological studies of large groups)'. The third is 'ideal-typical', as when we invoke the constructions of economic theory to see how closely the action corresponds to what a fully rational agent in single-minded pursuit of an economic goal would do. Actual cases are never so pure, and hence only approximate to the ideal type.

The messiness of this trio is made worse by being told presently that there are two sorts of ideal-type. Besides the perfectly *zweckrational* kind just mentioned, there is also an 'ideal-type' which delineates a classificatory concept like 'feudal', 'patrimonial', 'bureaucratic' or 'charismatic' by giving it a full internal coherence. Whereas the former economic ideal-type is 'ideal' in the sense that it is too pure to describe actual cases more than approximately, the latter conceptual ideal-type is 'ideal' in the sense that it imposes a misleading orderliness on what are often irrational phenomena. Relatedly, there is also scope for 'average types' of the kind found in empirical statistics, relying on general-isations which hold in practice. But these can be formulated clearly only where one is averaging 'differences of degree among qualitatively similar kinds of meaningful behaviour'. That makes their application doubtful when dealing with actions done from mixed motives.

Rather than burrow further into Weber, I shall try to assemble these pieces for myself from the epistemic standpoint of one seek-ing to understand rational role-play. There is one more Weberian distinction to bear in mind. In assigning action to a complex of meanings we produce explanation which is adequate at the level of meaning. In the end, however, explanation must also be ad-equate at the causal level. Weber seems to have something statisti-cal in view for the causal level (perhaps in the spirit of Hume's analysis of causation).

Without adequacy on the level of meaning, our generalisations remain mere statements of *statistical* probability, either not intelligible at all or only imperfectly intelligible... On the other hand, from the point of view of sociological knowledge, even the most certain adequacy on the level of meaning signifies an acceptable *causal* proposition only to the extent that evidence can be produced that there is a probability ... that the action in question *really* takes the course held to be meaningfully ad-equate. (Weber (1978), p. 15; italics in the original)

I take this to be a warning that to make action intelligible is only to find it a *possible* explanation, without thereby coming up with its *actual* explanation. It would seem that *Verstehen* governs poss-ible explanations and needs at least the reassurance which comes from causal support and perhaps supplementation by a distinc-tively causal explanation.

For Regulus, then, we start with a narrative and ask why it makes sense. The sense comes from two ideal-types, a conceptual one delineating the Roman Republic as a kind of society with heroic normative expectations, and an economic one showing why the action done solved a problem of choice. It is unlikely that either applies in full. The actual norms will not form a fully coherent fabric, and actual problem-solving is never pure calcu-lation. Also it is still unclear how the two types go together, given that there is still a tension between them. So we have more than one way to make the narrative credible, and hence must go on to ask which version is right. Weber calls for supporting empirical generalisations here but, although I agree that something more is needed, I think that we are in deeper epistemological water than generalisations can deal with.

It is time for the promised twist to the tale of Regulus which Cicero recounts so graphically and describes as a 'real event in our history'. The twist is that the event may not have happened at all. Modern authorities will have none of it. Mommsen's majestic *History of Rome*, for instance, calls the episode and its details 'incongruous embellishments, contrasting ill with sober and serious history' (1894, vol. II, p. 182n). J. H. Scullard (1935, p. 152n) holds that Regulus died in Carthage without ever returning to Rome. The yarn about his death by torture, he says, was a cover-up for the barbarity of his wife, who, on hearing that he had died, had some Carthaginian prisoners of war tortured to death. The modern view seems to be that Regulus was a convenient myth, rather like King Arthur and the Knights of the Round Table, which had found its way into schoolroom history by Cicero's time but has no claim to be taken for sober or serious history.

The twist makes it very clear that what needs explaining varies with what counts as a credible explanation, in ways which bristle with epistemological questions. Initially, we had a series of events from the third century BC and were trying to see how rational we could make them if we applied a model of rational role-play with due historical allowance for an alien social context. But this series of events cannot be what needs explaining, if it never happened. Attention shifts to Rome in the first century BC, when Cicero was writing. That Cicero could take the story for a 'real event in our history' needs a first-century explanation. Part of it would no doubt be that the legend was in circulation.[2] But, even granted that the Romans' attitude to the past was less systematic and more inspirational than ours, we still want to know why Regulus should have had the resonance of truth in the first century. (Think of the ups and downs of King Arthur as a real historical figure over the centuries for comparison.) This is a com-

[2] Witness, for instance, Horace *Odes* I.iii.5 and Livy's summary of the (missing) book XVIII of his *History* (*Periochae* XVIII).

plicated question, to do with legitimation as much as with causality, as I shall contend presently, and plainly different from the initial one. The explanandum is no longer Regulus' actions but Cicero's utterances.

Before galloping after this new fox, however, we should pause to ask how the moderns manage to have it over the ancients. Cicero was applying a test of plausibility to the stories, which he inherited; so do we. For example Scullard gives a report of the battle which Regulus lost which is just as much at several removes as is the discredited tale of a return to Rome. He does, admittedly, have some sources, like Valerius Maximus, where the battle occurs and the return to Rome is conspicuously absent. But, like any good historian, he is judging his sources, not copying them out. Advances in historical knowledge do not make a test of plausibility superfluous, since they employ one. It is not a mere matter of fact that Valerius Maximus would have mentioned Regulus' return to Rome, if it had happened. One can imagine Cicero's explanation of why a historian might not mention a real event too well known to need mentioning.

I point this out not to uphold the ancients against the moderns, or to raise a spectre of relativism, but to emphasise the work done by a notion of rationality in reconstructing actions as the result of desire plus belief. The formula $D + B \Rightarrow A$ has three variables. Of these, even A can be problematic. Weber's licence to use 'empathy', so that we can perceive who is doing what, does not extend to actions in the distant past or to descriptions in terms which the agents themselves would dispute or fail to understand. D and B are even more plainly problematic. Actions can result from desires and beliefs which strike observers as very odd, and an assurance that they will not have seemed odd to the agent is no help unless one can know how things seemed to the agent. More formally, given A and D, one can infer B, if one assumes that the agent is at least weakly rational; and, on that assumption, one can also infer D, given A and B. But, if one knows neither D nor B, then one can infer only that they form a pair which together explain why a weakly rational agent does A.

By 'weakly rational' I mean that A, D, B form a consistent trio: an agent with these desires and beliefs had a reason to do A. Even this much is cast in an external or objective form, on the grounds that, if the agent might take any pair of *D, B* as a subjective reason for *A*, the attempt to make sense of action is hopeless. But it is too weak to help much. Given *A* and *D*, there are all sorts of false beliefs which would make the trio consistent. Given *A* and *B*, there are all sorts of rum desires which would do the same. Given only *A*, there are any number of (*D, B*) pairs which would yield a consistent trio. Admittedly there are other ways of getting a fix on *D* and *B* separately. The beliefs which motivate will also be fairly consistent with the agent's other beliefs. His desires on one occasion will usually be consonant with those on other occasions, provided that he is weakly rational. But the same general question arises for extended sets of beliefs or desires. How do we identify the actual, as opposed to possible, members?

A tempting reply is simply 'ask the agents'. It does not even matter that they may be dead, if, like Cicero, they have left us a text. But we have to understand what they say or write. Philosophers will need no persuading that this is the original problem over again in perhaps more daunting form. Others may care to reflect on the Other Cultures problem in anthropology – the tuppence-coloured version of the penny-plain Other Minds problem. Actions in an alien setting are like texts in an alien language. To identify their meaning one must grasp the underlying system of thought. Access to the thought is through understanding the actions or texts. Intelligent bilinguals are not a walking solution, since there is the same point to be made about their rendering of one system in the language of another. If this is granted, then the puzzle is made only more graphic by being posed for two languages or cultures. It is a colourful version of the old philosophical problem of how one person can know how things stand from the internal point of view of another. If an intermediate case is wanted, the history of scientific thought provides one.[3]

The last chapter, on reasons and roles, adds a crucial complication of a different sort. An utterance is an action and hence often a move in a game. Although 'the acting individual attaches subjective meaning to it', it also 'takes account of the behaviour of others and is thereby oriented in its course'. The behaviour of others is often a matter of their roles in the context which sets

[3] For more on the theme of this paragraph see Wilson (1970) and Hollis and Lukes (1982).

their relationship to the acting individual. This calls for a more elaborate treatment of linguistic meaning than so far in evidence.[4] The starting point can usefully be to distinguish between an utterance's meaning and an utterer's meaning. To know what an utterance means, one must know (enough of) the rules of the language to identify the speech-act which has taken place. I take this to be a matter of *convention* in the way in which the identity of a chess move is one. The utterer's meaning is the *intention* to perform the speech-act, rather as *P-K5* might be both the move made and the move intended by the chess-player. Witness the example, this pair can come apart if the utterer or player holds false beliefs about the rules or fumbles or otherwise fails to perform what he intended to. Things can also go adrift if the conventions are indefinite, incomplete, incoherent or not fully shared by all persons involved. But I shall presume that, on the surface level, there is normally a match between the utterance's meaning, as given by convention, and the utterer's intention to convey it to others. Call this communication, achieved, basically, through a Weberian 'direct understanding' all round.

When it comes to 'explanatory understanding', the utterance's (or action's) meaning and the utterer's (or actor's) meaning start to diverge. Foreign policy decision-making is a neat example. The question on the official agenda is where the national interest lies. The proposals uttered and discussed are mostly addressed to this question and attacked or defended accordingly. The Defense Secretary is asked why he favours sending in troops and replies that any other course would be read by the Russians as weakness. The Secretary of State retorts that the use of American muscle would be a diplomatic disaster in the third world. Each has given a reason for or against a course of action. There is no guarantee that these reasons are in truth the utterer's underlying reasons. We can mark the point by calling the reasons which make the utterance appropriate in its context *legitimating reasons*.

One might fancy that legitimating reasons were unimportant

---

[4] What follows is hugely indebted to Quentin Skinner in person and through his work, some of which is listed in the bibliography. In particular, the point that an actor's professed reasons matter, even when they are not professed sincerely, is pure Skinner. It is splendidly put in his (1974) paper, which made a great impression on me.

to explanation, unless they coincided with the actor's motive in putting them forward. Quentin Skinner's readers know better. The legitimating language enables and constrains the power of the actors to effect their motives. If your motive in playing chess with me is to humiliate me, you will get nowhere unless you play better moves than I, by the public legitimating test of what makes a move a good one. The Secretary of State has to knock out the legitimating reasons for a military solution if he is to advance the interests of his own department by getting agreement to a diplomatic one. Once the terms of the game are set, the players may not challenge them or the public values (like the need for a strong America) enshrined in them. To pursue any discordant aims of their own, they must exploit ambiguities or come up with legitimate proposals which, so to speak, just happen to suit them too. The legitimate, or legitimating, language blends *zweckrational* with *wertrational* in fascinating ways. However cynical the participants, it remains crucial for what they can get away with.

The actors are not fools. They know what is afoot and will often signal their understanding. These, perhaps coded, signals are both an unofficial gloss on the official game and moves in other less official games going on simultaneously. The distinction which I have just drawn between legitimating reasons and motives need not be between public and private aims. The Secretary of State's motives are private in relation to the game of deciding the national interest but are legitimating reasons in the off-the-board game between the State Department and Defense Department. So there is a further question about why the Secretary of State is pushing for his department. Its answer need not be very private either. He may have several other concerns outside the State Department. How the trail ends depends partly on the person and partly on the account of human nature deemed finally explanatory. To avoid repeating the last chapter or anticipating the next, let us just say that it ends with his *real reasons*.

Power politics is an intricate example, and I do not imply that every social interchange is complex to the *n*th degree or that all human beings are infinitely tortuous. But I do suggest that everyday actors in everyday life commonly conduct second discourses, distinguishable from their official one. The official one continues to matter, because it enables and constrains the others. The others matter, because they account for how the actors pick their way through the indeterminate permissions of the official discourse. We need to understand both the legitimating reasons and the real reasons. (I do not call them 'motives', because that would suggest something different in kind from 'reasons' and essentially private in some philosophical sense.) In tabular form, *Verstehen* calls for a fourfold apparatus for adequacy at the level of meaning.

	Action's meaning	Actor's meaning
What?	conventions	intentions
Why?	legitimating reasons	real reasons

The epistemological problems of knowing that an interpretation is correct on all four counts are formidable, since answers to the two 'What?' questions often need justifying by reference to the two 'Why?'s. For example Cicero's *De Officiis* needs more than a Latin–English dictionary and an assumption that he meant what he said. He is trying to show that, wherever expediency seems to conflict with duty, it is only 'the specious appearance of expediency', since what is truly *utile* is always right. He uses his heaviest guns against what must therefore be stiff contemporary opposition. Regulus represents an age, mythical or not, when there was no puzzle explaining why people kept their oaths but only why they sometimes broke them. In first-century Rome, he feared, these priorities were fast reversing. We need this much not just for the larger task of making overall sense of the book in its period but also to be sure what *utile* means.

With the utterance's or action's meaning in partial variation with the utterer's or actor's meaning, we shall have to strengthen the rationality assumptions required for $D + B \Rightarrow A$. Weak rationality is not enough to avoid the hermeneutic circle, which comes into view when we note that the context of utterance or action is a conjecture, which we erect with explanatory intent. We need the conventions to identify the intentions and *vice versa*. We need both to get at the reasons and *vice versa*. Utterances and actions have meanings taken from a stock created by actors who use it. The circularity is not fatal in practice because one can work piecemeal by alternating between context and actor (or text's meaning and author's meaning), using conjectures about one to test hypotheses about the other. But this is possible only by relying on strong rationality assumptions to the effect that actors are moved by good reasons for their desires, beliefs and, hence, actions. In summary form the assumption is that human beings are rational, and the questions are what exactly this means and how we know.

Influenced by Weber, I think it means that social actions are solutions to problems of choice, which come close enough to ideal-type solutions to be thereby understood. At least, this is what I think it means for purposes of social science. The clearest examples remain those where there is a well-articulated ideal-type, as with economic theory, and I have to admit that situations in which the best course of action is more for judgement than for demonstration are less convincing. But, having said my piece on that score already, I simply adopt Weber's strategy of glossing adequacy at the level of meaning in terms of this kind of abstraction. The question of how we know that mankind has this rational character then divides into two.

Firstly, how do we know that economic theory and other ideal-type abstractions are a true analysis of what rationality means or implies for social life? Essentially this is the problem of *a priori* knowledge applied to the social sciences, and I stand by the answer given by von Mises ((1949) and (1960)) and endorsed by Hollis and Nell (1975). This is that formal systems consist of real definitions of elementary concepts, their implications and application rules governing *ceteris paribus* clauses. Examples of concepts which can be formalised in this way are number, mass, power and choice, although, witness the last two, there is room for argument about how. I cannot myself make sense of such disputes, unless they are about which of the candidates captures the truth of what the concept refers to. (Thus a conceptual definition of 'Power' is an attempt to say what power essentially is.) In other words we are dealing with Kantian conditions *a priori* of the possibility of finding a kind of describable order in social experience. I shall not press for this view here, since it is a contentious one needing more argument than there is space for, and the themes of this book do not demand it. But they are, I trust, consistent with it, and I think of the book as taking a hand in a dispute about the true conception of rationality.

The main alternatives to a Kantian view are positivism and pragmatism. The former, being wedded to an exhaustive and exclusive analytic/synthetic distinction, regards theoretical statements about rational action as either tautologies or empirical generalisations. The latter, rejecting the analytic/synthetic distinction, along with the idea that any word or concept could have a real definition, regards them as devices for working order into the flux of experience, to be judged for usefulness rather than truth. I shall not try to grapple with these rivals, but I mention them in preamble to the second part of the question about the rationality of mankind. How do we know that there in fact are rational agents, in the sense proposed?

The question challenges the use of ideal-type models for understanding the real world. Why assume that agents are perfectly rational, when we know that they are not? There is some case for a flat denial of the difficulty. This might be done by playing up the subjective element in utility theory and rational-choice theory, until all agents always do what seems to them best at the time and there is nothing more to be said. But I hope to have scotched this line by insisting that rationality involves more than subjective consistency. Another suggestion might be to play up the degree to which all action conforms to rules (or to what the agent takes the rules to be) and is always rational in this sense. But I hope to have given ample reason for refusing to let the rules absorb the agents. So I take it that there is a genuine puzzle about the gap between the ideal model and the actual world.

Positive economists often regard microeconomic theory as a good enough approximation to how the world works. Samuelson's articles in the *American Economic Review* (1963–5) are canonical. But they rely on a simple positivist view of nature and of natural science, which I judge to have been overtaken by the recent developments in the philosophy of natural science, which I mentioned in the opening chapter. In brief, they rely on there being theory-neutral facts of observation, and criteria for whether *ceteris paribus* conditions hold independent of the results of testing the generalisations which they protect. These presumptions are currently in so much trouble that the position needs rethinking. I shall not address the topic here, however, since they also rely on a continuity between natural and social science which my earlier chapters dispute.[5]

Samuelson's articles are a retort to Milton Friedman's (1953) argument that the 'realism' of an assumption is *solely* a matter of its predictive success. Microeconomic theory, and perfect competition models in particular, predict very well, according to Friedman, and are thereby vindicated. In this reckoning, the assumption that agents are rational is 'realistic' if and only if it yields good predictions of their economic and, indeed, other behaviour. I have always thought this a clever line for anyone who accepts the usual Humean rationale for Positive science since, given Hume's analysis of causation, the order in nature is solely one of reliable patterns. In that case what happens to latch on to the patterns successfully is best. But Friedman too has been overtaken by doubts about the independence of tests of predictions. In terms of his (1953) article, the upshot is to undermine the positivist theme of its earlier pages and to strengthen the pragmatist tendency of its later ones. If so, the case for assuming that agents are rational becomes that it fits in elegantly and usefully with the totality of our beliefs.

Pragmatism offers a short way with Weber's concern that explanations must be adequate also at the causal level. There is only the single question whether rational reconstructions of action conflict with anything else which we are disposed to believe about the social world. This relaxed view of the job of a social theory has evident attractions, enhanced by Quine's (1960) quickness of wit and deftness of prose. But it seems to me to be too relaxed about what we can accept as a reading of '$D + B \Rightarrow A$' in rendering action rational. Since I do not agree that *tout pardonner c'est tout comprendre*, I hold out for definite ways in which action can be irrational.

The question was how we know that there are rational agents,

---

[5] There is, of course, much more to be said on the topic of realism and abstraction in economics and on the wider topic of whether economics can or should be a positive science. For interesting recent argument see Blaug (1980), Caldwell (1982), Hutchison (1978), Katouzian (1980), Machlup (1978) and Stewart (1979). *Economics in Disarray* is the symptomatic title of Wiles and Routh (1984), which contains a lively set of papers on these issues.

in the sense embodied in ideal-types. My answer is that ideal-types are like an examination paper which no one is allowed to fail, even though not everyone scores full marks. No one fails, because we cannot understand action without at least a part score. Action cannot be non-rational, since we cannot ascribe intention to behaviour without reproducing at least some reason on the actor's part. Action cannot be very irrational, because we need warrant for believing that the reasons we ascribe were the agent's own, or at least likelier to have been his own than other possible reasons. But there is no need for full marks. Then the ideal-type solution to the actor's problem of choice becomes the yardstick for identifying departures, which require causal explanation.

This answer has to be nuanced to allow for the examiners' own frequent ignorance. Even economists are not omniscient, and, where the decision problem has the open texture of social or political role-playing, the very notion of possible full marks is suspect. But it is no part of my rationalist view that anyone has a full set of the Sibylline books. The examiners, like reflective onlookers of a game, have some advantages, but do not always see better than the players. Next year's examiners may disagree with them. Meanwhile, they have to carry out their task, since there is no other way of making sense of social life. The task is that of reasonably friendly examiners, who must bear in mind that other ages and cultures have a different context of rules and meanings. They must also be reasonably unfriendly to each other.

Friendliness is connected with adequacy at the levels of meaning and causation together. A rational reconstruction can be too friendly, in the sense that, although it is consistent with what the actor did, it does not correspond to the actor's own reasons. I am not trying to close the gap completely, since it seems to me implicit in there being separate persons, transparent neither to themselves nor to others. My conclusion is only that the more that can be done at the level of meaning and the less at the level of causation, the more of a sovereign artificer Adam will be. Methodologically, the more rational the action is, the easier it is to understand and explain it; so it pays to give the actors the benefit of the doubt.

There is still work to be done at the causal level for the parts of social life which understanding cannot reach. Firstly, where an actor's own reasons derive from irrational beliefs and desires, there is a causal question about the source of those beliefs and desires. 'Irrational' should not be confused with 'false'. One can hold a false belief for good reasons or a true belief for bad reasons. Whether fears are reasonable or unreasonable is not a simple matter of whether what is feared is truly dangerous. But there is some connection too. For instance in one of James Thurber's *Fables for our Time* a man finds a unicorn browsing among the tulips in his garden. He informs his wife, who, remarking with scorn that the unicorn is a mythical beast, summons the police and a psychiatrist, to have him certified. When they arrive, there is no unicorn and she asks him to confirm that he saw one. 'Of course not', he replies: 'the unicorn is a mythical beast.' So they lock her up instead and the man lives happily ever after. The question about the scope of understanding here is whether to send for a psychiatrist or a zookeeper. It is not a simple one of whether there was a unicorn or not (try it with a lion or escaped snake), but neither is the fact of the matter irrelevant. Psychiatrists and zookeepers represent different *sorts* of explanation of the man's performance.

Secondly, more goes on in social life than the actors, singly or plurally, realise. Psychology and sociology bring us a great deal of news about ourselves. Here too the scope for understanding by reference to models of rational action is not clear cut, granted that Cunning of Reason analyses of the summary of consequences extend the scope. But there are major theorists in both sciences whose work postulates forces in the unconscious or in the social system which operate beyond the reach of rational-decision models. Witness chapter 9 on functions and rules, I am happiest when such mechanisms can be construed so as to put them within human control. But I have not denied that much goes on behind our backs.

Thirdly, even when an action is done for good reasons which the actor recognised and we thus know why it was done, there are further, separate, causal questions to ask. For instance much of the history of technology is a success story of rational solutions to engineering problems. But that does not prevent interesting questions about the conditions for technological advances. *Verstehen* opens the enquiry, because that is how we set the questions, but it does not provide all the answers to all of them.

It will be seen that I am relating *Verstehen* to *Erklären* somewhat differently from Weber. In so far as he takes the causal level as statistical reassurance that the connections hypothesised are common, I do not object. There is indeed a problem in knowing that the possible reasons attributed to actors are their actual reasons and weight of numbers is, pragmatically, reassuring for explanation and handy for prediction. But the claim that statistical generalisations explain particular cases is another matter. In the current state of the philosophy of science there is no single or safe account of what is meant by 'causal explanation'. But Weber uses *Erklären* in the Humean spirit of the 'covering law model', thus making it explanatory to subsume a case under a generalisation for similar cases with similar initial conditions. I shall risk denying that rational actions have causal *explanations* in this sense or in any stronger one which appeals to a natural law to account for particular instances.

The chess-player who plays Q-K5 *ch* for the excellent reason that it gives him a smothered mate in five moves is doing what any good player would do in that position. But he does not do it *because* others would do it. There is no natural law of chess about the occurrence of smothered mates. Other good players would do the same simply because they would have the same good reason for doing it. The particular explains the general, not *vice versa*. Similarly I am disinclined to treat the economist's 'laws of supply and demand' as laws of nature which explain why demand falls and supply increases with a rise in price. If each supplier thereby has a similar good reason to raise output and each consumer similar good reason to vary his purchases, then that accounts for the systematic general result. When an economist hits on a new economic 'law', his discovery will prompt him to identify an unnoticed reason which has been moving a number of economic agents to do what is systematic in sum. Having identified this reason, he has explained the 'law'.

That contrasts with a natural science, where, I take it, there are still presumed to be laws of nature of an explanatory kind. There may well be some in the social world too, especially where social life is influenced by our biology or use of natural objects. AIDS is unmistakably a social fact, and the biological laws of its transmission and of the mutations of the virus affect people's behaviour. But I deny any presumption that social patterns are part of an explanatory causal order. Whether they turn out to be depends on their not being traceable to individual reasons and their collective consequences. AIDS affects people: what people know (or believe) about AIDS affects its spread.

In sum, the philosophical question of whether reasons are causes is best taken by steps. Good reasons *explain* action: they are why the agent did what he did. The explanation is not of the natural law form, however, since it does not work from the invariable or necessary generalisation to the particular case. If this distinction is accepted, it is a matter of indifference whether it is construed as one within the class of causal explanations or as one best marked by saying that reasons are not causes. 'Adequacy at the causal level' is thus finally of two sorts, one where understanding at the level of meaning reveals why the action was done, by reconstructing it successfully from within, and the other where the meaning-account had to be supplemented from without.

Conclusion

Even if Regulus' return to Carthage was not a 'real event in our history', it can still do duty for actions which puzzle us because the agent is deaf to expediency. Cicero tells us not to be puzzled. There is a difference between the false appearance of expediency and the true kind. It is truly expedient to do what is right, and, for an age where righteousness is the norm, it is easy to understand why people act rightly. The puzzle arises only when expediency and right come unglued.

These reflections in ethics are interesting also for the epistemology of *Verstehen*. I have been trying to extract a theory of understanding from clues offered by Weber's four kinds of action, two kinds of ideal-types and enigmatic distinction between the level of meaning and the causal level. The broad idea is that *Verstehen* takes an insider view with a mixture of empathy and suspicion.

The opening step is to identify the act by the agent's intention in its context of conventions. Empathy, meaning perception under an action-description, may suffice, if the enquirer already knows the conventions, but shades into more nuanced interpretation if intention or context is opaque. The next step is to recover the agent's reasons and judge his judgements, to see what is thereby accounted for and what needs further explanation. The process is complicated by the different character of the two ideal-type models. The 'economic' test for whether the actor allocated his resource efficiently would be roughly like an examination with model answers, were it not for the indeterminacies discussed in earlier chapters. The 'sociological' test for effective role-playing never was of that sort. But the enquirer must pass judgement, since the merit of the actor's reasons affects the residue for further explanation.

Weber's classification of actions into *zweckrational, wertrational*, traditional and affective is by now as fluid as he, in effect, suggests himself, when remarking that most actions are of mixed type. A rational role-player allocates resources efficiently but by a test of efficiency which relates to the norms governing his role. His role leaves him latitude to judge what is appropriate. He could not carry it out at all, were he unable to take settled customs for granted. Such customs include his own proven habits and other people's stable practices. One basic element in the stability of expectations is the unreflective desires and simple emotions which human beings share. A rational reconstruction needs usually to be of mixed type too.

Epistemologically the generic problem is Other Minds. I recommend tackling it by treating explanatory understanding (*erklärendes Verstehen*) as a form of inference to the best explanation. The best explanation of action is that the agent did it for good reasons which he recognised to be good. That many actions are as highly rational as this seems to me a precondition for detecting a meaningful order of plausible candidates. But the distinction between legitimating reasons and real reasons, coupled with the point that actors are incompletely transparent even to themselves, calls for watchfulness. I have been trying to make honest epistemology of the notion of understanding by giving to Rationality the epistemic work which the floppier concept of Meaning cannot manage. I cannot claim to have come up with anything as tidy as the hypothetic-deductive method.

Cicero says that it is truly expedient to do what is right. I agree that expediency is in some sense a moral concept. For purposes of social science this may imply only that actors who judge a course of action expedient are not merely calculating but also passing a normative judgement on the means available to them and indeed on themselves. Even that is methodologically interesting. At any rate it is interesting enough for present purposes. The deeper normative questions about rationality, morality and the demands of role will have to wait.

12

The Cunning of Reason III: self and society

Even in a market town the roles of town life furnish reasons for market behaviour. Market relations remain social relations, both when we scale the town up until it becomes a large, impersonal city, and when we scale it down until its rhythms harmonise with the natural world around it. They remain social relations also, if we vary the form of government to expand or shrink the public demands on private life. In Sparta, Salt Lake City or Peking there have been times when the gods of heaven or the state have declared all business public business. In Athens or Amsterdam, by contrast, the state takes only a tithe of social life and otherwise leaves citizens to their private purposes. But private purposes have their *mores*: grocers have neighbours, lovers play roles and there is honour among thieves. The rules vary from town to town and time to time. But, whatever they may be, they enable and constrain the life of the inhabitants. History matters greatly for understanding variations but, as Hume remarked, it informs of nothing new or strange in this particular.

That leaves unfinished business under three main headings. The first is the final, broad terms of settlement between rational choice and social agency. The second is the residual work, in the form of systematic features of social life thus unaccounted for, to be assigned to the Cunning of Reason. The third is a tantalising question about the self. I shall preface the agenda, however, with a word on social explanation and about the place of nature in the argument.

A social (or economic or political) theory is a general, first-hand attempt to explain what makes the social world (or some part of it) go round. A philosophical intervention is inferior in expertise but more quizzical about how the explanation works. There is no cosy division of labour here. Social theorists make philosophical commitments, and philosophers lay theoretical bets. This uneasy but, I trust, amiable relationship is illustrated by the 'Cunning of Reason' theme in the book. The social theorist picks a key but is left with systematic features unaccounted for. These features are as if the work of an unseen hand, meaning that they have an explanation but it lies beyond the theory's ken. He has two ways of dealing with them. One is to say that his key works *ceteris paribus*, as when the microeconomist sets his parameters so as to exclude political and social changes. The other is to put the key to further, less obvious and more ambitious use, as when the theory of rational economic choice is generalised to political and social life with the help of the theory of games. The former way is safer, but will serve only if the parameters mark a genuine boundary. The latter is riskier but livelier, and cannot be avoided where the boundary is artificial. It is 'the Cunning of Reason' to help him along by showing how a theory of individual, rational action can extend to patterns not willed by individuals.

The scope for the Cunning of Reason is thus relative to the theory proposed. It lies between what the theory explains directly and what is altogether beyond its ken. I have been arguing that microeconomics has to take the riskier path of Modern Political Economy, but that, in doing so, it asks too much of the Cunning of Reason. The main source of trouble is the need to allow for expectations. If they are merely those which a *zweckrational* economic agent derives by predicting what similar agents will do in the light of their similarly derived expectations, they are hopelessly indeterminate. They have no latent tendency to collective results which could then be fed back into the model as part of its *ex ante* apparatus. Conversely, if, prompted by the fact that economic agents usually belong to organisations, we add normative expectations, then the agents are no longer the individuals of microeconomics. What this implies for economics, for the scope of the Cunning of Reason and for the character of the self is the question of this chapter.

Someone may object that the question arises in this form only because I have construed rational choice so as to distinguish sharply between the natural and social worlds. Much of social life stems from the physical demands of hunger, sex, shelter and other animal promptings. Many emotions, conscious and unconscious, spring from this source. Hence the work being ascribed to the Cunning of Reason may belong more simply to nature. For example ethologists have claimed that humans, like other animals, have a 'territorial imperative' which accounts both for the collective aggression displayed in the search for *Lebensraum* and for the individual neuroses which go with overcrowding. This imperative and the need to reconcile aggressions can be argued to do much to explain cultural rules, for instance those governing warfare and property, and to render phenomena like imperialism predictable. Similarly, cultural and economic accompaniments to differences in gender are grounded in biological differences of sex, which might account, for instance, for the familiar double standards in sexual morality better than does some vague gesture to latent social consequences. The insistence that human life is importantly continuous with other animal life is at its most ambitious with sociobiology. But it also marks some brands of psychology and influences some theories, especially behavioural theories of cognitive development.

I mention this alternative starting point not to engage with it but to make the point that what is puzzling depends on the key one picks. A biological key would have accounted readily for behaviour which helps the survival of the human species but would have had trouble with action which involves symbols. Symbols are not a puzzle for a rational-choice theory, once utilities are broadened to include the moral and cultural value attaching to both means and ends. But it is a puzzle why rational agents resolve the indeterminacy of their expectations in ways which are not random. The puzzle is much helped by making the economic agents into rational role-players. But we still need to settle the implications for microeconomics and to see what is left to the Cunning of Reason. These are questions about what can (or cannot) be done with a hermeneutic key.

Since this is all very rarified, let me open the main agenda with the realities of an industrial dispute. Any hard-fought example will serve. I pick the British miners' strike of 1984. The massive conflict was an economic event on any definition of economics and, up to a point, could be described as a long negotiation to establish new wage levels in the mining industry. But the description is grotesque if it asks us to pretend that the economic sequence can be distinguished even in theory from its social and political surrounds. That is because the story can be told only in terms of expectations which cannot be split into calculative and normative. All parties who influenced what happened next – the miners, their families, their leaders, the National Coal Board, the government, other political groups, the police, the press – were influenced by what they expected both of others and from others. The crux throughout was whether the strike would crumble, remain solid or spread to reluctant pits. This was a question of loyalty but not of blind loyalty. Each miner was thinking partly in terms of his household budget and partly in terms of a wider morality. Linking the two were expectations, since both the likely settlement and the force of moral considerations depended on how many miners were willing to go to what lengths. This is not a piece of arcane theory but a point perfectly obvious to all involved. Loyalty was not a coefficient measurable in advance but an unknown depending on what would happen next, as governed by how loyal how many miners could be persuaded to be. Persuasion could (and did) fail both through clumsiness and through the counter-tactics of those trying to end the strike. There was a bitter, sometimes bloody, struggle to capture the legitimating language, in which actions could be proposed as keeping the faith. Crucially a second rival miners' union emerged in the Midlands, and the strike presently gave way to a return to work, although longer-run consequences remain to be seen.

This is a fairly neutral summary, which can be pressed in two directions, depending critically on the view one takes of the government's part. The government said initially, and continued to say officially, that they were not involved in this industrial business, except as the guardian of law and order. But, as the folklore phrase has it, 'They would say that, wouldn't they?' What the government meant, I think, is that they were trying to remove obstacles to a settlement which would reflect market forces. In that case the summary needs supplementing with more about the economics of coal. But, even so, the interpretation given to the demands of law and order and the attempts to impose this theory of market forces resulted in political interventions. Meanwhile, on the rival view that markets and market forces are inseparable from social relations and normative expectations, it follows simply that government is of course party to industrial disputes. In that case the summary needs supplementing with more of the social history of coal. Either way, however, we have an episode where so many of the principal actors were refusing to separate economic, political, social and moral considerations that this fact itself has to be included in the account which all actors had in their heads. It is central to any understanding which works from within.

The three questions of the chapter emerge simply. Firstly, what does the fusion of calculative and normative expectations imply for microeconomics? Secondly, what more matters than was in the actors' heads? (For instance, the miners' strike encouraged the growth of a national police force in a way congenial to the Cunning of Reason.) Thirdly, what finally has become of the self as a sovereign artificer, when the picture of rational role-play in a social world is complete? Although still making no pretence to be an economist, I turn first to microeconomics.

Rationality in economics

It cannot be sensible to begin microeconomic theory with Robinson Crusoe alone on an island, deciding whether to invest time and energy in making a fishing net (or with Adam choosing between distant mulberries and nearby figs). This isolated decision falls wholly outside the realm of action which, in Weber's phrase, 'takes account of the behaviour of others and is thereby oriented in its course'. Or, rather, in so far as it does not, it is because Crusoe has expectations about his tomorrow's self – an alarmingly philosophical thought for beginners. A basic, ideal-type case which abstracts from *social* action needs two agents: economics starts with the arrival of Man Friday (or when Adam is joined by Eve). This is a shorthand way of saying that, for an economic science which, as Robbins (1932) puts it, 'studies the allocation of scarce resources which have alternative uses', the basic event is exchange.

That would be mere pedantry if exchange consisted of two distinct actions, each explained by the subjective meaning which its performer attaches to his action. Just try conceiving of it in this way. Suppose that Crusoe and Friday have not detected each other's existence but have discovered that items deposited in a clearing in the middle of the island are mysteriously replaced by other items. If Crusoe, who has hens at his end of the island, leaves eggs, he finds that they disappear and are replaced by yams, which do not grow at his end. Friday makes the converse discovery. This sounds like exchange, because, from the outside, it looks like exchange. But, from the inside, each has merely stumbled on a mysteriously reliable fact of nature, that one thing can become another. For exchange to be involved, the reliability needs to be traced to a convention and hence, in effect, to expectations about price. It cannot occur until each detects the other and thereby orients his behaviour in its course.

But price is a normative concept, like contract, and one connected with questions not only of whether a good is worth buying and selling but also of whether it is worth producing. The desert island is again misleading in its suggestion that the typical economic concern is for food, rather than for the symbolic services of goods. One notices that in everyday social life even food has to do with more than square meals. All the world over, eating is a ceremonial event, full of fine distinctions between nutritionally similar items and buzzing with symbolic signals. That applies as much to a fly-blown bazaar as to the comestibles sold in high-class neighbourhoods. Also the producers and sellers have more in mind than money. They belong to social networks and are aware of being watched by fellow traders, neighbours, relatives, persons of influence and others who will still be there tomorrow to pass normative judgements. Even basic economic transactions are events in the social life of a community. To understand what is going on one must be able to read signals.

Economists would not, of course, deny that market events are social events. Their distinction between the economic picture and its social frame is an analytical device, justified by its predictive power and the scope which it creates for elegant mathematics.

Even if it works better for money markets than for labour markets, it claims to have enough merit to rely on wherever people exchange desirables at a price. But, although I respect this view, and especially for the beauty of its accompanying mathematics, it conflicts with all the main arguments of earlier chapters.

Predictive power is suspect as soon as predictions are declared to be issued *ceteris paribus* or provided that there is no interference with the normal working of the economic process. Such *ceteris paribus* clauses are by way of analogy with natural science; and the analogy is spurious. For instance, a biologist might predict the size of the future rabbit population, *ceteris paribus*, and find his figure wildly wrong because landowners have taken to massacring rabbits. His prediction would not be thereby at fault. That is because rabbits and landowners belong to cleanly divided realms, where boundary-crossing is intervention. Landowners are not rabbits (or foxes), and rabbits do not read newspapers. There is no such boundary between the economic and the social or political. The 'normal working of the economic process' *includes* the tax laws, the status system, the prevailing moralities and the current political scene. Such matters are interwoven in the minds of the agents whose actions are being predicted. The economic process produces, among other things, newspapers and television, which help in the weaving. These are reasons (distinct from chapter 7's reasons for saying that expectations involve decision as well as prediction) for denying that economic *ceteris paribus* clauses work as in natural science. Their job is not so much to exclude interference with a system from outside it as to stipulate social continuity in the integrated realm where the economic transactions occur.

What lets the economist assume continuity in the social games, granted that the players can and often do change the rules? The best orthodox answer, I think, remains the one offered in the name of Modern Political Economy. If *homo economicus* is everywhere, then social continuity assumptions are all of a piece with standard microeconomic and game-theory assumptions. In particular government is not an alien force, as landowners are alien to rabbits, but another set of 'economic' agents. Once the analytic device of abstracting to *homo economicus* is seen to be a way not of dividing up a seamless web but of picking out a universal key to understanding action, one may as well try to make a virtue of its universality. Then *ceteris paribus* clauses become, less problematically, a way of considering overlapping markets one at a time.

But to remove the boundary in one direction is to remove it in the other. The line is cleared for the opposite contention that *homo sociologicus* is everywhere, with social action primary and economic action an interesting case of it. Not even economic man lives by bread alone, and this is a point about his assessment of means as much as about his self-monitoring of preferences. The line heads for a more traditional political economy and arguments about the formal modelling of the productive process, which I grasp too little to pursue.[1] Enough has been said, however, to sketch in the sort of more old-fashioned agents who inhabit this seamless world.

Crucially, they are still rational agents who choose and are still to be understood in the Weberian manner by constructing ideal-type – and hence normative – solutions to problems of allocation. Since they are role-playing agents, however, the final notion of rationality is one which merges *zweckrational* with *wertrational*. The governing concept is that of a good reason for action, even if the philosophical gain threatens to be at the expense of the economist's tidy mathematics. I cannot deny that role-related reasons for action are messier than quantifiable reasons. But the need for them is pervasive. For instance a firm trying to decide where to locate its branches has a tidy, perhaps computable, puzzle about times, distances, optimal dispersion and other interrelated variables. It also has a conundrum about unquantifiables like the good will of local government authorities, ease of recruitment, neighbourhood amenities and larger trends, ranging from changes in planning regulations to changes in political control. Roughly the conundrum is about the character of the game, and the puzzle about the choice of moves within it. The firm's reasons must range over both. Its agents must be clever about the latter, shrewd about the former and able to justify themselves in a community which passes moral judgements.

I sum up with two parallels from ethics and a final word on rationality. The point of the parallels is that to know what prin-

---

[1] For a further, if still prefatory, discussion, see Hargreaves-Heap and Hollis (1984).

ciples an agent should act on is not always to know what he should do. This indeterminacy is, of course, disappointing, but may help to excuse a final messiness in the notion of rationality as applied to social life and hence in the scope finally left for the Cunning of Reason.

Ethics too has trouble with expectations, which it sometimes tackles by proposing that a moral agent acts rightly if he follows the rules (or scheme of duties) which would be for the best if followed by all. Thus if 'tell the truth' were among the categorical imperatives or ideal utilitarian rules, each agent should always tell the truth. But what if the agent knows that others do not comply? It is simply not plain that partial or near compliance with the ideal rules is second best to perfect compliance. It may be that the moral theory of the second best prescribes different rules for morally obedient agents dealing with morally disobedient others. Perhaps one should lie like a trooper to troopers. If so, an indeterminacy creeps into the notion of a morally good reason for action, in echo of disputes about whether what would be rational in a perfectly competitive market is relevant to action in an imperfect one.

Then again, it is only on optimistic assumptions that a moral agent faced with conflicting claims can rely on there being a unique, coherent set of best rules to steer by. If there is more than one coherent set, we find the snag in the previous paragraph cropping up even in the ideal case as soon as he needs to know what other agents are likely to do. If there is no coherent set, because moral claims can be radically plural, then even knowing what others will do may not be enough to settle the right course of action. Either way, the notion of a morally good reason is again indeterminate, in echo of what was said earlier about role-related reasons for action. Yet the *Verstehen* recipe for understanding is to identify what it would be rational for the agent to do, so as to identify what failures of rationality need explaining. On the whole, I think, the best epistemological strategy is optimism – a denial in theory that there are ultimate incommensurabilities. But I am all too aware that in practice this is whistling in the dark.

My final word on rationality subdivides for the ideal and second-best cases. In the ideal case the agent is Kantian from both a philosophy of mind and a moral standpoint. Knowing that other agents, who are relevantly like him, will act from the same reasons, he does what is likeliest to realise what he and they collectively have most reason to value. Where this formula yields more than one course of action, there is a co-ordination problem to be solved by creating a salient, as recommended by game-theory. Where other groups of rational agents with different but overlapping interests are involved, there is a bargaining problem to be referred to that branch of economic theory. Where the game is zero-sum and the best strategy for his group varies with what they expect from rival groups, the ideal case becomes tricky. This possibility points into the heart of political philosophy, I shall suggest in a moment, and in particular to Rousseau. Meanwhile the language for analysing the ideal case is one of universalisable external reasons, which move a rational agent because he recognises them.

The second-best case occurs whenever the rational agent cannot expect that doing what he would do in the ideal case will be for the best. It subdivides into two satisficing problems. Where the snag is that other agents are imperfectly rational, he bets on what they will in fact do and, as in chess, plays the man rather than the board. This is not always a matter of approximating to the ideal. Just as double bluff fails against a fool, so, in general, it can be a rotten idea to play refined moves in coarse situations. That is a reprise of the contrast at the end of chapter 8 between elegant blueprint decision-making and shrewd political judgement. Shrewdness is a satisficing rather than maximising quality, one learnt and justified by experience. One is left with an uneasy suspicion that a practical theory of the second best requires the rational agent to have a touch of luck for when he comes to justify himself afterwards.

The other satisficing problem is set by roles which do not fully harmonise. Whether it is in theory radical and so could occur even in an ideal society is an old question in political theory, connected with ideas of justice. But it certainly occurs in practice. The rational agent, I suggest, satisfices with an eye to the forum in which it will be most urgent to justify himself afterwards, while thus leaving something over to satisfy other claims with. Here a model which relies on the neatness of calculation and the approximate neatness of a single role is threatened with practical chaos.

For once, however, practical thoughts come to the rescue. Chaos is as intolerable to the actors as to the theorist. So the actors have devices for serialising and compartmentalising their roles, and each is aware that others have them. Theory can make grateful use of this fact by including it in the model which it discerns in the actors' heads. To be rational is still to do what is likely enough to be justifiable when one is called to account, and action can still be understood in terms of good (enough) reasons for it.

Second-best cases are the stuff of the unideal world which we inhabit, where imperfect rationality is related to the distribution of power. I do not mean to imply that power always distorts, as anarchists, libertarians and utopians are wont to maintain. But power which creates and relies on uneven information sets problems for clear-headed agents dealing with less clear-headed ones. Half a loaf is better than no bread; but it is not easy to decide when to stop holding out for more, at the risk of getting less. The snag, summarily put, is that the best is often the enemy of the good; pursuit of the best, or acting as if in an ideal-type world where the best could be achieved, can cost one even a good solution. For practical purposes we need a rational-actor theory of the good which is not overshadowed by a theory of the best.

The Cunning of Reason

There is a final messiness about the concept of rational action, both because second-best solutions are prone to be indefinite and various and because the instrumental has been merged with the expressive. It spills over into the residual task assigned to the Cunning of Reason. All the same, it is a smaller, less arbitrary residue than is left by the standard instrumental model of rational-choice and game-theory.

There the boundary between the economic and the social also falls between actors' economic expectations and their social expectations. The Cunning of Reason is then left whatever is governed by social expectations, to be dealt with in systematic ways which need have nothing to do with the working of markets. This, I have argued, is to overwork the idea of unintended or latent consequences. Modern Political Economy agrees and makes a virtue of the fact that normative expectations influence economic behaviour. But I have spent enough time saying why I refuse the corrective.

With normative expectations included, more consequences are intended or foreseen by the agents, and there is more in the model to account for latent ones. But the upshot is an increased messiness which comes from making the agents finite social actors. Consequences can be deemed latent on three rather different grounds. One is that they are unforeseen – a simple criterion for the moment of decision but complicated for a longer time period in which some actors may notice them and may or may not try to do something about them. Secondly, although foreseen, they may be unwanted, as when a monetarist government reduces inflation in ways which they foresee will cause unemployment but which they believe themselves powerless to prevent. Thirdly, although foreseen and wanted, they may be not openly avowable, as when a new law whose manifest purpose is to compel secret ballots before strikes occur has a latent function of reducing wage-levels by weakening the grip of trade unions. Adding the thought that what is latent for some actors may not be latent for others, we are left without a clear point at which the Cunning of Reason takes over. For instance American foreign policy in, say, the Middle East or Latin America has effects which the White House denies responsibility for. This does not always prevent the suspicion that there is more to it or that some agencies knew more than others or that the result involved the efforts of several hands pulling different ways. Perhaps the whole story could be unravelled and traced to its origins, or perhaps the ifs and buts of history prevent a complete analysis.

In any case I do not doubt that actions have many consequences, which are systematic but initially unnoticed by everyone. They can be deemed the work of the Cunning of Reason if, when they surface, they are found to be the collective effects of individually rational decisions taken by role-players in the course of games which the theory has identified. In other words a theory of social action can be credited with being able to account for social change, provided that the changes result determinately from choices by agents of the sort portrayed. The chief sources of change, which I have picked out, are the creative character of roles, the influence of the available past and the tendency to over-shoot collectively in the individual pursuit of positional goods. I fear that there may be more to it, even after adding in the un-noticed effects of technology, which, although I have not dis-cussed them, presumably suit the attempt to trace social facts to human decisions. If the fear is well founded, there are still system-atic features of society and social change which this book cannot put down to the Cunning of Reason. While waiting to have them pointed out, I rest my case for a revised individualism. In a sen-tence, Adam (singular and plural) is the prime mover of social life, enabled and constrained by rules which evolve in response to the combined effect of choices. Since the prime mover is only par-tially sighted, the combined effects are full of surprises sprung by the Cunning of Reason.

Unsociable sociality

Who, finally, is Adam? He is no longer the abstract, economically rational individual of standard rational-choice theory and game-theory, even after switching from a Humean to a Kantian analysis of motivation. He is too much the role-player for that. But neither has he been absorbed into the collectives and organis-ations where he plays his parts. Even granted that obedience to expectations includes a creative latitude, marked by distance within roles and ingenuity between them, I have still not made him just a participant in his place and period. He is more of an his-torical figure than economic individualism would have it, but less than is claimed by historical determinism. By divine command, relayed by Pico della Mirandola at the start, I have placed him at the centre of the social world and made him neither heavenly nor earthly, neither mortal nor immortal. That sets an elusive question about the self.

It is a many-sided question, which I shall not try to tackle exhaustively. For instance our bodily concerns matter more than I have admitted. Aristotle defined man as the rational animal, and I have not tried to come to terms with the long line of Aristotelian thinking before setting our animal nature aside in order to con-centrate on the hermeneutics of culture. Equally my silence about psychology does not spring from a belief that psychology can be parcelled out between biology, sociology and economics. But even animal concerns which touch our identity (in some intimate sense of that difficult word) are cultural too. For example, nature issues pretty standard sexual equipment and a pretty general urge to use it; yet the variations on the mating game are amazing. The emotions stirred in the seraglio, the church social and the drive-in movie may have common promptings, but they differ in ways which cannot be nature's. There is much to ponder in the interplay of nature and culture. But, if the self is not just the sum of its roles, it is not thereby the sum of roles, body and psyche. The final question is about self and agency.

It will stand out more sharply if we recall that there seem to be wide cultural variations on the concept of the self. Some tribal cultures appear to regard a person as identical with his ancestors and descendants, his identity somehow an extrusion of a corporate clan extending over generations. Some religions, like Buddhism, so diffuse the self into experience or community relationships that only the grammar of the first person singular lets an agent refer to himself. Our own stout individualism has emerged from a cultural trail which, apparently, starts in Homer (role without self), and leads through Roman law (persons as property owners) and Christian theology (the soul as the form of the body), before settling down to protestant and Cartesian ideas of *res cogitans* (bodiless self without role). There is nothing evidently universal or philosophically undisputed about the concept of a person as a *substantia individua rationalis*.

All the same, the cultural variation is ambiguous, and not only because one can always ask which culture has the truth. It is ambiguous also because there is latitude in interpretation. Take the suggestion that Ancient Greece thought in terms of role without self and consider Sophocles' *Antigone*, written in the fifth century BC. The play is set in Thebes, in the aftermath of the civil war between Eteocles and Polynices, the sons of Oedipus. Both have been slain and Eteocles, the rightful king, has been duly buried. The throne has passed to Kreon, their uncle and the new head of the royal house. In accordance with custom, Kreon has forbidden the burial of the traitor Polynices, whose body lies rotting outside the walls. Yet family honour demands burial and Antigone, their sister, must decide which law to obey. She opts for what she takes to be the higher law and performs the burial rites. Kreon responds by following what he takes to be the higher law and has her walled up alive to die. He relents, but by then she is dead, together with her lover, who is Kreon's son. The ancient curse on the royal house of Thebes has destroyed them all.

The characters of the play are *dramatis personae* in the old sense of 'masks' or complete embodiments of role. Yet Antigone and Kreon *choose* their doomed paths. At least, that is how I read the anguished passages where they debate their courses of action. This need not imply that they were brought down by an arrogance (*hybris*) born of moral failings, or that other choices would have saved them. But it does imply that Sophocles is thinking in terms of individual agency. So does he conceive of an active self distinct from character-parts and roles? With roles so pervasive, the answer cannot be a simple yes. But, since he recognises moral conflict both within and between roles, it cannot be a simple no. Moreover, in keeping with what has been said about *Verstehen*, we should bear it in mind that any answer imposes our ideas as well as identifying his.

My own view is that Sophocles makes very defensible sense in the terms of chapter 10, where I presented public persons as (more or less) rational stewards of offices. That is not a final answer about the self, because chapter 10 did not contain one. But it means that there is no clear historical tale to tell. The story does not exactly start in a world of role without self. It does not exactly end in a modern world of self distinct from role, as I shall repeat in a moment. Besides, even if the tale were clear, it would not settle the truth about the self. This remark will offend relativists, who hold that history and anthropology have no right, duty or need to judge between the varied conceptions by which different cultures organise their experience. It can seem absurdly parochial to regard Sophocles as a candidate for a 1987 Modern Philosophy prize. I retort, however, that each conception includes a claim to have the truth about the human condition; and the relativist, who judges these claims to be of merely local significance, is pretending to an Olympian standpoint of his own. *Verstehen*, I have argued, works by judging the actor's own understanding against a universal standard. Since I have not claimed that the modern interpreter always has the right answers, I can consistently hold that the field for the 1987 philosophy prize is a formidable one, drawn from many ages and cultures. To award the prize is, of course, asking for trouble. But to pose epistemological questions about how explanations work is already to raise questions of truth. The philosopher, although standing behind the front line of social theory, has no safe or honest position completely to the rear. So I shall end by trying to award the prize.

Humanist portraits of Adam which catch anything of Pico's sovereign artificer will display an individualism of some sort. The possible range is wide. Most obviously in keeping with Pico is the one from Sartre's *Existentialism and Humanism*: 'In life a man commits himself, draws his own portrait, and there is nothing but that portrait' ((1973), p. 42). To show that he truly means *nothing* but that portrait, he cites the dilemma of a young Frenchman who must decide, after the fall of France in 1940, whether to stay and look after his mother or to join the Free French forces in England. There can be no hiding behind moral authorities of any kind, Sartre says, since the choice of a guide is an open choice and it is bad faith to pretend otherwise. Authorities include not only those of church and state but also those of inner feeling or conscience. So insistent is he that the self has complete *carte blanche* that, paradoxically, it seems to me, the resulting portrait cannot be of the self. If Adam is identified with pure, notional will, there is literally nothing but the portrait and hence nothing to make one version more authentic than another. All explanation of Adam's choice of ends and means is then an account of failures of authenticity, thus restoring the claims of a kind of social understanding, which existentialism deems misconceived.

If Adam is to be responsible for his own portrait, he will need to be able to paint a responsible portrait – one for which he has reasons, which need no further reasons. That is also the condition for his being a sovereign artificer accessible to a social science. There is this much to be said for an 'economic' individualism which takes a set of preferences as given. But, as I have tried to say, we need to ask further about the self, which has these motivating preferences. The principal 'economic' answers stem from Hobbes and from Hume. Hobbes presents man as a physical machine with a self-preserving urge (*conatus*) to make life safe and commodious. Hume looks into his own breast and finds nothing more than a bundle of perceptions (including sentiments). Although these answers differ instructively, both yield a desire-driven account of social action and a contractarian theory of social institutions. But, if I am granted my reasons for holding that it takes more than consistent desires plus an information-processing device to make the self active, both these variants of 'economic' individualism abolish the individual.

Once again Kant seems to me more promising. *The Critique of Pure Reason* addresses the 'scandal' that no one could explain how the mind, presented only with experienced phenomena, knows that there exists a causal order of enduring physical objects. Kant's idea is that the mind is an active judge, marshalling the phenomena under concepts and categories derived by reflecting on how objectivity is possible. The key is the 'transcendental unity of apperception' – a unity among the fragments of consciousness which the mind understands to be its own unity, even though not directly presented with itself in its consciousness. The enduring quality of things perceived resides in the perceiving, judging self. This epistemological individualism postulates a self which connects with Kant's ethical theory of the moral agent as a reflective individual, moved by external reasons, in the form of categorical imperatives of duty. A moral agent treats others as moral agents too – as ends, never merely as means to his own ends. It is this style of individualism, rather than contractarian backscratching, which is embodied in declarations of the rights of man.

I do not find Kant's epistemological-cum-ethical individualism robust enough for understanding social life. He bids us overcome the unsociable streak in our 'unsociable sociality' through the exercise of a morally good will. It seems to me that a good will is not enough. We must also consider what social institutions are needed, if we are to exist and flourish as persons, where 'person' is a social concept suited to social understanding. The link between a political philosophy of institutions and a social epistemology of persons might, I hope, be forged transcendentally in the Kantian manner. Like physical objects, the actions and interactions of social life are 'phenomena' – occurrences whose meaning and connection are not given in experience. As we construct the physical world by judging what concepts the phenomena fall under, so we make sense of social occurrences by judging what people are doing in what capacity. We refer the events to a system of social positions, which, although not given in social experience, we know to be there. We come to inherit the social system by learning to act intelligently within it, and thereby learn how to change it too. This requires a continuity of the acting self, by analogy with the unity of the thinking (or 'apperceiving') self in perceptual and causal judgement, but with the difference that we can shape the social world, far beyond the small tinkering which the natural world allows us. The self, this time a social agent, is not an empirical 'me' but an active 'I'. It stands outside its knowledge of its (agent's) place in the social system, and is known transcendentally, in that understanding presupposes it. Its activity is what makes social life possible.

Antigone's dilemma is not a problem of joint decision posed for two separate role-players, one of whom has a sister's duty to bury her brother, while the other has a subject's duty to leave a traitor unburied. It is a dilemma facing a single agent. This is made no clearer by adding that the problem faces a single individual will. Indeed, if it means adding the Sartrean admonition that she would be in bad faith if she took either duty (or both) as inescapable, it amounts to saying that it matters not one whit which way she goes. Sophocles' comment is, I think, that she *is* both Polynices' sister and Kreon's subject and that ultimate dilemmas destroy the agent, because reasons for action deriving from each source are self-cancelling in combination. At any rate, the tragedy makes sense in these terms by giving us a notion of a person whose choices are doomed, without trying to identify the self with the will. I cannot see that we need more, or gain anything by adding a pure ego as a gloss on what it is for the same actor to have conflicting duties.

Pure ego thus seems to me an illusion. But it is a plausible illusion, when conjured up against the opposite limiting case. Durkheim remarks at the end of the *Rules of Sociological Method*, 'Individual human natures are merely the indeterminate material which the social factor moulds and transforms.' I have argued so strenuously against overworking the 'social factor' in this determinist way that a pure, independent ego may seem the necessary corrective. But there is no call for one if the social factor is not a moulding force but an arena where role-players learn and shape their relationships. A self robust enough to resist being absorbed into the social system need not be so independent that it vanishes into darkest privacy. On the contrary, it belongs in the arena, where its identity is at stake.

This line has an air of trying to have something both ways – of thinking in terms of a contract, which is not a contract, between individuals, who are not individuals. Well, yes, it does. I am taking up Rousseau's suggestion that the social contract creates the persons who, so to speak, make it. He remarks in *Le Contrat social*:

> The passage from the state of nature to the civil state produces a remarkable change in the individual. It substitutes justice for instinct in his behaviour, and gives his actions a moral basis which was formerly lacking ... [H]e must now consult his reason and not merely respond to the promptings of desire. (book I, chapter VIII)

The paragraph draws up a balance sheet for assessing the advantages of this brand of social contract and ends by declaring that membership of civil society transforms the individual 'from a limited and stupid animal into an intelligent being and a Man'. Citizenship, he then notes, also offers 'Moral Freedom, which makes a man his own master. For to be subject to appetite is to be a slave, while to obey the laws laid down by society is to be free.'

The political implications are extremely murky, not least because Rousseau is speaking of utopian conditions, where the chains of existing corrupt societies have been broken and where the general will emerges because each citizen seeks the good of all. That makes it very unclear what obligations, if any, citizens owe in imperfect, actual societies. But his notion that there are two kinds of individuals is significant for social understanding also. On the one hand there are those governed by private will and personal interest, who are moved by the promptings of desire. On the other there are citizens who consult their reason and are moved by their duties as subjects. The latter kind can flourish only amid just institutions, since they constitute themselves citizens only by creating such institutions. I cannot pretend that there is any easy way with the obvious circularity. But I endorse Rousseau's suggestion that one cannot conceive of individuals prior to the institutions which they live by and shape. In every form of society individuals have reasons for their will, and these reasons vary with the form of institutions. A market society is not an exception, but one where the institutions absolve individuals from having to justify the pursuit of private advantage. No actual societies are so fragmented that mutual trust and moral concern are wholly vulnerable to bargain-hunting. Indeed, the argument of earlier chapters implies that none could be, because normative expectations cannot depend solely on shared predictions and survive. Actual societies vary in the success with which they manage to allow citizens the freedom to express what they have reason to value; and the variations are crucial for adequacy of understanding at the levels of meaning and causation.

Our latterday world, then, differs from Sophocles' not because the Renaissance invented the individual but because it offers larger scope for self-creation. I do not refer to the new alphabet of self-improvement, ranging from aversion therapy, biorhythms, colonic irrigation, dianetics and encounter groups to yoga and Zen. I mean that we are now born into fewer of the roles which come to constitute us and choose more of the partners with whom we play and change the game. In part this has come about because we have learnt that it is possible. In part it has become possible because we now believe it possible. But it is not risk-free. Antigone might now escape self-destruction by opting out of the game which the gods set her to play. Instead, however, she might be marked down for motiveless killing by strangers on the streets of an impersonal city. The Cunning of Reason can make as much mischief in the new world as in the old.

Conclusion

The social sciences are not just labourers, or philosophy just an underlabourer, in the attempt to discover the truth about Adam. They also put ideas into Adam's head. Some of these ideas strengthen his power to be his own sovereign artificer. Others distance him perilously from his handiwork. But at least they have helped him to see better what is in the world, by showing him his own activity. Although we shall still surely die, we have less excuse for not knowing good and evil, if we understand the limits of our individual sovereignty.

I rashly undertook to award the 1987 Modern Philosophy prize. Very well; let it be divided among Kant, Rousseau and Sophocles.

Bibliography

Allison, G. 1971. *Essence of Decision*. Boston, Little, Brown
Arrow, K. J. 1951. *Social Choice and Individual Values*. New York, Wiley
Axelrod, R. 1984. *The Evolution of Cooperation*. New York, Basic Books
Ayer, A. J. 1969. Man as a Subject for Science. In *Metaphysics and Commonsense*. London, Macmillan
Barry, B. 1970. *Sociologists, Economists and Democracy*. University of Chicago Press
Barry, B. and Hardin, R., eds. 1982. *Rational Man and Irrational Society?* Beverly Hills, Sage
Becker, G. 1976. *The Economic Approach to Human Behaviour*. University of Chicago Press
Bernstein, R. J. 1979. *The Restructuring of Social and Political Theory*. London, Methuen
Bhaskar, R. 1979. *The Possibility of Naturalism*. Brighton, Harvester
Blau, P. 1964. *Exchange and Power in Social Life*. London, Wiley
Blaug, M. 1980. *The Methodology of Economics*. Cambridge University Press
Blum, L. A. 1980. *Friendship, Altruism and Morality*. London, Routledge & Kegan Paul
Bond, E. J. 1983. *Reason and Value*. Cambridge University Press
Buchanan, J. M. and Tullock, G. 1962. *The Calculus of Consent*. University of Michigan Press
Caldwell, B. 1982. *Beyond Positivism: Economic Methodology in the Twentieth Century*. London, Allen & Unwin
Carrithers, M., Collins, S. and Lukes, S., eds. 1985. *The Category of the Person*. Cambridge University Press
Cornford, F. M. 1908. *Microcosmographia Academica : Being a Guide for the Young Academic Politician*. London, Bowes & Bowes

Dallmayr, F. R. and McCarthy, T. A., eds. 1977. *Understanding and Social Enquiry*. University of Notre Dame Press

Davidson, D. 1980. *Essays on Actions and Events*. Oxford University Press

Dilthey, W. 1926. *Gesammelte Werke*, edited by B. Groethuysen, esp. vol. vii. Stuttgart, Teubner Verlag

Downs, A. 1957. *An Economic Theory of Democracy*. New York, Harper and Row

Dyke, C. 1981. *Philosophy of Economics*. Englewood Cliffs, Prentice-Hall

Edgeworth, F. Y. 1881. *Mathematical Psychics*. London, Kegan Paul

Elster, J. 1978. *Logic and Society*. New York, Wiley

    1983a. *Explaining Technical Change*. Cambridge University Press

    1983b. *Sour Grapes*. Cambridge University Press

    1984. *Ulysses and the Sirens*. Cambridge University Press

Elster, J., ed. 1986. *The Multiple Self*. Cambridge University Press

Elster, J. and Hylland, A., eds. 1986. *Foundations of Social Choice Theory*. Cambridge University Press

Emmet, D. 1966. *Rules, Roles and Relations*. London, Macmillan

    1972. *Functions, Purposes and Powers*. 2nd edition, London, Macmillan

    1982. *The Moral Prism*. London, Macmillan

Friedman, M. 1953. The Methodology of Positive Economics. In *Essays in Positive Economics*. University of Chicago Press

Frohlich, N. and Oppenheimer, J. A. 1978. *Modern Political Economy*. Englewood Cliffs, Prentice-Hall

Gellner, E. 1979. *Spectacles and Predicaments*. Cambridge University Press

Giddens, A. 1976. *New Rules of Sociological Method*. New York, Basic Books

    1979. *Central Problems in Social Theory*. London, Macmillan

    1984. *The Constitution of Society*. Cambridge, Polity Press

Goodin, R. E. 1976. *The Politics of Rational Man*. London, Wiley

    1985. *Protecting the Vulnerable*. University of Chicago Press

    1986. Laundering Preferences. In Elster and Hylland, eds. (1986)

Habermas, J. 1984. *The Theory of Communicative Action*, trans. T. McCarthy. Boston, Mass., Beacon Press

Hahn, F. 1981. Reflections on the Invisible Hand. *University of Warwick Economic Research Papers*, no. 196

    1982. *Money and Inflation*. Oxford, Basil Blackwell

Hahn, F. and Hollis, M., eds. 1979. *Philosophy and Economic Theory*. Oxford University Press

Hardin, R. 1982. *Collective Action*. Johns Hopkins University Press

Hargreaves-Heap, S. 1985. Why Economists Disagree. *Capital and Class*, **26**

Hargreaves-Heap, S. and Hollis, M. 1984. Bread and Circumstances: The Need for Political Economy. In D. Whynes, ed., *What is Political Economy?* Oxford, Basil Blackwell

1987. Great Expectations. *Tijdschrift voor Politieke Ekonomie*
Harré, R. 1979. *Social Being*. Oxford, Basil Blackwell
   1983. *Personal Being*. Oxford, Basil Blackwell
Harrison, R., ed. 1979. *Rational Action*. Cambridge University Press
Harsanyi, J. 1977. *Rational Behaviour and Bargaining Equilibrium in Games and Social Situations*. Cambridge University Press
Hawthorn, G. 1976. *Enlightenment and Despair*. Cambridge University Press.
Heath, A. 1976. *Rational Choice and Social Exchange*. Cambridge University Press
Hegel, G. W. F. 1955. *Die Vernunft in der Geschichte*. Hamburg
   1975. *Hegel's Logic*. Part I of *The Encyclopedia of the Philosophical Sciences*, translated by W. Wallace. Oxford University Press
Hirsch, F. 1977. *Social Limits to Growth*. London, Routledge & Kegan Paul
Hollis, M. 1977. *Models of Man : Philosophical Thoughts on Social Action*. Cambridge University Press
   1979. Rational Man and Social Science. In Harrison, ed. (1979)
   1981. Economic Man and Original Sin. *Political Studies*, **xxix**, no. 2
   1982. Education as a Positional Good. *Journal of Philosophy of Education*, **16**, no. 2
   1983. Rational Preferences. *Philosophical Forum*, **XIV**
   1985a. Positional Goods. In A. Phillips Griffiths, ed., *Philosophy and Practice*. Cambridge University Press
   1985b. Of Masks and Men. In M. Carrithers *et. al.*, eds. (1985)
Hollis, M. and Lukes, S., eds. 1982. *Rationality and Relativism*. Oxford, Basil Blackwell
Hollis, M. and Nell, E. 1975. *Rational Economic Man*. Cambridge University Press
Hollis, M. and Smith, S. 1986. Roles and Reasons in Foreign Policy Decision-Making. *British Journal of Political Science*, **XVI**
Hutchison, T. 1977. *Knowledge and Ignorance in Economics*. Oxford, Basil Blackwell
   1978. *On Revolutions and Progress in Economic Knowledge*. Cambridge University Press
Katouzian, H. 1980. *Ideology and Method in Economics*. London, Philip Allen
Keynes, J. M. 1936. *The General Theory of Employment Interest and Money*. London, Macmillan
Krupp, S. R. 1965. Equilibrium Theory in Economics and in Function Analysis as Types of Explanation. In D. Martindale, ed., *Functionalism in the Social Sciences*. Philadelphia, American Academy of Political and Social Science
Latsis, S., ed. 1976. *Method and Appraisal in Economics*. Cambridge University Press

Lewis, D. 1969. *Convention: A Philosophical Study*. Harvard University Press

1979. Prisoner's Dilemma is a Newcomb Problem. *Philosophy and Public Affairs*, **VIII**, 3

Luce, R. D., and Raiffa, H. 1957. *Games and Decisions*. New York, Wiley

Lukes, S. 1968. Methodological Individualism Reconsidered. *British Journal of Sociology*, **XIX**

1973. *Individualism*. Oxford, Basil Blackwell

1974. *Power: A Radical View*. London, Macmillan

1977. *Essays in Social Theory*. London, Macmillan

Lukes, S., ed. 1986. *Power*. Oxford, Basil Blackwell

Macdonald, G. and Pettit, P. 1981. *Semantics and Social Science*. London, Routledge & Kegan Paul

Machlup, F. 1978. *Methodology of Economics and Other Social Sciences*. New York, Academic Press

Macintyre, A. 1981. *After Virtue*. London, Duckworth

March, J. G. and Simon, H. A. 1958. *Organisations*. New York, Wiley

Margolis, J. 1982. *Selfishness, Altruism and Rationality*. Cambridge University Press

Marsh, C. 1984a. Back on the Bandwagon: The Effect of Opinion Polls on Public Opinion. *British Journal of Political Science*, **XV**, 1, 51–74

1984b. Do Polls Affect What People Think? In C. F. Turner and E. Martin, eds., *Surveying Subjective Phenomena*, vol. 2. New York, Russell Sage, pp. 565–91

Marx, K. 1979. The Eighteenth Brumaire of Louis Napoleon. In Marx and Engels, *Collected Works*, vol. 11. London, Lawrence & Wishart

Mellor, H. 1983. Objective Decision Making, *Social Theory and Practice*, **9**

Mises, L. von. 1949. *Human Action*. London, William Hodge

1960. *Epistemological Problems of Economics*. Princeton University Press

Mommsen, T. 1894. *The History of Rome*. London

Morgenthau, H. 1948. *Politics Among Nations*. New York, Knopff

Muth, J. F. 1961. Rational Expectations and the Theory of Price Movements. *Econometrica*, **29**

Nagel, E. 1963. Assumptions in Economic Theory. *American Economic Review*, **53**

Nagel, T. 1970. *The Possibility of Altruism*. Oxford University Press

Nussbaum, M. 1986. *The Fragility of Goodness*. Cambridge University Press

O'Hagan, T. 1984. *The End of Law?* Oxford, Basil Blackwell

Olson, M. 1965. *The Logic of Collective Action*. Harvard University Press

Parfit, D. 1984. *Reasons and Persons*. Oxford University Press

Parsons, T. 1951. *The Social System*. Glencoe, The Free Press

1968. *The Structure of Social Action*. New York, The Free Press

Pettit, P. 1986. Free Riding and Foul Dealing. *The Journal of Philosophy*, **LXXXIII**, no. 7

Quine, W. v. O. 1953. Two Dogmas of Empiricism. In *From a Logical Point of View*. Harvard University Press
  1960. *Word and Object*. MIT Press

Rapoport, A. 1966. *Two-Person Game Theory*. University of Michigan Press

Rawls, J. 1971. *A Theory of Justice*. Oxford University Press

Regan, D. H. 1980. *Utilitarianism and Cooperation*. Oxford, Clarendon Press

Robbins, L. 1932. *An Essay on the Nature and Significance of Economic Science*. London, Macmillan (2nd edition, 1935)

Rosenberg, A. 1976. *Microeconomic Laws*. University of Pittsburgh Press

Runciman, W. G. 1983. *A Treatise on Social Theory Volume I: The Methodology of Social Theory*. Cambridge University Press

Samuelson, P. A. 1963. Discussion: Problems of Methodology. *American Economic Review*, **53** (supp.)
  1964. Theory and Realism: A Reply. *American Economic Review*, **54**
  1965. Professor Samuelson on Theory and Realism: A Reply. *American Economic Review*, **55**

Sandel, M. J. 1982. *Liberalism and the Limits of Justice*. Cambridge University Press

Sartre, J.-P. 1973. *Existentialism and Humanism*. London, Methuen

Schelling, T. C. 1978. *Micromotives and Macrobehavior*. New York, W. W. Norton
  1984. *Choice and Consequence*. Harvard University Press

Schick, F. 1984. *Having Reasons: An Essay on Rationality and Sociality*. Princeton University Press

Schutz, A. 1972. *The Phenomenology of the Social World*. London, Heinemann

Scullard, H. H. 1935. *A History of the Roman World*. London, Methuen

Sen, A. K. 1970. *Collective Choice and Social Welfare*. London, Oliver & Boyd
  1977. Rational Fools: A Critique of the Behavioural Foundations of Economic Theory. *Philosophy and Public Affairs*, **6**, 317–44, reprinted in Hahn and Hollis, eds. (1979)
  1982. *Choice, Welfare and Measurement*. Oxford, Basil Blackwell
  1983. The Profit Motive. *Lloyds Bank Review*, no. **147**
  1985. *Well-being, Agency and Freedom: The Dewey Lectures 1984*. New York, The Journal of Philosophy Inc.

Sen, A. K. and Williams, B. A. O., eds. 1982. *Utilitarianism and Beyond*. Cambridge University Press

Shackle, G. L. S. 1973. *Epistemics and Economics*. Cambridge University Press

Sheffrin, S. M. 1983. *Rational Expectations*. Cambridge University Press
Simon, H. A. 1957. *Models of Man*. New York, Wiley
  1969. *The Science of the Artificial*. MIT Press
  1976. From Substantive to Procedural Rationality. In Latsis, ed.
    (1976), reprinted in Hahn and Hollis, eds. (1979)
Skinner, Q. 1972. 'Social Meaning' and the Explanation of Social
    Action. In P. Laslett *et al.*, eds., *Philosophy, Politics and Society IV*.
    Oxford, Basil Blackwell
  1974. The Principles and Practice of Opposition. In N. McKendrick,
    ed., *Historical Perspectives*. London, Europa
  1978. *The Foundations of Modern Political Thought*. Cambridge
    University Press
  1984. The Paradoxes of Political Liberty. In *The Tanner Lectures on
    Human Values for 1984–5*. Harvard University Press
Slote, M. 1983. *Goods and Virtues*. Oxford, Clarendon Press
Smith, A. 1970. *The Wealth of Nations*. Harmondsworth, Middlesex,
    Penguin
Smith, S. 1985. Groupthink and the Hostage Rescue Mission. *British
    Journal of Political Science*, **XV**
  1987. The Tradition of International Relations as a Social Science. In
    A. Dorsch and G. Legare, eds., *Paradigm Hegemony and International
    Relations*. Ottowa, Carleton University Press
Stewart, I. M. T. 1979. *Reasoning and Method in Economics*. London,
    McGraw-Hill
Taylor, C. 1971. Interpretation and the Sciences of Man. *Review of
    Metaphysics*, **25**
  1979. *Hegel and Modern Society*. Cambridge University Press
  1985. *Collected Papers*. Cambridge University Press
Taylor, M. 1987. *The Possibility of Cooperation*. Cambridge University
    Press
Ullman-Margalit, E. 1977. *The Emergence of Norms*. Oxford, Clarendon
    Press
Weber, M. 1922. *Economy and Society*, ed. G. Roth and C. Wittich.
    Berkeley, University of California Press
  1978. *Weber: Selections in Translation*, edited by G. Runciman,
    translated by E. Matthews. Cambridge University Press
Wiles, P. and Routh, G., eds. 1984. *Economics in Disarray*. Oxford, Basil
    Blackwell
Williams, B. A. O. 1981. *Moral Luck*. Cambridge University Press
Wilson, B. R., ed. 1970. *Rationality*. Oxford, Basil Blackwell
Winch, P. 1958. *The Idea of a Social Science*. London, Routledge & Kegan
    Paul
Wittgenstein, L. 1953. *Philosophical Investigations*. Oxford, Basil
    Blackwell

Index